MW01194380

Gangs of the El Paso–Juárez Borderland

Mike Tapia

GANGS OF THE EL PASO-JUÁREZ BORDERLAND

a history

University of New Mexico Press | Albuquerque

Names: Tapia, Mike, 1974– author.

Title: Gangs of the El Paso–Juárez borderland: a history / Mike Tapia.

Description: First edition. | Albuquerque: University of New Mexico
  Press, 2019. | Includes bibliographical references and index.

Identifiers: LCCN 2019030170 (print) | ISBN 9780826361097 (cloth) |
  ISBN 9780826361103 (e-book)

Subjects: LCSH: Gangs—Texas, West. | Gangs—New Mexico. | Gangs—
  Mexico—Chihuahua (State) | Mexican-American Border Region—
  History. | Mexican-American Border Region—Social conditions.

Classification: LCC HV6437. T37 2019 (print) | LCC HV6437 (e-book) |
  DDC 364.106/6097216—dc23

LC record available at https://lccn.loc.gov/2019030170

LC e-book record available at https://lccn.loc.gov/2019030171

COVER ILLUSTRATIONS

top El Paso © 4kodiak / istockphoto.com.

middle Varrio Meadow Trece Gang Members. Meadow Trece
  O.G.s, 1990s. Photos courtesy of J. Franco, Sunland Park Police
  Department.

bottom A group mugshot photo of several Juárez-based juvenile
  delinquents in the 1920s. Photo courtesy of Bob Chessey, El Paso.

TEXT AND COVER DESIGN | Mindy Basinger Hill

COMPOSED IN 10.25/14pt Minion Pro × 25p6

TO RAQUEL, SOPHIA, OLIVIA, HENRY (AND BABY-P).

You all mean the world to me.

CONTENTS

ACKNOWLEDGMENTS

The author would like to thank the following for their assistance on this project. Early in the process were Chris Barela, Vicki Hooser, and Lt. Howie at the Doña Ana County Jail; Lt. Blanco and the gang unit at the New Mexico Southern Correctional Facility; and Robert Flores, James Nance, and Wendy Wisneski at El Paso County Jail. Michelle Carreon and Danny Gonzales of El Paso Public Library's Border Heritage desk were amazing, along with our mutual friend and noted local historian Fred Morales. Thanks also to David Flores and Claudia Rivers from UTEP Library's Special Collections department.

From the law enforcement community (both retired and current), thanks to Jay Wisner, Danny Garcia, Joe Bob Sellers, Ruben Genera, Jeff Gibson, Mary Lou Carrillo, Tommy Cisneros, El "Ray-Ray" Lucero, David Borunda, Steve Nance, Jon Day, Pearce Wilbur, Eric Flores, Arturo Guerrero, Paul Lujan, and Jeremy Story.

At New Mexico State University (NMSU), border violence writer and asylum activist Molly Molloy was always super with feedback on early drafts and other consultation. Research assistants Deborah Blalock and Aleena Jackson toiled away at archives, as did El Freddy de la Bowie. Thanks to the College of Arts and Sciences for always supporting my work and related travel.

And of course, *gracias a todos los vatos y rucas* from the Borderland region *que me esquiñaron*. It all started with El Pete Vargas, *y tambien se aventaron el* Andy "Rhino" Muñoz, El Juan Mendoza, El Matt "Chichi" Juárez *y su carnal* Frank Juárez. Thanks to Chuy Medrano, Danny "Smiley" Barreras, Oscar "El Pachucon" Gonzales, Jesse Gutierrez, the Lucero family and Deandra, Jimmy Barela, Angel Hernandez, Julian Cardona de Juaritos, and Jesse "El Spooky" de L.A./El Chuco. *Mi nino* Tony *y mi* "Compa Ron" Valenzuela *tambien son chingones*. El Eugene Pettes, Sergio Hernandez, Stephanie Varela, and Adrian Vigil are damn *firme gente* from that city of Crosses who helped tremendously. I hope you all enjoy this final product.

Gangs of the El Paso–Juárez Borderland

INTRODUCTION

The El Paso–Juárez Borderland as Place and Its Criminal Subcultures

Place can sometimes be difficult to define. El Paso, Texas, and Cd. Juárez, Chihuahua, share physical, historical, cultural, familial, and, to some extent, economic space. Yet, in many respects, the first-meets-third world contrast between them is striking. In other instances, it is difficult to distinguish between the two places. A "sister cities" metaphor is often used by local cultural and business elites to describe them, but it competes with a powerful "totally different places" narrative among the general population. Juárez and El Paso and, residually, its entire region are wrought with contradictions that are often difficult to analyze and make sense of. The implications this has for criminal and delinquent subculture formation is one such area.

This work is focused on the region encompassing west Texas, southern New Mexico, and northern Chihuahua, Mexico. It is a case study examining the past 100 years of historical developments there through a criminological lens. The area contains some 3 million people anchored by the binational metroplex of El Paso–Juárez. The easternmost point of this borderland region is the Ft. Hancock port of entry about 50 miles east of El Paso–Juárez. En route are a series of small agricultural border towns straddling the border that include Socorro, San Elizario, Clint, Fabens, Tornillo, and Acala (see a layout of the borderland region in fig. 0.1). On the Mexican side of this lower valley area are the badlands—the notorious eastern Valle de Juárez, known during the recent *guerra* (i.e., drug gang war) as a stronghold of the Sinaloa cartel (US Dept. of Justice 2011). Across the border at Ft. Hancock is El Porvenir, a town of about 3,000 people, serving as the rural portion of Praxedis Guerrero. Both places had a mass population exodus in 2010 due to chronic drug war violence, leaving a total estimated range of between 5,000 and 7,000 people there today.[1]

The westernmost part of this borderland region is Columbus, New Mexico. It is an official port of entry with Puerto Palomas, a small town of about

3,000 to 4,000 people on the Chihuahua, Mexico, side. Situated some 80 miles west of El Paso–Juárez, this location is as active as any other for drug, weapon, and human smuggling across the border. Much like El Paso–Juárez, it was a strategic locale for Pancho Villa and opposing forces during the Mexican Revolution roughly 100 years ago and it remains a hotspot for lawlessness on the border. These places have retained their importance over time as key geographic nodes in what has become a highly militarized and politicized border region.

In 2008 the entire police force of Palomas abandoned their posts and resigned in unison, fleeing drug-gang retribution (Bowden 2010). In 2011, the mayor of Columbus, its police chief, and a city councilman were arrested on gun-smuggling charges in an operation that fed the drug cartels on the Palomas side (Campoy and Eaton 2011). In a typical example of how crime networks tend to stretch across the entire region, the guns originated in Chaparral, New Mexico, 90 miles west of Columbus, between Las Cruces, New Mexico and El Paso, Texas (see fig. 0.1). This book is filled with many such examples of the crisscrossing clandestine links that exist in all directions in the area.

From east to west, this 130-mile border region contains five official ports of entry: Ft. Hancock, Tornillo, El Paso, Santa Theresa, and Columbus-Palomas. El Paso alone has six of Texas's 11 international land-port bridges, each facilitating some combination of daily commercial, vehicular, and pedestrian traffic. This region is the most reinforced area of "homeland security" along the entire US–Mexico border (Millman 2007) and sees a higher volume of trade than any border sector (Texas Comptroller 2017). Nonetheless, as an unnatural, manmade barrier, it will never be as effective at keeping the two countries as separate as it purports. The interconnectedness of the various locales in this region are as old as the settlements themselves, and it remains an implausible goal to keep their exchanges separate based on the international boundary. In the midst of the Trump administration's hard-line anti-immigration policies as the backdrop, my purpose is to offer a historical view of this borderland region's criminal subcultures and adaptations to the political boundary on both sides of the law.

The place furthest from the actual border with Mexico, but that is a vital part of this region's anatomy, is Las Cruces, New Mexico, about 50 miles northwest of El Paso–Juárez on Interstate 10. This growing city of just over 100,000 people is connected to the heart of the region in terms of its culture, infrastructure (e.g., media outlets and public utilities), and social networks,

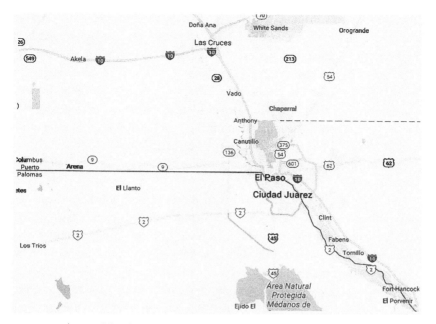

FIGURE 0.1 | Map of the El Paso–Juárez borderland region.
Credit: Map data © 2018 Google, INEGI.

both normative and criminal. It therefore is included in this study of historical dynamics and other features of the region in the context of its street gangs and related subcultures. The issues of Mexican immigration, border security, and related topics have been extensively covered in the media and explored by academics and other writers. Some even argue it has been overdone (Olson, Shirk, and Selee 2010). However, it has seldom if ever been analyzed with a sociohistorical framework that is focused exclusively on its street-level criminological elements. That is the primary contribution of this book.

Barrio Gangs and the Borderland

Barrio gangs date at least as far back as the 1920s in most Mexican American (Chicano) communities in the United States (Bogardus 1943; Vigil 1988). As I have stated elsewhere, they are well studied in California but not in many other places (Tapia 2017). Notable exceptions include the literature for San Antonio (Montejano 2010; Valdez 2005; Valdez et al. 2009), Denver (Durán

2013), Tucson (Cummings 2003), and Washington State (Moreno 2006) to name a few. El Paso, Texas, is regarded by academics and much of the lay public as the birthplace of the zoot suit *pachuco*, the original Chicano youth street subculture. This title arguably belongs as much to Cd. Juárez as it does to El Paso, an issue that is discussed in chapters 1 and 4. But it is interesting that there is not much published academic work on such topics for this locale. Several important exceptions include Coltharp (1965), Duran (2018), Garcia (1995), and Gundur (2018). Among these, none is solely focused on the history and evolution of barrio gangs in this binational metroplex or its broader region.

The chronology I cover begins with the neighborhood-based societies of poor, streetwise El Paso youth in the 1920s and 1930s, moving through the decades to examine changes in each distinct era of this durable barrio gang subculture. Each chapter takes a different major population center in the region in turn, profiling local gang histories and their importance in the larger setting, including its modern criminal networks. I detail the primary gangs in each place and the network linkages that exist among them across this unique borderland region. I treat these topics with criminological frameworks, juxtaposing my findings with those of related works, and compare them to those involving Chicano gangs in other regions. This approach allows me to address questions of continuity and change in the timeline of barrio gangs across the Southwest more generally.

Traditional barrio gang subculture has undergone more changes in the last 10 to 15 years than it has in the several decades prior, and the rather drastic changes suggest it may be headed for extinction. For example, these groups no longer seem to congregate on street corners and posture in public to claim turf against their proximate competitors, which is a break from decades of this cultural norm (Gundur 2017; Quiñones 2014). There are examples of this offered at each research site. A basic impetus for the work, then, is to help preserve some of the history of this once-abundant feature of the Mexican American experience, a fixture in US–Chicano (and Mexican border) communities for about the past 100 years. The migration of gang-involved individuals and families in the Southwest has been a strong feature shaping the gang norms of each locale in the study. In tracing the history of such gang elements, anthropological snippets of urban Chicano culture are elucidated along the way.

Finally, the borderland is a salient sociopolitical topic, especially in terms of public safety, crime, drugs, and "homeland security." The role of geography is particularly important in the unique formation, structure, and intensity of borderland gangs versus that found in the nation's nonborder locales. Ironically, the actual threats to public safety posed by criminal organizations on the US side of the borderland are minimal. Among large US cities, El Paso, in particular, has had one of the lowest violent crime rates for decades, most recently ranked as the second safest (*El Paso Herald Post* 2017). Its gang subcultures are therefore overvilified, but they are not completely benign. I specify the conditions under which they pose(d) an actual threat to public safety with a historical approach that comes to present day.

Methods and Influences

The information in this book comes from a wide variety of sources. It includes newspaper archives, police records, public and classified intelligence reports from local and federal agencies, insights and information from other published scholarly work, the archived records of interventionists and community activists, and interviews of people knowledgeable about the book's various subtopics. The borderland region is interesting in that drugs, gangs, and clandestine, underworld elements are endemic; camouflaged, but often in plain sight. Therefore, many rich sources of information abound, even in unlikely places. As Campbell (2009) notes, most every native or longtime resident of the region either remembers, or knows firsthand, of something or someone of relevance to the street gang-drug nexus. This also applies to members of local law enforcement who grew up in the barrio and who became highly effective at their jobs due to their prior familiarity with its networks and methods of operation. Often, their familiarity with these elements comes from within their own kin.

I drew on oral histories of South El Paso residents contained in a special collection of the University of Texas at El Paso (UTEP) library that are rich in detail about barrio life in by-gone eras. I collected brief oral histories of my own from retired members of law enforcement and other border dwellers. I also drew on the published work of Father Harold Rahm and Robert Weber (1958) who worked with gang youth in South El Paso in the early 1950s. The investigative writing of the late Charles Bowden (2002), while not academic in nature per se, documents decades of borderland drug-scene dynamics in one case, spun around the family story of the region's former DEA chief.

These and other intellectual ventures back and forth across the Juárez–El Paso border illustrated the macrolevel relationships involving the US and Mexican governments, down to the microlevel tactical maneuvers of *sicarios* working for the Juárez cartel (Molloy and Bowden 2012).

Academic works about the borderland's underworld have also demonstrated the mundaneness of its drug cultures. In *Drug War Zone: Frontline Dispatches from the Streets of El Paso and Juárez* (2009), Howard Campbell, an anthropologist at UTEP, illustrates this. He offers a very broad view of drug-smuggling history that includes case studies of street-level dealers on both sides of the border, of modern hybrid drug cultures in El Paso embedded in normative networks, and in typical teen behaviors. He also includes the perceptions of longtime county and federal law enforcement agents working on border drug interdiction. In his archival work, old Juárez drug dealers are depicted, and although these portions are very thin compared to my work, he was also able to interview insiders to the barrio gang scenes of the 1960s through the 1980s.

Former New Mexico State University (at Las Cruces) sociologist Robert Durán's book *Gang Paradox: Inequality and Miracles on the U.S.–Mexico Border* (2018) offers an alternative look at similar topics. As is Durán's style in other major works, it is a macrosociological, historical take on the creation, existence, and meaning of gangs in El Paso and the broader region. Durán's thesis is that gangs are borne from the forces of discrimination and the resultant subcultures that emerge in the lower working class. He writes about the moral panics created by the press and law enforcement that mislead the public about threats to public safety. Durán's work is framed by a strong social justice orientation that views the emergence of *pachuco* border gangs as a type of resistance.

Gundur (2018; 2019) is one of very few scholars (perhaps the only one so far) to address the history and evolution of the region's most notorious modern gang, the Barrio Azteca. He does so in the context of recent changes in prison gang structure and the implications of such changes on the order of the street, topics that I also address here and elsewhere (Tapia, Sparks, and Miller 2014). Although these authors and I have all written about borderland crime dynamics using similar types of sources and frameworks, the results are substantially different, and each is insightful in its own way. I attempt to bring many of these elements together in this book.

Chapter 1 offers a brief history of south El Paso neighborhoods and its gangs going back to the 1920s. I draw on archived interviews of south El Paso residents who spoke of this era's vibrant community life, its ethnic relations, and street subcultures. The published work and personal insights of the learned El Paso historian Fred Morales were extremely helpful in guiding the chapter. Newspaper archives and Father Rahm's (1958) work also provided much insight to these issues. I build a timeline that moves through the decades, following trends and changes in the character of El Paso barrio gangs through the 1960s. This chronology sets up a foundation for the modern groups handled in later chapters, depicting the formation of the most menacing of current groups such as the Sureño Trece, the Chuco Tangos, and the Barrio Azteca.

Taking the same approach for the nearby cities of Las Cruces and Anthony, New Mexico, chapters 2 and 3 describe their gang histories and the network linkages that exist across the borderland region. Over the past several decades, El Paso, Anthony, and Las Cruces have seen gangs transplanted from California, Chicago, and Juárez, and the latter's westernmost impoverished *colonias* (shanty towns), such as Anapra. In chapter 2, I profile some of the earliest known groups to emerge in Las Cruces, based on discussions with former gang members, retired law enforcement, and other community members who witnessed these developments. I then build a timeline that runs to current day, as street-gang issues have remained salient in Las Cruces until quite recently. I offer a broad description of the gang dynamics that took shape there over time. Often it embodies archetypal Chicano gang elements that are found in other larger southwestern cities, and at times it shows characteristics that are unique to the small city context.

Anthony is a small community (population 15,000) located halfway between El Paso County (population 840,000) and Las Cruces in Doña Ana County, New Mexico (population 215,000). As it sits right on the state boundary, half of Anthony is in Texas and half is in New Mexico. It is surrounded by a series of smaller communities that straddle the state line and that surprisingly have street-gang histories of their own dating back to the 1960s. Chapter 3 profiles this community and others in its proximity with respect to their gang origins and networks to other places in the region. Chaparral, New Mexico (population 20,000), for example, sits across Interstate-10 from Anthony, and is hidden eight miles into a mountain range off the highway. Its gang networks stem from nearby northeast El Paso, Anthony, and Las Cruces.

Sunland Park, New Mexico, is situated between El Paso, Texas, and Santa Teresa, New Mexico, bordering with Anapra, an impoverished colonia of western Juárez. Sunland Park, therefore, represents the convergence of a tri-state area and shares its gang networks with all of these locations. Prior to the fortifying of the border in that area in the late 1970s, and prior to the establishment of the municipality of Sunland Park in 1983, it was known only as Anapra, and it was spread across both sides of the US-Mexico border. These communities in and around Anthony comprise the connective tissue among the three major urban centers in the region—El Paso, Las Cruces, and Juárez—and it is evidenced in their delinquent networks and subcultures.

Chapter 4 focuses on Cd. Juárez, describing its symbiotic relationship with El Paso and challenging the "sister city" trope that is commonly used by politicians, the business community, and culture scholars. It traces the history of these "sin cities" to the Prohibition era. It characterizes the types of banditry, delinquency, and gangsterism that predominated on both sides of the river as a shared underworld subculture. Gradual changes in gang structure and the radical spike of Juárez's violence level to record heights in 2010 are detailed in search of an explanation for this shift. The contemporary work of Mexican sociologists and journalists is reviewed and considered in this assessment of record-setting drug-gang violence in Juárez. Spillover effects into El Paso, or other places in the United States, and more notably, the paradoxical lack thereof are also discussed at length.

Chapter 5 details the contemporary gang landscape in El Paso using police data as its starting point. A paradox is identified wherein police claim "gang crime is at a record high" in 2017, yet the city's violent crime rates continue to be among the lowest in the United States. The literature on Latino violence is reviewed in search of an explanation for this contradiction. El Paso's modern gang issues (1980s–current), its hotspots, its notorious gangs, and both inter- and intra-ethnic group conflicts involving its black gangs are detailed. The chapter ends with a profile of the evolution of the most intense and sophisticated street-prison hybrid gang to ever emerge in El Paso. Its historical ties to drug gangs in Juárez and its more recent formal mergers are described as the catalysts in its creation. Competition from other allied forces on both sides of the international border are also detailed.

The final chapter sums up the lessons learned from examining the criminological dynamics of this unique border region over time. It begins by resisting the glorification of gang life in the face of the social ills that produce it and that result from it. The role of geography in producing unique gang subcultures, the meaning of *place*, and the bifurcation of the region by the border are also expounded. Relatedly, the paradox of the abundant gang presence and subculture, accompanied by low violence rates in El Paso, and the contrast of Juárez's profuse violence adds to the region's complexity. The network features of gangs across the borderland region and its intricacies are further considered. Recent shifts in Chicano gang structures and the nuances of gang developments in this region vis-à-vis neighboring regions to the east and the west are also laid out. The book closes with several observations about the most recent changes occurring among gang millennials.

ONE

The Early Barrio Gangs of El Paso, Texas
1920s to 1960s

Introduction

Perhaps because it is the largest and oldest adjacent border city to Mexico, El Paso's barrio gang history goes back further than that of any other US city. A careful analysis of this place and its early delinquent street gangs is therefore a critical starting point. El Paso is well known by scholars of various disciplines (e.g., literature, history, ethnic studies, sociology) to be the birthplace of the zoot suit pachuco (e.g., Coltharp 1965; Garcia 1995; Ornstein 1983). Most would say this is an ancestor to the lowrider *cholo* and that both are predecessors of the modern-day Chicano gang member. Others might argue that each subculture is distinct and not all of them are necessarily criminogenic. Nonetheless, the overlap among them is undeniable. The epicenter of such urban subcultures and their street activities for roughly the past century has been south-central El Paso, with particular roots in the two barrios still known today as Chihuahuita and Segundo Barrio. Part of this chapter depicts gang turf in these areas in the 1950s and 1960s—the heyday of barrio gangs.

This chapter begins with a brief history of these neighborhoods and its gangs going back to the 1920s and 1930s. I draw on oral histories of south El Paso residents from this era, on the work of Father Harold Rahm (1958) who worked with gang youth in south El Paso in the early 1950s, and on the work of self-taught El Paso historian Fred Morales, who grew up in Chihuahuita. His books and photos illuminate the earliest groups of delinquent youth in south El Paso, going back to about 1910. Newspaper archives from this era also provide much insight to these issues. This chapter's timeline follows trends and changes in the character of El Paso barrio gangs from about 1915 through the 1960s.

El Chuco–Juaritos as the Epicenter

Most major cities in the southwestern United States have become well-known sites of Chicano gang activity. Los Angeles has come to be known as the capital city in this regard, with Fresno, Oakland, and San Diego not far behind. San Antonio, Houston, and Dallas are also rather intense sites of Chicano gang activity, as are Tucson, Albuquerque, and Chicago in the Midwest. Historically speaking, however, the barrio street counterculture in these places does not rival that of El Paso, Texas, and its Mexican sister city, Ciudad Juárez, Chihuahua. That is, El Paso is well known by scholars, old pachucos, and the lay public alike as the most profound context for the development of the pachuco and cholo subcultures. The widely known Chicano slang title that El Paso has acquired over time, for example, is "El Chuco" (Burciaga 1992; Torres 2010), which speaks volumes about this history.

For her doctoral dissertation in linguistics at UTEP, Lurline Coltharp (1965) describes the pachuco language and subculture, which, in 1930s Juárez and south El Paso, was known as the *tirilón* style. There is no agreed upon origin and exact meaning of *tirilón* among historians, linguists, and anthropologists who have studied the region but it is generally equated to early pachuco zoot suiters. According to historian Fred Morales, this was the name of one of the first known street gangs in El Paso, located at *los cinco infiernos*, the five tenements on the 900 block of South Chihuahua Street (Morales 2017). While this may be true, UTEP's oral histories and other research items suggest it was a generic name that Mexicans gave to delinquent street characters of the border region from the late 1920s through the 1950s (UTEP 1978, 1974). It is interesting that the region's primary modern criminal syndicate, the Barrio Azteca, currently uses the term *tirilon* to refer to the rank of lieutenant in the organization. As Chicano prison gangs are known to indoctrinate themselves on the historical and cultural aspects of their ancestors, this is by no means a coincidence.

It is common knowledge among Latino culture scholars and local enthusiasts that the zoot suit style was made popular in the early 1940s by Mexican actor and Juárez resident German Valdez via his famous character Tin Tan. Of the various Mexican actors who channeled the pachuco persona of the region at the time, it was Valdez's upbringing as a teen in Juárez–El Paso that made him the most genuine and, thus, the best at doing it (Guzman 2017). Eighty years later, the style is still celebrated in the region, with zoot suit–

FIGURE 1.1A | *left* | German Valdez as Tin-Tan.
Credit: https://www.pinterest.com/thezombielennon/tin-tan/.

FIGURE 1.1B | *right* | Popular actor/comedian from the El Paso–Juárez region Jaime Manzano, a.k.a. El Pecas, who appeared in *El Pocho* (i.e., an Americanized or US-born Mexican). Here he is pictured with Pedro Infante (left), one of Mexico's most famous actor/singers of all time. Credit: Mateo San Roman.

themed clubs, festivals, and other events in El Paso, Juárez, and Las Cruces (Ruelas 2017; Sanchez 2016).[1] There is even a bronze statue of Tin Tan called El Pachuco de Oro in Juárez's downtown market square, and a building on Mariscal Street dedicated to German Valdez's portrayal of this type of borderland dweller on the silver screen.

Chihuahuita

Chihuahuita is El Paso's oldest barrio per se,[2] dating back to 1814, and situated as close to downtown Cd. Juárez as can be on the US side of the border. It was once known simply as Census Tract 18 and was the first neighborhood ward to be designated by urban pioneers in South El Paso in 1886 (Morales 2007). It was characterized as having poor, unsanitary conditions in the 1920s and 1930s and generally described as "crumbling and decaying" in that era (Uhl and Meglorino 1993). Most of its residents were refugees from the northern border state of Chihuahua fleeing the dangers of Mexican revolutionary movements in the region. Timmons (1990, 218) called it the "worst barrio slum in the U.S.," plagued by starvation, disease, and crime. Its streets were not paved until after World War II. According to Uhl and Meglorino (1993, 5) in the 1940s pachuco gangs were abundant in Chihuahuita, "with tourists and Fort Bliss soldiers as their favorite victims."[3] Some of the known gangs from the area in the 1930s and 1940s were the Wyoming Street, Oregon Street, Campbell Street, and South Mesa gangs (Rahm 1958; UTEP 1974, 1979).[4]

El Segundo Barrio[5]

As the name implies, Segundo Barrio (i.e., the second ward) is the second oldest urban settlement in south El Paso (Morales 2007). Despite Chihuahuita's reputation as a rough neighborhood, Segundo is without a doubt the name and place most equated with pachuco and barrio gang elements in the borderland region. Some of its known landmarks include Aoy School (i.e., the Mexican school), Guillen Middle School, Bowie High School, the Armijo Community Center, Alamito housing projects, and the Catholic Churches of Sagrado Corazon and San Ignacio. One oral history interviewee spoke of the atmosphere in the mid-1920s in Segundo (UTEP 1979):

> *Cada calle tenía su grupo de jovenes.* (Every street had a group of kids). We were all "Sandlotters" who played ball against the other barrios like from Chihuahuita. Habían Los Tigres de Oregon Street, Los Indios de la Florence, and a group from San Antonio Street (i.e., La Sana). *En ese tiempo, no habían* (At that time, there were no) youth rec centers, *así como el de* (like that of) San Juan. So we just hung out on street corners.

Segundo became as notorious of a barrio as East Los Angeles, and this is not coincidental as it has a very strong cultural and practical tie to that place (more on this below). To this day, Chicano gang affiliations of the most serious type are still equated with, if not still based in, Segundo. The El Paso Police Department's (EPPD) gang unit currently lists three groups claiming affiliation to the neighborhood. Segundo Barrio is listed in their current gang database with 75 members. This group likely represents a gang that is four or five generations old and thus now has ties to prison gangs and cartel members in the region.[6] The Segundo Barrio Kings are also listed in the database with 43 members. The size of this group implies that it is a serious gang that is also likely several generations old. The affiliation to the Kings (the Chicago-influenced People Nation) suggests it grew out of the vast gang proliferation years of the 1980s and 1990s. They are one of about 15 to 20 sets of Kings across the city. Finally, the Second Ward Killers are listed in the current EPPD gang database but with only four members.

Early Barrio Gangs

Various sources of information have been useful to estimate how far back the barrio street gangs of El Paso go and how serious a problem they were viewed to be. One of the earliest published academic accounts that mentions El Paso's slum gangs is Frederick Thrasher's 1927 book *The Gang*. Thrasher, the most renowned US street-gang researcher at the time, had received a report in 1925 from a colleague working in El Paso named Roy E. Dickerson. He noted that El Paso gangs "in the Mexican areas had been around for eight or nine years" (380), placing their origin around 1916 by his measure. Dickerson further noted 300–400 gang boys ages 15–18 across 20–25 gangs, each with a leader and involved in variety of crimes.[7]

One of the first newspaper accounts of street gangs operating in south and central El Paso gave brief descriptions of several of the most problematic groups, their activities, and their locations (*El Paso Herald Post* 1920). The first was identified as a group who regularly congregated at "14th street [*sic*] between Santa Fe and El Paso St., who engaged in robbing wagons and taking the loot across the bridge to Juarez" (4).[8] A second group could be found at Finley and Estrella Streets, described as five young men and two adults involved in bootlegging and burglary.[9] A gunfight ensued between them and police in an apprehension attempt, resulting in two of the gang members' deaths (4). Another bootlegging and burglary gang's headquarters was located at San Antonio and Piedras. A group of desperados who regularly congregated at Fourth and Ochoa that police disbanded for "rowdyism" shot at police when they returned to their vehicles. A gang of "miscellaneous thieves" was also located at 9th and Chihuahua. Toward central El Paso were the Grant Avenue Boys, five of whom were sent to state reform school. Finally, a bicycle stealing ring was described as a group of young negroes and Mexicans, but no specific location was given.

While gangs were viewed as a nuisance by the larger community and, at times, engaged in lethal violence (*El Paso Herald Post* 1934a), it didn't appear to be a huge priority in the early 1930s. One of several opinion editorials appearing in the local newspaper in the early and mid-1930s referred to south El Paso's delinquent youth gangs as a longtime "outdoor sport . . . and

FIGURE 1.2 | A group of boys in *Segundo Barrio*, ca. 1910. Credit: Photo courtesy of the El Paso Public Library, Otis A. Aultman Collection.

problem," with one commentator stating that trying to get rid of them would only displace the fights and other problems "uptown" (Conner 1935, 4). The Good Will Boys Club was a delinquency intervention agency in south El Paso at that time. When the county threatened to cut its budget in 1933, there was an outpouring of support from the community, vouching for the rapport the director had with some of the city's youth gang leaders, with whom he regularly negotiated to help control delinquency (*El Paso Herald Post* 1933a).

One notable case involved two rival gang leaders in south El Paso, Aurelio "Capone" Chavez and Edmundo Romero, both 17 years old. A barber named Mateo Marmolejo was seriously injured when he tried to break up a gang fight between the two unnamed gangs led by these boys. Capone denied ordering his crew to jump Marmolejo and negotiated with police to drop the charges in exchange for exerting his influence to quell gang violence against innocent victims in south El Paso. Even juvenile bureau officers had to admit to Capone's influence among these groups, stating "his word is law [out here]" (*El Paso Herald Post* 1932a). Romero, who was also charged, took issue with this characterization, boasting *he* was the toughest guy in south El Paso. The director of the Good Will Boys Club, H. E. Williams, worked with both gangs to call a truce and collectively deter gang-related violence. Around this time, District Attorney Jackson estimated there were 100 gang-involved boys in south El Paso (*El Paso Herald Post* 1936a).

It appears that tolerance of youth gangs by the community began to wear thin just prior to the advent of the zoot suit pachuco era in the late 1930s and early 1940s. Even church officials who traditionally worked with and helped barrio gang youth complained about the lack of police attention as public disorder increased near the church (*El Paso Herald Post* 1936b, 1939). Another example occurred in 1938 when Judge Langford of the Police Court dramatically increased fines for loitering and other youth gang-related offenses after a physical confrontation between gang boys and a youth bureau officer at El Paso and Overland Streets (*El Paso Herald Post* 1938a). The delinquent intensity of the 1930s youth gangs in El Paso and the extent of problems they caused are revisited below.

Identifying the Gangs

Harold Rahm, a Catholic priest assigned to south El Paso's Sacred Heart of Mary parish in 1952, worked with gang boys of the area until his departure in 1964 and wrote a book about his experience. *Office in the Alley: Report on a Project with Gang Youngsters* (1958) chronicles the development of the intervention program, including many insights and observations of the youth gang culture in Segundo Barrio at that time. Aside from being a great primer for doing street-level gang intervention in poor Chicano communities, it contains information on the actual gangs themselves much like an anthropological study would. It turns out to be one of the few quality resources in existence for documenting a relatively early era in the timeline of El Paso's gang subculture.

In describing the general structure of area gangs, Rahm notes how the newspaper often mentioned south El Paso's "number gangs," since many early gangs named themselves after the numbered streets there. Rahm explains that by the 1950s, gang hangouts were often different from the place the gang originally claimed as its turf. They roamed about the inner city and situated themselves in more interesting or higher profile locations where they postured against rivals and competed for turf such as at Frontera Park and Armijo Park. Local pool halls such as The Emporium were also popular hangouts for gang youth, going back to the 1930s (*El Paso Herald Post* 1936c).

The gang landscape in Segundo in the 1950s was described as being divided into several major camps. About one quarter of the neighborhood was controlled by the 7xs, who were a small, older group of teens with a fierce reputation. They hung around the Alamito housing projects on St. Vrain Street and along Hill and Tays Streets. The 14s were the "pee-wee" group to the 7xs,[10] and one of their important allies was the 4Fs of South Mesa Street. This group reportedly took its name from the 4-F classification the boys in this section of south El Paso received in the selective service. Since they all hung out together on street corners, the pool hall, and the bar, they began to become known as a gang. In the 1950s they were a second-generation gang and, according to Rahm, "nobody knew what became of the original 4Fs, or even what their names were" (39).

Another section of the neighborhood was run by the Little 9s, who, like their rivals, the 7xs, were a small, older, fiercer group of teens and young men. They claimed Frontera Park and the general area around Fifth Street and Oregon Street as their turf. The Lucky 13s were the pee-wees to the Little 9s. An important ally to these groups were the Charms. Another reputable east El Paso gang in the early 1950s was 2-x, who were suspected of stealing grenades from Ft. Bliss and being involved in a series of shootings (*El Paso Herald Post* 1951a). Rahm found it peculiar that all gang names were in English, considering that most of these boys spoke a great deal of Spanish. Compare this to Tapia (2017), who shows that the majority of 1950s barrio gangs in San Antonio used group names in Spanish.

Here is a more complete list of active gangs in south El Paso in the 1950s according to Father Rahm's work with the church's intervention center.

Canal Kids (CKs), a.k.a. La Canal	Happy Wanderers	[O]K-9[11]
	[King] Cobras	Park St. (Parkers)
Charms	King Gamblers	Rebels
DDT's (a.k.a. El Diablo)	KKs	Rhythm Devils
	Lads & Mads	Road Blockers
Durango St. a.k.a. Duranguito	Little 9s	TPM
	Little 10s	X9s

But other sources reported a greater number of active gangs. In a 1956 newspaper article, a juvenile probation department official stated that his office and police were investigating 50 active juvenile gangs in the city (Montgomery 1956) and that altogether they had "reached the greatest numerical status in history" by then. The early 1950s was also identified as a period

FIGURE 1.3A AND B | Two Generations of [Varrio] King Cobra Members.
On the left are former members of the King Cobras from Juárez–South El Paso, taken in the 1960s. On the right are future members of the gang Varrio King Cobra taken in the 1970s. By the 1990s, this gang dynasty had transplanted to Las Cruces, New Mexico. Credit: Photo courtesy of Andres "Rhino" Muñoz.

when street gangs were particularly active (McVicar 1960; Montgomery 1956). There was a brief lull after a series of interventions by various segments of the community, but it seems to have come back with a vengeance in the mid-1950s.

While the information recorded by Rahm and frequent newspaper stories depict the general atmosphere and help to document some of the active gangs of the time, primarily it provided a snapshot of the groups in existence in the mid-1950s. With the exception of the 4Fs, not much is offered in the way of the history or earlier manifestations of the gangs. Another rich source of information has, therefore, been the oral histories of residents of south El Paso in the 1920s through 1940s, who named the gangs of that era.

One interviewee named Beto was born in 1928 and listed the south El Paso gangs that existed in the mid- to late 1940s. He echoed some of the gangs mentioned by another, older interviewee from Segundo Barrio (see discussion above), such as the Florence Street and Oregon Street gangs. But he also added the Campbell Street gang at 5th and Campbell, the 9th Street gang, Park Street gang, the Charles gang, and the Mesa gang. Another interviewee, Guillermo Balderas, who was born in El Paso in 1910, spoke of the 1940s gangs that tried to recruit his son. They approached him saying, "You've

either gotta join Tortilla Flat, OK 9, OK 7, or South Mesa" (UTEP 1974).[12]
Fred Morales (2017) notes that the Clovers hung around the tenements at
the corner of Eighth and El Paso Streets in the late 1940s.

Street-Gang Intensity

Relative to their boisterous behavior in prior eras, by the late 1950s, south
El Paso's street gangs were said to have gone underground (McVicar 1960).
One of the issues identified by police was what we refer to today as the street
code of "no snitching." In south El Paso, police referred to this as the *quién
sabe?* syndrome. This had various implications for criminal victimizations.
It was the refrain heard from juvenile victims of gang warfare, who refused
to name their assailants, usually because the victim and his gang planned
to retaliate and didn't want police meddling in their business. Merchants
also often refused to identify or press charges against gang youth who had
victimized them for fear of retaliation. To solve these crimes, police relied
on their familiarity with gang turf and on "lists of individual members kept
on file" (McVicar 1960, 3).

Compare this to some of the south El Paso youth-gang incidents making
the news in the early 1930s, when group leaders involved in petty crimes
often snitched on each other (*El Paso Herald Post* 1933b). Also, unless they
were the younger members of adult gangs, the intensity of the street-gang
context in decades prior did not seem as high as it became in the 1950s. The
early 1930s seems to have had the more genuine character of impoverished
youth competing with other barrios in sports, or milling about, creating
mischief (UTEP 1979). See, for example, the typical 1930s delinquency newspaper headline: "Eight Boys Arrested for Stealing Fruit" (*El Paso Herald Post*
1933c) or "5 Boys Jailed for Burglaries," where the boys ranged in age from 6
to 13 (*El Paso Herald Post* 1934b). One story of debatable seriousness involved
a "youthful automobile driver" joyriding around south El Paso, swerving
toward young pedestrians to scare them into jumping out of the way (*El
Paso Herald Post* 1931a).

A member of one of El Paso's old merchant families, Lee Shamaley, was
interviewed about early 1930s era gangs:

> They were tough. They'd jump you and beat you up and take your
> pocket money if you were a kid from outside their territory and
> wandered in there. They'd sneak up to Sunset Heights to steal, and

we'd have royal battles driving them away. But there was no killings
or attempted ones . . . no firearms and knives like they use now.
(Ahlgren 1981)

Consider, however, some of the other gang stories making the news in the
1930s. These call into question this more idyllic, if not romanticized, era of
innocent street-corner play groups. There was a gang of boys either luring
or forcing girls into the desert to be sexually assaulted, victimizing at least 30
teenagers over several years across two age cohorts of boys (*El Paso Herald
Post* 1938b). In another case, during the trial of Bernardo Guzman, then age
20 and accused of murdering a nongang gentleman in an attempted robbery, younger members of his gang engaged in witness intimidation (*El Paso
Herald Post* 1936d). See also the headline "Gang Attacks Man," in which a
juvenile gang used iron chains to attack and rob a passerby in south El Paso,
"the fourth [such occurrence] in a week" (*El Paso Herald Post* 1936e). A topic
that continues to detail the early El Paso gangs' subculture is to tie them to
their LA counterparts in the era of the pachucos.

Los Pachucos: The El Paso–LA Connection

For Chicanos, there is a normative historic migration stream between El Paso
and Los Angeles, for familial and work reasons primarily. Any native resident
of El Paso can attest to this fact. Ornstein (1983) notes that the pachuco subculture originated in El Paso and migrated to Los Angeles where it caught
on and flourished in the early 1940s. One anthropologist working in El Paso
claimed that the pachuco delinquents left El Paso for California, but "they left
many imitators behind" (Braddy 1960). Mario Garcia (1995) also documents
the sustained cross-migration of gang culture and shared networks between
El Paso and Los Angeles, dating back to the 1920s. He discusses how some LA
gangs originated in El Paso, naming Los de la Siete, (7th Street gang), Los de
la Quinta (5th Street), and Los de la Hill (Hill Street) in particular.[13]

Archives in the Institute of Oral History at UTEP contain a wealth of
information on the south El Paso–Los Angeles connection, especially in the
context of pachuco subculture transference between the two places. One
interviewee from the Campbell Street gang in El Paso, who disclosed his
street name as Diablo, talked about jumping a train as a stowaway to California (Califas) with his comrades in the mid-1940s and finding street gangs
in central LA comprised purely of youth from El Paso (UTEP 1978). Another

example of the reciprocal influence between El Paso and LA was the late 1940s El Paso gang called Tortilla Flat, named in an oral history interview (UTEP 1974). This was the name of a popular 1935 novel by John Steinbeck, but, according to some, a gang by that name didn't appear in Compton, California, until the 1960s (United Gangs 2010; Valdemar 2008), suggesting it may have originated in El Paso.[14]

The pachuco subculture that originated in El Paso caught on quickly in California and thus became more commonly associated with the latter than the former. Many of Lurline Coltharp's (1965, 1975) interviewees in south El Paso in the early 1960s and early 1970s, for example, equated the tirilones to California natives. This is a point of confusion for many in the borderland region when discussing these issues. The steady migration of El Paso's pachuco youth to Los Angeles often prompted the LAPD to make inquiries of their El Paso counterparts to identify gangs and solve cases (*El Paso Herald Post* 1943a). However, police seemed to falsely believe there was a gang called the Pachucos spread across the country, when it was actually a stylistic fad among street-oriented Chicano youth of the Southwest. As a result, they were "unable to link" the gang activities of West Coast pachucos to those in El Paso, despite the "remarkable similarity" between them in dress, hairstyles, speech, and weapons (*El Paso Herald Post* 1943b).[15]

The reciprocal influence of El Paso and LA's early barrio gangs is evident, but by the mid-1950s it had spread to other large communities in the Southwest and beyond to other regions. Although not as prominent of a connection, the pachuco influence traveled 550 miles east of El Paso, to San Antonio. A 1955 newspaper article was written about the spread of pachuco-style gangs "from L.A.," where a juvenile bureau officer explained that local barrio gangs are simply imitators of the style of dress, speech, and delinquent attitude, but that he wished they were actually more organized, like LA gangs. (*San Antonio Light* 1955). *Pachuquismo* also tended to be spread by young GIs from the borderland or LA who were stationed elsewhere throughout the United States. By this time, it was understood by LAPD to be a subculture "have[ing] no formal organization, rules, dues, [etc.] . . . The fellow who is the toughest and talks the best is the leader" (Associated Press 1954).

In the modern era, the dominance of the California gang influence on El Paso, on other southwestern cities, and the nation is clear. This book's chapters on the origins of Chicano gangs in Las Cruces and Anthony, New Mexico, for example, show a strong California influence on modern manifestations. Today, we see the widespread emulation of Sureño Trece (SUR-13), southern California's dominant Chicano adult and juvenile prison-street hybrid gang, as the most abundant gang in most large southwestern cities. This is also true of their rivals, the Norteño-14s from northern California, whose reach is not as extensive as that of the Sureños, but is national in scope nonetheless. Tapia (2014) found both of these gangs as far north as Indianapolis in 2009, and they had been there for more than a decade already. This type of gang migration—both real and emulated—is similar to the spread of the LA Bloods and Crips "brand names" in the 1980s and 1990s across the nation (Decker and Van Winkle 1996). The influence of Folk and People Nations were also prominent in the proliferation of gang subculture in this era (Hagedorn 1988).

The 1950s in Detail

As El Paso was said to have a serious juvenile gang problem in the early 1950s (McVicar 1960; Montgomery 1956), there was no shortage of political attention to them. For example, a grand jury was assembled in June 1950 to probe the issue of citywide "Rat Packs" (youth gangs).[16] Testimony from school and police personnel revealed that many of the youth participating in vandalism and other forms of antisocial behavior were poorly supervised privileged kids from "north of the tracks" (*El Paso Herald Post* 1950). This seems counterintuitive, given most of what was known about the causes of youth gang behavior and the historical problems the poor areas had experienced. Perhaps it was a pretext to more aggressively address gang issues in those areas.

In the impoverished south El Paso area, a shooting in August 1951 was attributed to a gang war that had broken out between the 7-X, 2-N, and [Lucky] 13 gangs (*El Paso Herald Post* 1951b). It caused police to sweep south El Paso for any youth bearing marks of gang membership—often a tattoo between the thumb and forefinger (*El Paso Herald Post* 1943a), resulting in 30 youth being picked up for questioning. The city had a curfew at this time, which was not very effective in this case, but assisted in rounding up a very active northeast side gang called the Dukes in the year prior.[17]

Of the 1951 roundup, EPPD Captain Lessor stated, "This is the beginning of the end of gang wars in El Paso." But gang violence continued to rise in El Paso for the next year or two. A juvenile probation officer confirmed that gangs were active in most El Paso high schools, citing 1952 as the height of the gang epidemic, reduced to "almost nil" by 1954 (*El Paso Herald Post* 1956). As in many cities, the prevalence and severity of the youth gang issue

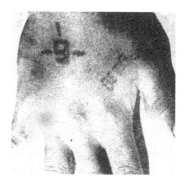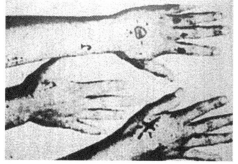

FIGURE 1.4 | 1950s Pachuco tattoos as shown in the newspaper. Credits: (left) *El Paso Herald Post*, August 24, 1951, p. 1; (right) *El Paso Herald Post*, August 27, 1954, p. 1.

in El Paso was debated at length in the media, and misrepresented in many cases, depending on the context. Gang prevalence is notoriously difficult to measure due to the lack of a good definition of *gang* and *gang member*, the constant shifting of gang structure and norms, and the many variations present among youth subcultures.[18] Estimates of the number of gangs, members, and gang-related crimes in a given place tend to vary immensely, depending on the investigators, their purpose and vantage point, and method of assessment.

On January 31, 1956, three separate stories appeared in the newspaper regarding the resurgence of youth-gang activity. Gangs were now operating in high schools, yet there was staunch denial of this by school officials, who displaced the blame and implored police to handle the issue in the community. An assistant principal at Burgess High School referred to the groups as underground organizations after incidents of vandalism were directed at the school and at his home (a Molotov Cocktail was thrown at the latter). He suspected a group called the Gamblers was behind it, but the district superintendent would not concede it was a gang-related incident. This "underground" group was known to wear black jackets with *Gamblers* embroidered in Old English letters on the back (*El Paso Herald Post* 1956).[19]

Las "Cholas": Girls in Gangs

While gang activity is male driven and male centric in most research and media depictions, it is well known that females are an integral part of Latino gang life (Sikes 1997; Valdez 2007). Female participation in gang activity

FIGURE. 1.5 | Molotov cocktail remnants. Credit: *El Paso Herald Post*, 1956, January 31, p. 1.

has no doubt been a constant feature of El Paso's youth gangs but only documented since about 1950. One of the first newspaper depictions of their roles was titled "Girls in Rat Packs Carry Weapons" (Finley 1950). The author used this report as a forum to address a broader spectrum of issues central to female gang studies in subsequent decades. One of El Paso's most disruptive gangs of the era, the Dukes, had a female counterpart called the "Duchesses." Female auxiliaries became common in schools throughout the 1950s (*El Paso Herald Post* 1956) and beyond. The female members of 7-x reportedly served as lookouts on burglaries and other property crimes (Finley 1950). The girls' roles in boy gangs were also to carry and conceal weapons, drugs, and other loot, as male officers were usually not authorized to search them. They also furnished alibis for the boys' whereabouts when they were crime suspects.

Today initiation rituals for females are widely written about in gang literature with some evidence to support that having sex with boys in the gang is often expected or required as one of several options for initiation (Miller 2001; Sikes 1997; Valdez 2007). Even in the early stages of gang development, there were rumors hashed among police officers that this occurred within El Paso's youth gangs. However, Police Chief Wolverton disagreed publicly, stating there were girlfriends and female family members involved in the gangs but sex as initiation was pure rumor. Finley's 1950 report also addresses the timeless gang cultural norm that boys fight over girls. Dating boys from different gangs as a precursor to violence is a staple in the published literature and lay knowledge on female gang involvement.

Gang girls were also found to be violent toward each other. One incident exclusively involving teen gang-girl violence occurred in the summer of 1957, in the lower valley by the newly built Bel Air High School. A 16-year-old member of the Little Darlings girls gang viciously slashed a 15-year-old member of the Baby Dolls, requiring some 130 stitches to close three wounds. The victim's address was given as a south El Paso location (*El Paso Herald Post* 1957a), although these gangs were both said to be from the East Side's Hacienda Heights neighborhood where the incident occurred (*El Paso Herald Post* 1957b).[20] Her attacker was sentenced to the state's juvenile correctional facility for girls in Gainesville, Texas.

Finley's report on gang girls covered broader aspects of the gang landscape in El Paso. He notes there were four large gangs operating in the South Side: 7-X, Lucky 13, OK-9, and Old Ft. Bliss (a.k.a. El Fuerte, near the western outskirts of Juárez). This is one example of the misinformation that often accompanies "knowledge" of gangs and their activities. There were likely far more gangs of a decent size in the South Side at that time. Of these four mentioned, OK-9 was the oldest recognizable name as a longstanding gang, with Old Ft. Bliss as the name given to a military post near Anapra that predates the current location of the Ft. Bliss Army Base in the northeast part of town. If OK-9 was durable, it was also likely that the following list of 1930s and 1940s gangs were also still active in 1950 when Finley wrote his article:

Campbell Street	Ninth Street	Tigres de
Charles Street	OK 7	Oregon Street
the Clovers	San Antonio	Tortilla Flat
Hill Street	Street (La Sana	Wyoming Street
Los Indios de	in 1960s)	
Florence Street	South Mesa	

Cigarettes, marijuana, and Sneaky Pete liquor use was said to be commonplace among the gangs of the day. Crude weapons such as chains, knives, brass knuckles, and homemade zip guns were the most often used instruments in fights. Handball, or *rebóte*, was a popular pastime as there were many of these courts throughout the barrio.[21] Of the relative calm among the youth gang scene at the time, Detective White of EPPD commented, "The toughest teenage gangsters are either in reformatories or in prison" (Finley 1950). Nonetheless, the peace did not last long.

FIGURE 1.6 | Confiscated street gang weapons. Credit: *El Paso Herald Post*, February 25, 1958, p. 1.

Barrio Warfare Expands and Intensifies

When examining the growing intensity of the juvenile street-gangs' activities and assaults throughout the 1950s, most would assume that they were less lethal than today's gangs. However, even though the sophistication of weapons is not what we have today, the violence was becoming comparably serious. Below is a sample of relevant headlines randomly taken from the *El Paso Herald Post* newspaper during the late 1950s into the 1960s, offering details of assaults, murders, and random acts of violence.

"Boy Won't Tell Who Stabbed Him" (South Mesa Street, August 12, 1957)

"Murder Charges Filed: Youth Chases His Enemy, Knifes Him" (June 3, 1959)

"Police Confiscate Shotgun: 2 Refuse to Explain Bullet Injuries" (South EP, January 16, 1960)

"1957 Gang Slaying Feud Sparks Battle; Child 4 Wounded" (South EP, March 28, 1960)

"Boy Stabbed in Gang Fight" (San Elizario, May 16, 1960)

"Two Stabbed in Gang Fight Near El Paso High School"
   (December 21, 1963)
"Gang Beatings Send Two Men to Hospital" (Ysleta, January 19, 1963)
"Five Youths Stabbed in South EP Brawl" (Ice-picks, broken bottles,
   November 18, 1963)
"Police Probe Shooting, Fight Link" (South EP drive-by and stabbings,
   April 5, 1965)
"Shooting Believed Part of Series of Gang Attacks" (Sherman
   Projects, May 24, 1965)
"Youth Stabbed in Gang Brawl" (Near Ysleta High School,
   September 18, 1965)
"Violence Rises in E.P. Teen Gangs" (Large brawl, San Juan Center
   in Central EP, April 19, 1967)
"Gang Attacks Youths in City Park" (Memorial Park, Central EP, June
   13, 1967)
"Teenage Gangs Assault Four" (Random violence, black and Chicano
   youth, October 7, 1967)
"Roaming Gang Fights Break Out" (Northeast EP, January 19, 1969)

These incidents are only a small sample of the several dozen throughout
the period that were reported in the newspaper. In the 1960s gang activity
became more prevalent in the barrio than ever before. Many more gangs than
have been noted so far had formed across the city. With a few exceptions, the
gangs discussed in the section below were the most reputable groups known
to be active in central and south El Paso in the 1960s. This information comes
from interviews of south-central El Paso barrio dwellers who were youth at
that time and from published accounts in books and newspapers.

Figure 1.7 shows a map of 1960s gang turf in south-central El Paso. The
intersection of I-10 and Alameda Avenue (center left) marks the turf of the
Beeboppers, who were documented in Rojas (2007), in Campbell (2009),
and recalled by several interviewees in the current study who were teens
in the 1960s. Members used black jackets that said *Beeboppers* and most
lived on Hammett, Pera, and Latta Streets near Zavala Elementary, and in
Diablo turf (just below them on the map). Also shown are the Red Eagles,
who hung out at El Luga, a popular corner store in that neighborhood.
This corner was a well-known *conexión* (connection) where heroin users
and dealers hung out. Several contemporary versions of the gang were the
Luga Losers and Los Stones de Lugas. The latter is still listed in the EPPD

gang database with 21 members and on the popular social media web page Chucotown Streetlife.

South of these groups were the Paisano Street housing projects near the El Paso Coliseum. They were home to several groups listed in figure 1.7 (the Panthers, Devils or Angels, Nazis, and the Destroyers). The majority of the projects were claimed by Del Diablo Territory (DDT), one of El Paso's oldest and more notorious barrio gangs (further detailed below).[22] Southeast of them were the Valverde Frogs and the (Dolan) Rebels, adjacent groups who claimed turf near Our Lady of the Light Catholic Church.[23] The nearby Sherman Housing Projects, built in the early 1950s, would host a formidable barrio gang soon thereafter. Also shown is Clardy Fox who claimed the general area south of Delta Avenue to the Border Freeway.[24] The Ascarate Copperheads were a nearby group from the Henderson Elementary School area, also listed in Campbell (2009, 86–87). The Psychos were reportedly the parent group to the Trojans, both also from this part of town, with most of these gang members attending Burgess High School.

In the center of figure 1.7, by Jefferson High School, is Barrio La Roca on Alberta Street near Thomason Hospital (Ahlgren 1981; Campbell 2009), and further east on Paisano Boulevard was Barrio Sobaco. This area was also documented in Campbell (2009) as a conexión near the San Juan barrio. The Sobaco area was essentially comprised of a row of about 15 adobe homes. Fred Morales (2017) specifies their turf extended to an old brewery on Chelsea Street, near the Sambrano Addition neighborhood and the San Juan Community Center. Also in that vicinity were the Lucky Lords, considered the San Juan barrio's old gang, later to become Los Sanjuaneros and eventually Varrio San Juan (VSJ).

While their turf is slightly off the map to the left, the Scorpions gang goes back to the 1950s when they had a serious rivalry with X-14 (shown on the left side of the map). Their clashes involved numerous attacks and retaliations, some lethal (*El Paso Herald Post* 1958a). They were also known as the Cypress Street Scorpions, claiming Barrio Park on Finley Street. To the far left of the map is the turf of one of their enemies, Los Fonzies, who were active in Bowie High School.

Finally, the upper-left-hand corner of figure 1.7 marks the beginning of the Five Points area in Central El Paso. Shown are the Scavengers, while off the map to the north are the still reputable Varrio Grand-View (VGV), claiming Grand-View Park. This group is a durable, multigenerational gang with 13 members still listed on the EPPD gang list, who have spread to the

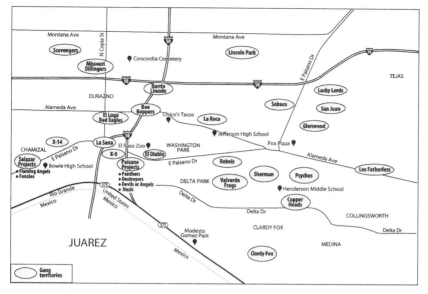

FIGURE 1.7 | South-central El Paso gang turf, 1960s–1970s.
Credit: Isabelle Burke.

east side of town. Five Points has remained a salient gang area over time, with more recently formed groups. The Five Points Kings was formed in the 1980s and still have 21 members in the EPPD database. A 1990s gang called Varrio Chico Trece (VCT) existed around the Memorial Park area. They appear to be a transplant or an extension of the gang Barrio Chico Trece (BCT) from Colonia Anahuac in Juárez (see chapter 4). There is also a Barrio Chico-13 gang from San Clemente, California (Morales 2008), that may have influenced the formation of the El Paso–Juárez sets or vice-versa.

The gangs mapped in figure 1.9 get back to the barrio's epicenter, showing the active groups in Segundo Barrio and Chihuahuita in the 1960s. They included Rio Linda on the southern portion of Park Street and west of the Peyton Meat Packing Plant, a well-known landmark in that area. Close by were the Jokers near another major Segundo Barrio landmark, Bowie High School. North of them were the Saints from El Pujido neighborhood located at Overland and Ladrillo Streets. The (Neuman) Raiders were on Leon Street and Neuman, and the Myrtle Street Muertos were from the adjacent Magof-fin area.[25] Slightly off the map to the north, Los Durangos' turf was roughly the intersection of Overland and Durango Streets. This neighborhood is currently the center of a heated political and legal battle between the City of

El Paso and a group of preservationists seeking to designate the neighborhood's buildings as historic to save them from demolition to make way for a civic arena (Perez 2017).

Toward the center of figure 1.9, the Alamito housing projects on St. Vrain Street had a resident gang, documented in Lopez-Stafford (1996). The Kansas All-Stars claimed the corner of Fifth and Kansas Streets. The Blue Stars hung out in the alley between El Paso and Santa Fe, bordered by Third and Fourth Streets. The Shamrocks, who were named by Campbell (2009) as a Segundo Barrio gang, occupied the corner at Fourth Street and Mesa Avenue (Morales 2017). For details of this gang's history, see Birge (1962). The Alley Cats (documented in Frank Ahlgren's newspaper article in 1981) hung out in the alley behind El Paso and Oregon Streets, run by the Marin brothers. Below them on the map were the Oregon Eagles at the 1000 block of South Oregon. Campbell (2009) notes the apartments there, near a now-defunct flea market, was a conexión.

While this was the Eagles' turf in the 1960s and 1970s, recall that Los Tigres de Oregon Street started out as sandlotters there in the 1930s (UTEP

FIGURE 1.8 | *Los Vatos de la Canal*, ca. 1972. Credit: Photo courtesy of Fred Morales.

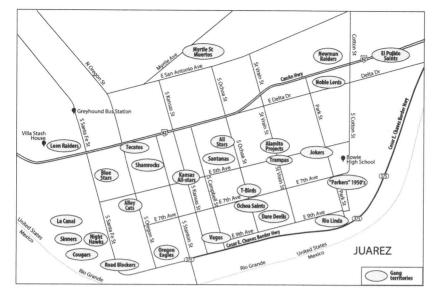

FIGURE. 1.9 | *Segundo Barrio* and *Chihuahuita* Gang Turf, 1960s–1970s.
Credit: Isabelle Burke.

1979). Tapia (2017) documents that Chicano gangs occupying the same turf over successive generations tend to update their gang's name to be more consistent with the times. We also see this with the younger faction of Park Street becoming the Jokers in the 1960s.

Several Chihuahuita gangs (lower-left-hand corner of fig. 1.9) were also listed in Rahm's (1958) inventory of the 1950s South Side gangs, and these exhibited considerable durability. One of these was La Canal from Canal Road, listed in Rahm as the Canal Kids. The street takes its name from the landmark Franklin Canal in south El Paso, which winds for about 30 miles across numerous El Paso neighborhoods to the east of the city. The neighborhood's most well-known gang, the Cougars (a.k.a. La Chihuahuita) came out of the tenements known as Los Presidios on the 900 block of South Chihuahua. There were also the Roadblockers on Santa Fe and Ninth Streets who were named in Rahm's 1950s inventory. Finally, the Parkers from the 1950s were found on the opposite end of Park Street as the Rio Linda bunch (see fig. 1.9).

El Puente Negro (just off the map in fig. 1.9, to the left) was a late 1960s Juárez-based gang that straddled the border crossing in Chihuahuita. They were documented in a 1972 newspaper article as a "glue sniffing gang of alien juveniles, led by 'El Raton'" who commit acts of vandalism and burglaries in south El Paso (Villalobos 1972). They were also noted in a 1993 article about the Chihuahuita neighborhood appearing in UTEP's student newspaper, *The Prospector*.[26] Details of their drug- and human-smuggling operation were also offered in Howard Campbell's (2009) work on El Paso–Juárez as a historical drug corridor. He writes that they competed with the gang from the Chihuahuita Apartments (i.e., the Cougars) over this hustle.[27] Several interviewees noted two crossings, one on South Chihuahua Street and one on South Oregon Street and, therefore, there were two Puente Negro klicks, PN-1, a.k.a. The River Boys (Morales 2017), and PN-2 just west of them.[28] The Puente Negro-1 gang remained salient for many years, as told by Chuy, who is familiar with this crossing and gang life in the area.

> This gang smuggled drugs and people across to the U.S. They have a bad reputation with local gangs because of their dirty plays. They are notorious for robbing their customers and anyone that passed through their turf.

El Paso's Most Notorious Barrio Gangs

Some of the traditional turf-based gangs or barrios depicted in the maps in figures 1.7 and 1.9 reached notoriety in modern El Paso urban folklore. These groups lasted several decades at a minimum, but in some cases multiple generations, and many have remnants still in existence today. One of these is the Thunderbirds, a.k.a. the T-Birds, from Ochoa and Seventh Street in Segundo Barrio (fig. 1.9). They were El Paso's largest gang in the 1970s and 1980s, anchored at the Armijo Recreation Center, where they began in 1965 (Ahlgren 1981). A violent melee between the Corrales brothers of the T-Birds and a group of *tecatos*[29] at the Armijo Center in 1972 resulted in several deaths and critical injuries (*Las Cruces Sun News* 1972; Moore 1976). The T-Birds are still listed in the current EPPD gang database with 14 members, an indication that some of their old members are still active in criminal activity.[30] As large and reputable as the T-Birds were, they became one of several feeder groups to the Barrio Azteca, El Paso–Juárez's primary street-prison hybrid gang since the late 1980s (see chapter 5).

One of the oldest El Paso gangs was once known as X-9 on Hammett Street in El Barrio Del Diablo (see fig. 1.7). This gang, from the southeastern side of the inner city on the US border crossing via the Puente Libre (i.e.,

FIGURE 1.10A AND B | The *Puente Negro* Bridges in *Chihuahuita*.
Credit: Author's photos.

the "Free" Bridge, today known as the Bridge of the Americas), was originally bordered by Boone, Delta, and Paisano Streets. The barrio's influence eventually extended it past Washington Park, bordering on Barrio La Roca. To the south toward Juárez, San Xavier Church was a part of it, extending it even further across Delta Avenue. The barrio's home base was the (now remodeled) Paisano housing projects, and some of its main landmarks were Zavala Elementary, the El Paso County Coliseum, the El Paso Zoo, Washington Park, and the Dudley "Dome" Baseball Field, home of the professional minor league team, the El Paso Diablos, until 1989.

The area gang known to mark its territory as "DDT" for "Del Diablo Territory" goes at least as far back as the 1940s (see Rahm 1958), but it is likely older. The only other gang from the area that is perhaps as old was from the neighborhood behind the water treatment plant and was known as Las Pompas (Morales 2017). A story about the first cohort of Diablo members appears in Rojas (2007) naming Fernando de la Vega as a smuggler who was shot in the leg by the border patrol in 1932 and returned after prison with a signature limp, making him easily recognizable around the barrio. In the late 1950s, the resident gang of El Diablo had epic battles with rivals from the nearby Sherman housing projects, who marked their turf as "DST" for "Del Sherman Territory."[31] About 1967, a group of El Diablo members, including the Astorgas and the Minjares, beat up the vice principal at Jefferson High School, "Mr. Willis," who, in Rojas (2007) and in unpublished, oral history accounts was said to be a bigoted teacher there.

Another proximate rival was Los Fatherless (LFL), which is arguably the single most notorious modern barrio gang to emerge from El Paso. Their original turf area from the Alameda-Paisano intersection near Fox Plaza extended east on Alameda Avenue to Ascarate Park (see fig. 1.7).[32] These three groups, Del Diablo, T-Birds, and Fatherless, are among El Paso's most reputable modern (1970s–1990s) turf-based gangs, and were precursors to the Barrio Azteca prison gang, which, in turn, eventually came to dominate street-level drug sales from the 1990s forward. Los Fatherless is currently listed in the EPPD gang database with 93 members, suggesting that of the classic barrio gangs, they have remained the most durable and relevant.

In inventorying El Paso's quintessential barrio gangs, the history of the old pachuco-style gangs from Chihuahuita, while now obsolete, should not be overlooked.[33] Barrio Lincoln and Varrio San Juan from Central El Paso are also part of the classic set of gangs in the city. Another of the groups arguably belonging to this class of El Paso barrio gangs is White Fence. Although this gang has its roots in East Los Angeles, they have been in El Paso for decades and are formidable rivals of some of the groups listed above.[34] Currently, they have ten members listed in the EPPD gang database. Varrio Glenwood Street (VGS) also belongs to this class of gangs, originally a Central El Paso gang (see fig. 1.7) but now with sets in the East Side and essentially throughout the city. Like the Fatherless, they are a true intergenerational gang with 98 current members. They were first documented in a 1965 newspaper article in the *Herald Post* titled "Valley Thugs Worry Police." In 1996, three died in a shootout on Glenwood Street after a gang party (McArthur 1996). Their most serious rival as of about the year 2000 is a Juárez-based transplant gang called 19th Street.

A final set of reputable gangs began more recently (1970s through 1990s). These groups include Los Midnite Locos (LML), Lopez-Maravilla (LMV), Varrio Grand View (VGV), Varrio Hacienda Heights, Logan Heights, Big Hazard, Alvarez Kings, Varrio Northeast, Florencia-13, Gran Varrio Pachuco (GVP), Calavera/Barraca, Varrio Los Kennedys, Los Ortiz Brothers (LOB), Puro Barrio Salazar (PBS), and Barrio Los Compadres (BLC).

TWO

A Gang History of Las Cruces, New Mexico

Introduction

As a small- to-medium-sized college town with agriculture, the government sector, and a state university as its primary economic drivers, Chicano barrio gangs in Las Cruces (a.k.a. the city of crosses) are a relatively recent phenomenon, compared to other larger cities in the southwestern region. The barrio gang histories of El Paso, Albuquerque, and Tucson, for example, are much older than that of Las Cruces. Still, the poverty rate in Las Cruces is about twice the national average, with 24.4 percent of all persons living in poverty (US Census Bureau 2019a) and perhaps as a result, it developed a criminal gang subculture of considerable intensity.

In most US cities, street-gang violence peaked in the early to mid-1990s. While these issues were well underway by then in Las Cruces, they seem to have peaked slightly later and sustained for a longer period than in most places. For example, whereas gang units in most large cities were initiated in the late 1980s and early 1990s (Kennedy 2009), to include nearby El Paso (Kirk 1993), in Las Cruces, one did not officially form until 2005.[1]

The city's geographic position within the borderland region has made it susceptible to gang influences from nearly all directions. It is three hours south of Albuquerque, a city with longstanding Chicano barrios and a notable history of gang delinquency (Santiago Baca 1986). It is three hours east of Tucson, which has pachuco and cholo subcultures similar to that of El Paso–Juárez in prevalence and intensity (Cummings 2003). This chapter makes evident that Las Cruces's modern gangs have a strong California influence as well. Finally, its most proximate and obvious gang influences come from El Paso–Juárez, less than one hour southeast of the city.

In this chapter, I first profile some of the earliest known groups to emerge in Las Cruces, based on discussions with former gang members, retired law enforcement, and other community members who witnessed these developments. I then build a timeline that runs to current day, as street-gang issues have remained salient in Las Cruces until very recently. Gang colors and affiliations, for example, were still publicly flaunted until about 2010, with media reports of upticks in gang violence as recent as 2011 (KFOX News 2011) and graffiti issues through 2012 (*Las Cruces Sun News* 2012). This chapter offers a broad description of the gang dynamics that took shape in Las Cruces over time. Often it embodies elements that are found in other larger southwestern cities, and at times it shows characteristics that are unique to the small-city context.

Early Delinquency in Las Cruces

A survey of delinquency in New Mexico in 1957 reported that levels were manageable and not a major cause for concern but that it was a growing issue (Rooker 1957). At that time, only Alamogordo, Raton, and Roswell reported gang activity, with the chief juvenile probation officer in Las Cruces, Ken Barnhill, stating that in his district, delinquency was "by no means out of hand." One of the first juvenile gang incidents to be documented in newsprint in Las Cruces was a gang rumble in 1959 that was broken up by police in the Food Mart parking lot on Church Street in the center of town (*Las Cruces Sun News* 1959). The names of several of the youth who were already on probation were printed, and none of them were Hispanic surnames (Bahan, Brown, Perdue, and Waller).

In the 1950s Las Cruces's black and Chicano youth were seemingly as much into sports, dancehall bands, and fast cars as they were into mischief.[2] The Pettes brothers, for example, possessed many mainstream talents in music and sports but were reputable streetwise youth nonetheless. Figure 2.1 shows several of the musical bands the Pettes brothers were members of as teens (top) and two other popular area bands (bottom). There was, however, a reputable delinquent Chicano group from the historic Mesquite District neighborhood in Central Las Cruces in the late 1950s who was part of the social scene and well known to police.

THE MODIES

Retired Las Cruces police officer Joe Bob Sellers (2017) recalls a large delinquent group of Chicanos called the Modies dating back to the late 1950s. They were located in the Central Las Cruces area encompassing north Mesquite, north Tornillo, and Campo Streets, and were led by the Compolla brothers,

FIGURE 2.1A, B, C, AND D |
Late 1950s teen beebop bands in
southern New Mexico.
top to bottom (a) The Alligators,
Las Cruces, 1958; (b) The Saints,
Las Cruces, 1959; (c) The Big
Beats, Mesilla, 1960; (d) The
Royal Tones, Silver City, 1960.
Credit: Photos courtesy of
Eugene Pettes, Las Cruces.

their extended family, and other friends in the neighborhood. Efren Modesto Compolla, age 80, is still referred to by his peers as "Modie." By most accounts, the Modies was a car club whose members engaged in drinking, fighting, and other minor forms of delinquency. Other Las Cruces car clubs from the era were the City Gents, the Eliminators, the Sultans, the Panthers, and later, the Drifters. Some of these groups' favorite hangouts were the Circle on Tornillo Street behind Booker T. Washington Elementary School, Saucedo Hall in Mesilla, and other dancehalls in San Miguel, an adjacent town in the Anthony valley known for its sock hops. For older teens, the Welcome Inn and Guadalajara Bar in Las Cruces were also popular spots with much action.

The origins of the Modies group name remains somewhat a mystery. For some it refers to the now classic cars they worked on (i.e., Moties ~ Motor ~ Moties), a longstanding hobby in Chicano culture. Other interviewees who remember the group assumed the name was a reference to smoking marijuana (i.e., *mota* in Spanish slang ~ Moties), and it was probably meant to be ambiguous. Still others claim that it was named after Modesto Compolla, a leader of the group, hence "Modie." Several core members of this group included Gil Molina, Ysidro Gonzales, Jesse Rodriguez, the Pettes brothers, the Zamora brothers, the Baca brothers, and the Hernandez brothers. These were some of the earliest known streetwise Chicano and black youth in Las Cruces, and most are still living. One of its older members, Angel "Bobby" Hernandez, was found dead in a drainage ditch (*Las Cruces Sun News* 1968) under suspicious circumstances. The now retired police officers who investigated his death noted that he was involved in an altercation at the Welcome Inn bar with known subjects from another old Las Cruces barrio, Chivatown, prior to his body being found, but the case was never solved.

THE DESERT RASCALS

Another of the oldest documented delinquent groups in Las Cruces is the Desert Rascals, who were associated with a boys group home in Central Las Cruces called the Desert Rascals. This group home held both foster youth and delinquent youth sent to live there by the district court. The home for "wayward youth with poor home lives" (Smith 1969, 1) was established in 1963, eventually housing up to 33 boys and regularly feeding about a dozen more in a lunch program. In 1969 it moved from the far west Las Cruces Fairgrounds area off Picacho Avenue to 346 North Mesquite Street in the east-central part of town (*Las Cruces Sun News* 1969c). At that time, it housed 15 boys. The move was brought on by the new director, who felt the boys were stigmatized by being placed "out in the desert" in far west Las Cruces to keep them away from the city. He argued that, instead, they needed to be properly socialized and integrated within the city. Several interviewees, including Pedro and David, recall being afraid to walk by the new centralized location because the boys housed there were prone to jump area youth to rob them of their money or other goods.

THE 45-ERS

The 45-ers was a group of about 15–20 Mexicanos centrally located around Kline Park in the old Mesquite Historical District. This is near the current Weed and Seed program and Eastside Community Center, both used for early interventions with impoverished youth at risk for delinquency. By all accounts, in the late 1970s, the 45-ers were one of the first turf-oriented barrio gangs to emerge in Las Cruces.[3] They were described as a group of cholos and pachucos who were territorial and aggressive. Given they were also described with derogatory terms such as *mojados* or *juareños* (i.e., wetbacks from Juárez) by gang members who came of age in the next generation, it is clear they were from older families who settled in Las Cruces from the lower-working classes of El Paso–Juárez. This exemplifies how the Chicano gang subculture easily migrated to Las Cruces from bigger cities (more on this topic below). The city is only about fifty miles from the El Paso–Juárez border.

It is not known when the 45-ers ceased to exist. One retired police officer says, "not past the early 1980s," but younger interviewees, who were in their teens in the early 1990s, stated they were still around then. One source said they changed their name to Los Home Boys (LHB-13). While the Las Cruces Police Department Gang Unit has Home Boyz listed in their own comprehensive inventory of Las Cruces street gangs, LHB was also a well-known lower valley El Paso gang in the 1980s. Here again, it is uncertain whether there were ties between these groups. It is quite a generic name for a Chicano street gang and, therefore, is possibly coincidental. However, a middle-aged former member of a gang called Natural High noted that one of the 45-er's leaders, Oscar Mares, now deceased, was indeed from El Paso. There are various confirmed gang ties between Las Cruces and El Paso that are documented later in this chapter and throughout the book.

That the first Chicano barrio-style gangs would not emerge in Las Cruces until the 1970s tells us something about the culture of the city. At the time, the population of Las Cruces was approximately 45,000 (US Census 1982). It has traditionally been a college town, anchored by New Mexico State University (NMSU), and therefore is not a typical southwestern city in terms of its demographics. Of the city' population, 57 percent is Hispanic, with 37.5 percent white (US Census Bureau 2019a). NMSU's student population is about 15,000, a large portion of whom are temporary residents from outside the city and tend to be from middle-class families, regardless of race or ethnicity. El Paso, Texas, by contrast, is six times larger, with a much higher proportion of Latinos (80 percent) and where the barrio-gang subculture goes back to the 1920s. Thus, by virtue of its large university and agricultural background, the proportion of middle-class whites in Las Cruces is large compared to other cities in the region.

EAST SIDE LOCOS

The most notorious Chicano barrio gang to emerge in Las Cruces was the East Side Locos (ESL) in the early to mid-1980s. Their predecessors were hard-rock/heavy-metal enthusiasts of the late 1970s referred to as "rockers" or "freaks" by the youth of that era. Some of these Central and East Side groups were Los Vagos, Shades of Brown, the Stone-Freaks, the Dragons, the Royal Chicanos, and Natural High.[4] The Kids was a group of about twenty Latino students at Zia Middle School (West Side) and Las Cruces High School in the late 1970s and 1980s. Their appearance was that of a rocker-cholo hybrid, wearing denim jackets with *The Kids* printed on the back in graffiti-styled lettering (Howie 2017; Meeks 2008).

The Dragons were another known gang from that era with turf on Organ Street in east-central Las Cruces, who fought against both Los Vagos and the Royal Chicanos for turf near Bowman and Tornillo Streets in Central Las Cruces. These groups' younger siblings attended Alameda and Court Elementary Schools, extending their conflicts to those settings. All of these precursors were cliquish groups that engaged in violent confrontations but had not yet developed the character of barrio gangs per se. By comparison, from their inception, the 45-ers appeared to be steeped in the cholo gangster subculture of the era, clearly influenced by El Paso's style, often said to be the birthplace of the pachuco (Obregon-Pagan 2003).[5] The East Siders also eventually adopted the lowrider culture of borderland Chicano gangs that was commonplace in the 1980s.

Since their emergence in the late 1970s to early 1980s, the East Side Locos remained the dominant gang in Las Cruces for the next three decades. Throughout this period, they were the largest gang with the strongest

FIGURE 2.2 | The East Side Locos gang assembled at the funeral of Rudy "Chava" Lucero, the gang's founder, 1996. Credit: Photo courtesy of Nancy (Lucero) Herrera, Las Cruces.

FIGURE 2.3 | The East Side Loks. Credit: Photo courtesy of Las Cruces Police Department Gang Unit.

leadership, making them a household name among police and the general community. Some of their members were from California and brought the intense norms of the California Chicano gangs with them. The East Side operation became the focus of an FBI-led investigation attempting to dismantle it in 1998 (Associated Press 1998). One of the gang's leaders at the time, Mike Montoya, a.k.a. Uncle Mike, was said to be trafficking about two to three kilograms of cocaine per week.

Despite the arrests of Montoya and 17 associates, including his wife Ber-

FIGURE 2.4 | Credit: Photo courtesy of Las Cruces Police Department Gang Unit.

tha, the East Siders did not fade away. The gang has bounced back from major setbacks, including a rash of suicides and murders of several of its core members, one of which was that of its founder, Rudy "Chava" Lucero. Later, Chava's younger brother, William "Chili Dog" Lucero, 36, was murdered by younger gang members in a fistfight that escalated to a shooting (Meeks 2011). Since that time, several large subsets have developed, such as the Dog Pound, Cruces' Most Wanted, and the East Side Loks. ESL is, therefore, a resilient, multigenerational gang that continues to replenish its ranks over time. The Luceros, the Valenzuelas, the Saenz, and the Roman families were some of the founding ("O.G.") families for East Side. Younger known families in the modern era include the Manzanarez, the Garcez, Trujillos, and Calvillos. Many former members have gone to prison and joined the Syndicato de Nuevo Mexico (SNM) prison gang, the Sureño Trece (SUR-13) gang, a street-to-prison hybrid called the Cruces Boys, and the Bandidos biker gang, all currently major players in southern New Mexico's organized crime.

Several Doña Ana County jail officers claim the ESL are sparse now and "keep to themselves." Others claim the younger generations are going strong and still recruiting. While East Siders adopted the color green at some point in the late 1990s, there are at least two large sets of East Side Crips who wear blue and black.[6] There is also a set of East Side Bloods, who presumably wear red. The East Side Loks continue to use the traditional color green. As seen in figure 2.4, modern ESL graffiti sometimes incorporates the number 13, implying a connection to, or an association with SUR-13 nation, perhaps the largest current gang affiliation in Las Cruces today (e.g., see gang officer testimony in *United States v. Archuleta* 2013). However, when SUR-13 first emerged in Las Cruces in the late 1990s, there were violent conflicts between them and the ESL.

According to the LCPD's gang unit, ESL lacks formal structure today, but O.G.s are respected and looked to for guidance while younger members are considered pee-wees. This is consistent with the archetypal Chicano gang structure in the literature (Vigil 1988). LCPD and county and state corrections officers note that many East Siders became Cruces Boys once they were incarcerated (more on this group below).

WEST SIDE

Although they did not have the number of members the East Siders had in the mid-1990s, their rivals, the West Siders, represent a longstanding and formidable Las Cruces gang tradition. Like ESL, there were various subsets comprising a larger group, which by some accounts are still active and recruiting. There have been numerous violent incidents between various subbranches of the East and West Siders over the years. However, it is worth noting that Las Cruces's small size contributes to lots of co-offending and even friendships that formed across gang lines, in some cases due to pregang ties. Today, these friendships form based on past associations, often even among former adversaries. This is rather common to find in the modern age, providing some evidence that "gang banging [as it was once known] is dead" as I suggest in the book's introduction and as addressed further in the closing chapter.

Some of the earlier West Sider O.G. families included the Saucedas, the Madrids, the Norwoods, and Gabe and Charlie Garcia. The Zamarripas is a family with several core members in more recent years. In one early notable incident, after a police chase and a standoff involving his alleged brandishing of a knife, Gabe Garcia, age 20, was shot dead by Officer Terrazas of the LCPD in Apodaca Park in August 1971 (*Las Cruces Sun News* 1971). This set off a series of protests by Chicano activists, claiming excessive force was used against the youth.

A notorious 1990s subset of West Siders was the West Side Nasty Boys. An alleged member of theirs, Jesse Avalos, was one of two codefendants who were convicted of the abduction and murder of an 18-year-old female student at NMSU in 1998 (Associated Press News 2000). El Paso also had a Nasty Boys gang, known as South Side NB-13. Given these two cities' proximity, and the accuracy of their direction per gang names relative to each other (Las Cruces is west of El Paso), these groups were likely affiliated. The El Paso faction was much larger and far more reputable than the Las Cruces set, however (details in chapter 5).

Smaller gangs that developed on the west side of town between the late 1990s and 2010 include Pocos Pero Locos, Los Pelones,[7] and 6th St. Although West Siders typically use blue as their color, there is a large set of West Side Bloods.[8] In this regard, the general vicinities of Las Cruces and their corresponding gang affiliations (e.g., East, West, North, and Central Sides) are actually comprised of a convoluted patchwork of subsets that claim various gang nations and colors. Individual gang histories, their influences from external groups, mainly from California and El Paso–Juárez, and their subsequent politics define these local affiliations. Only those intimately familiar with these nuances and changes therein (insiders and police) can offer a good overview of the landscape at any given time. Gangs are purposely secretive and elusive social groups with structures and affiliations that are prone to change with internal and external street politics. In Las Cruces, some of this is clearly also driven by the rudimentary nature of gangs in a small city.

8 BALL POSSE / PURO OCHO

While it became one of Las Cruces's most reputable drug "crews" (a small, unified group), EBP's formation and rise to notoriety in the early 1990s was reactionary, as told by one of its O.G.s. The two families that are most associated with its early leadership are the Vargas and Morales families. Like many Las Cruces Chicano gangs, EBP was begun by a California-based family member who moved to Las Cruces in the late 1980s. Many large southwestern cities, at one time or another, had a gang called 8 Ball Posse, to include El Paso's northeast and Lower Valley sets and the San Antonio, Texas, set, who gained their fame in a book by Gini Sikes (1997). The gang's origins are thought to be traced to Varrio Norwalk, a large, decades-old barrio gang territory in southeast LA County (Morales 2008).

EBP started as a relatively benign group in Las Cruces, caught up in the gang craze that was sweeping across the United States largely influenced by the California subculture, rap music, and movies like *Colors* (1988). One of the Vargas brothers had a run-in with an African American set of the Bloods (also said to have moved from LA). These Bloods began partying regularly with some girls who lived in 8 Ball crew's territory, Nevada Street in

Chiva Town, and it led to several conflicts. The black gangsters intimidated the younger, less experienced group of local gangsters with drive-bys and armed assaults on individual members, namely along Solano Street near 8 Ball's turf. Pete Vargas, who had military training and who had been recently released from a short prison sentence, then reorganized the EBP, equipping them to go on the offensive against the black gangsters and to compete with the bigger Chicano groups such as the East Siders.

Known from that point on as Puro Ocho (used by most sets of EBP across the United States), the crew earned their fierce reputation by drug dealing, conducting home invasions on other gangs, and attacking rivals in ambush-style assaults. The intensity of the crew diminished over time, but like most Las Cruces-based gangs, 8 Ball is still somewhat regarded as an entity because it was family-based to start. Younger family members continue to have a faint, informal affiliation to EBP, making it an intergenerational group, similar to the archetype in the Chicano gang literature.

DOÑANEROS / DOÑA ANA BOYS / NORTH SIDE DOÑA ANA (NSDA)

One of the older and most durable Chicano gang traditions is set in the northwestern portion of the city, extending into central Doña Ana County. The Doñaneros were originally based out of the "Valley" in the Mayfield High School area, but other landmarks in their turf extend as far east as the Doña Ana boxing gym, Columbia Elementary, and Vista Middle School. Originally, the Doñaneros were not known to use a gang color, but about a decade after the gang emerged in the 1980s, they adopted the color blue. While they were originally a turf-oriented group that by many accounts kept to themselves, they began to resemble a typical modern street gang over time. Some of the well-known families associated with this group are the Madrids, the Clarks, and the Saenz.[9] A well-known crew that emerged from within the larger group in the late 1990s was known as 40 oz.

As the Doñaneros were a large gang, in the early 2000s, there was a split within competing factions of the group, organized on the basis of turf and family ties, which basically broke down to the old school Clarks versus the newer group, the Saenz. The newer faction is known as North Side DA, which is a loaded affiliation. First, *North Side* implies both the north-central part of Doña Ana County, which is less urbanized than the original turf areas of the group. Second, and perhaps more important, *North* refers to an affiliation to the Norteño gang nation, rooted in Bakersfield and other parts of northern California, who exclusively wear the color red. Their natural enemies are

Sureños, who favor the color blue. Apparently, the split that occurred within the Doñaneros was serious enough that one faction completely flipped to claim allegiance to the natural enemy, perhaps in part to declare war against the other. It is also likely that its leadership—the Saenzs in particular—had prior affiliations to Norteños in California, as there are many former California residents among Las Cruces's underclass and working-class populations. Representatives of the sheriff and police departments described that the split led to members of the same family targeting each other in violent encounters within a close area of Doña Ana.

One recent high profile case was the murder of East Sider Sal "Chico" Garcez by Joe Torrez, a local mixed martial arts fighter and member of NSDA. It was a controversial case stemming from a New Year's Eve party, leading to trash talking and ending with the stabbing death of 25-year-old Garcez at Torrez's mobile home in Doña Ana County. Four male and two female members of the East Side Locos (all relatives) drove up to Torrez's home to begin a fight. Due to this fact, Torrez was acquitted of Garcez's murder on a claim of self-defense. The controversy of the case involves the autopsy report, which allegedly shows that Garcez sustained numerous stab wounds from several different blades and a slit throat (Anderson 2014). The implication is that it was a set-up or an ambush orchestrated by the NSDA.

OLDER, LOCALE-BASED GROUPS

Chicano gangs are notoriously turf-based (Moore, Vigil, and Garcia 1983; Montejano 2010; Tapia 2015). Las Cruces's gangs do not exactly adhere to that archetype, a topic that is discussed further below. There are, however, several areas of the city and county where there is a strong sense of pride, loyalty, and nativism among the delinquent Chicano youth who grew up there. In some cases, there are specific barrio gangs associated with these areas, but in most others, it is not apparent.[10] In each case, however, there is certainly a tradition of solidarity among the delinquent youth in those areas that is recognized by other, well-organized gangs that are not necessarily turf based. Some of these areas include Fair Acres to the far west of the city, Butterfield Park (BFP) to the far east, Moongate also to the far east, Los Mesilleros from the incorporated town of Mesilla to the southwest, and Los Mesquiteros from a southern suburb of Las Cruces.[11]

The Modern Chicano Street Gangs

VARRIO KING COBRA (VKC)

The Varrio King Cobras (vkc) in Las Cruces migrated and evolved from an El Paso–Juárez–based gang in the 1950s called the King Cobras (identified in chapter 1 as a Segundo Barrio gang).[12] The version in Las Cruces represents one of the first serious modern gangs to emerge there in the vast gang proliferation years of the late 1980s and 1990s. This was a period in which the street gang phenomenon was sweeping across the nation and became most violent. In a city that mainly adopted an affiliation to the southern-based gang nation, that is, Sureño and Crip-type gangs that used the color blue, the vkc were known as "red-raggers," with an implied affiliation to Norteños and the Bloods.

While the Crips and Bloods are clearly African American gangs, in a small city where the gang craze had just hit, and with teenagers as its main participants, there was initially much confusion about how colors should correspond to affiliations. Complicating the matter is that gansta rap is a big part of the subculture, diluting the ethnic identity of Chicano gangs and supplanting loyalty to the barrio with that of the hood or the set. These traditional elements are hybridized in most Chicano street gangs today, even in large cities like San Antonio (Tapia 2017). While vkc was a Chicano-dominated gang, at least one of its known core members in the late 1990s was of black Mexican mixed heritage, which perhaps contributed to their hybrid ethnic identity—typical of the race-ethnic makeup of Las Cruces gangs.

Of the modern gangs, the vkc was one of the largest, fiercest, and most well-organized groups, heavily influenced by California Norteño families from the Oakland–East Bay area. They were involved in numerous violent conflicts with other groups, namely the ESL set Cruces Most Wanted (CMW), the Mesquiteros who enrolled in Las Cruces High School, and the West Sider set Pocos Pero Locos. As is typical of the high-risk lifestyles of gang youth, some of their members met their fate in drive-by shootings, up-close violent encounters, car accidents, and suicides. While gang turf is seldom clearly demarcated in Las Cruces, there was a critical mass of vkc members in the 1990s and early 2000s in the Young's Park/Lynn Middle School area (east-central Las Cruces), and another on Mesquite Street in the east-center of town. But like most other Las Cruces gangs, they had members spread throughout the city.

The vkc is a traditional Chicano barrio gang in that they are a multigen-

FIGURE 2.5A AND B | Varrio King Cobra members. (a) Several core members of vкc, 1992; (b) a former vкc Leader, Andy "Rhino" Muñoz, in 2011, us Federal Prison, Bastrop, Texas. Credit: Photos courtesy of Andres "Rhino" Muñoz.

erational, hierarchical gang. They serve as the parent group to several red-rag affiliated groups of pee-wees that they either associated with and/or took under their wing in the 1990s. One of these is North Side Pomona-14 (NSP-14), which was initiated by a Las Cruces native who moved to California for long enough to gain familiarity or affiliation with the genuine North Side Pomona gang, a well-known but now defunct group from the San Gabriel Valley (Morales 2008). Consistent with the distortions of affiliations that often occur when youth street subcultures travel to new locations, the literature on Pomona-based gangs states they are SUR-13 affiliated, the natural enemy of their Las Cruces Norte-14 affiliation. This is not surprising, as the group's founders were very young, starting out in Zia Middle School where they recruited from graffiti tagging crews such as Out Causing Kaos (OCK) and party crews like Kings Making Trouble (KMT).

The A-Ks is another red-ragger/Norte/Bloods group that were junior affiliates to the vкc. The crew's ambiguous name cleverly refers to both Alcoholics Krew and the powerful assault rifle that is a prized resource among violent street gangs.[13] The group had a close affiliation to Triple 6, a more violent crew having an implied fascination with Satanism.[14] Although these groups do not appear on the LCPD historical gang inventory, they lasted from the late 1990s to about 2005 and were reputable groups among street-oriented youth. One incident that brought them notoriety occurred when a known

FIGURE 2.6 | Several core members of the A-KS, ca 1998.
Credit: Photo courtesy of Adrian Vigil, Las Cruces (far right).

member of Triple 6, David Trujillo, age 20, escaped from the Doña Ana County jail. He had been booked on separate counts of armed robbery and drive-by shooting (*Amarillo Globe News* 2001).

The Valley Cartel Crew (VCC) is one of the more notorious of the junior allies of the VKC. Of the various groups that started out as offshoots of the VKC, they became the most serious and had the most longevity. One of the ways in which VCC stood out among modern gangs is they had a legitimate claim to turf with distinct boundaries on the west side of town off of Picacho Avenue, bordered by Brown Street, Sixth Street, Second Street, and Melendrez Street (Flores 2017). Unless they have been absorbed by groups like the prison-street hybrid the Cruces Boys, they may still exist today. Some members of the VCC either had preexisting ties or developed ties to an adult prison gang in El Paso and, therefore, by extension, to drug cartel members in Juárez.[15] This represents the maximum type of evolution in criminal sophistication of a street gang that becomes possible by virtue of their geographic placement in the borderland-region's metro complex.

The escalation of a Las Cruces–based street gang up the criminal network hierarchy in the region is thought to be a rarity.[16] It is difficult to know how common this really is, however, or to know what the extent of the ties between street gangs and, ultimately, borderland drug cartels are. Both law enforcement and gang members themselves are known to exaggerate these connections, each for their own reasons. While some members of law enforcement admit to their limitations in gang intelligence, others may glorify the crime fighter role or decide to err on the side of caution and assume such ties exist. Gang members often exaggerate the extent of their criminal sophistication to glorify their lifestyle, its seriousness, and its payoff. By the same token, however, some are wise enough to camouflage their activities and play down those connections. The nature of gang organizations is, therefore, truly a secretive, underworld phenomenon that is shrouded in hearsay and uncertainty. The more apparent ties that exist between certain El Paso groups and Juárez-based drug cartels are detailed in chapter 5.

SOUTH SIDE ROYAL KNIGHTS (SSRN)

The South Side Royal Knights (SSRN) are another of the modern gangs that formed in the vast proliferation years of the gang craze in Las Cruces. While it is tempting to classify their formation and early structure as genuinely homegrown, it is the reference to South Side that suggests it too is marked by the southern California influence. In this sense, it again typifies the founders' unfamiliarity with, or preferential adaptation of the gang toward, the Sureño Nation. For example, the group did not originally use the number 13 in its name, despite its implied affiliation to Sureño Trece (a.k.a. SUR-13).[17] In fact, one sheriff's detective stated SSRN often fought against the Sureños when the latter first emerged in the city in the early 2000s. In keeping with the permeation of SUR-13 subculture, and the widespread self-proclaimed affiliation of locally formed groups to that Nation, SSRN eventually did begin to associate with the number 13.

While they were not as large of a group as VKC, the SSRNs did have a membership count of about 30 to 40 members spread throughout the city. By all accounts, their home turf was around Apodaca Park (northeast Las Cruces), but this area has also been said to be part of ESL, making most turf boundary assessments unreliable. There were a large group of SSRNs living on Moongate Street, for example, which is more than five miles from the centralized area around Apodaca Park. An adjacent area to this disputed turf was that of the Central Side gang, but its boundaries were not well defined. In many cases, within the same family, one sibling may belong to the red VKC gang, another to the blue SSRN gang, while their cousin may be a Central Sider or ESL member.

CENTRAL SIDE

Although not much information came to light in this study about the Central Side gang, they were definitely a known group, likely with ties to El Paso, as there were still three different sets of Central Side in EPPD's list of active gangs in 2018. A former supervision officer from a state agency who wished to remain anonymous recalled some serious issues between Central Siders, East Siders, and SSRNs living in the same neighborhood in the mid-1990s.

> We had several members from all three gangs living off of Solano from Ash Street to Apodaca Park, in the public housing complex and in the mobile homes across from the park. One client's family had to move the living room to a back bedroom as their house had been shot up so often. Other youth stopped attending school for fear of being targeted, so school officials worked with them at home to obtain a GED.

Thus, in terms of networks, turf, and loyalties, the unique characteristics of Chicano gangs in this small city often defy those structural elements seen in the gang literature, or in larger cities. At first, this tends to give the impression that so-called gang life in Las Cruces was more benign than in major cities. These were essentially the findings of a brief ethnographic field study on Las Cruces youth gangs published more than 25 years ago (Mays, Winfree, and Jackson, 1993). However, since then, the gang elements of intergenerational continuity, lethal violence, and dedication to the gang lifestyle have remained intact, creating another interesting case study in gang research on small to mid-size cities (similar to Fleisher's 1997 work on the Freemont Hustlers from Kansas City, for example). While Mays et al. (1993) is the first and only known published fieldwork examination of youth gangs in Las Cruces, it is a limited view, having interviewed only 22 youth referred by schools and gang officers, and with little historical context provided.[18]

THE CADDY BOYZ

The Caddy Boyz were a group of brothers, the Almarazes, who were transplants from Mariana Maravilla, one of the many notorious East LA Maravilla barrios. One source stated they got their name because they favored Cadillac symbols, equipping their vehicles with conversion kits before graduating to genuine Cadillacs and other flashy vehicles afforded from drug profits. The family also had a very recognizable, large dually truck with expensive rims and stereo system that they were known for. While they were on law enforcement's radar for some time, initial raids on their home in the east Mesa were unsuccessful (Chuy #2). The family had several Mexican restaurants in the central city from which they were known to sell dope.[19] A cousin of theirs was killed in Juárez, which led most to assume that the family had a direct link to drug suppliers there.

The group's activities eventually resulted in federal drug charges against several of the brothers. In one high-profile case, two of the brothers, Carlos and Armando, were among 21 defendants charged in a raid at the Welcome Inn bar in Las Cruces (Peerman 1999). At the time, the bar was run by Mike Gonzales Jr. and Sr., who were both law enforcement officers, employed by multiple agencies in the region over the years. Many consider this to have been a set-up by an overzealous prosecutor's office, intent on harming the Gonzaleses due to differences in political party affiliations and other such factors. Similar to Las Cruces's 8 Ball Posse, the Caddy Boyz were not a street gang per se, but more of a family-run drug crew, known to exact vengeance on competitors in the drug trade when needed.

NO JOKE POSSE (NJP)

No Joke Posse (NJP) was a crew of 7 to 10 youth active in Lynn Middle School and Oñate High School from about 1987 to 1991. Their colors were blue and black and their enemies were VKC and ESL. It was a mixed-race (black and Chicano) gang that lasted only a few years until several of its core members were incarcerated in New Mexico's oldest and largest youth prison for boys, Springer Correctional Center in the far northeastern corner of the state. While there, NJP members met other delinquent youth from Las Cruces and formed friendships that transcended their street-gang affiliations. Although the next generation of NJP pee-wees anxiously awaited their chance to "rep" the gang, its founders' new associations and opportunities led them to disband after their release from the boys school. Several of its members graduated to drug and human smuggling and eventually served federal sentences for these crimes. One former member of NJP, Juan Mendoza (pictured in fig. 2.7 as a teen), is now the founder and director of a behavioral health counseling agency in Las Cruces, using his life's experience to redirect clients of the local criminal justice system.

BROWN PRIDE LOCOS (BPL)

Sgt. Rob Gutierrez of the LCPD notes that in 2003 the BPL's territory was in east-central Las Cruces, where they controlled Klein Park, as had the 45-ers

FIGURE 2.7 | Credit: Photo courtesy of Juan Mendoza, Las Cruces.

in a prior generation and the Modies before them. Their turf was bordered by Campo Street to the west, Lohman Avenue to the south, Spruce Avenue to the north, and North Tornillo Street to the east. They exclusively wore the color brown—pants, shirts, and bandanas—and were considered a pee-wee affiliate of the Sureños. They sold drugs to support their own drug habits but "were not a very organized group." They also committed opportunistic burglaries and thefts in their own neighborhood. As told by Sgt. Gutierrez, ESL began to encroach on their turf around 2009, which drove BPL to other areas. Construction of the East Side Community Center created more police presence in the central-east side. Eventually, gang activity in the area diminished altogether.

Sgt. Eric Flores of the sheriff's office also noted that one or more sets of Brown Pride were present in the east Mesa area to the far east of the city following I-70. They were most prominent in the Amber Mesa area off of Holman and Blue Topaz Roads. They were also affiliated with SUR-13. Others have noted that there was a party crew in Las Cruces named Brown Pride. This created some controversy in the street-oriented youth community about which was the "real" Brown Pride group, and it led to conflicts between the gang and the party crew.

Sureño Trece (SUR-13) and Gang Migration

One of the most abundant gang affiliations across the United States today is Sureño Trece (a.k.a SUR-13). With origins in southern California, this is probably the most prolific Latino street gang in the nation. Youth and young adults claiming allegiance to SUR-13 are likely present in all 50 states

(Morales 2008). This does not mean that the groups are all part of the same extensive network; rather it is often a popular gang for Latinos to emulate at the local level.

When a local street gang adopts the name of a Nation such as the Crips, the Bloods, or the SUR-13, the implication is that they are a set of the larger gang. While there may have been a connection to a SUR-13 gang in some locale distant from L.A. by one or more members starting a set in a new place, seldom were they sent to do so. Rather, when the families of gang-involved youth relocate, elements of the gang subculture tend to travel with them in inadvertent transplantation rather than purposeful franchising. The transplanted cultural elements include clothing/colors, language, hand signs, credo, and the rules and regulations of the group. Familiarity with these elements enables individuals to start up a set of the group in the new locale without the knowledge or permission of a parent group in the place of origin.[20]

For the most part, the gang's subcultural elements tend to travel relatively well, that is, they tend to stay mostly intact when they become transplanted to a new locale. This is especially true of the modern era, where the process is assisted by Internet-based information that is available to all youth regardless of social class. In prior eras, cultural elements became distorted as they traveled, as seen with the examples of California-influenced Las Cruces gangs in the 1980s and 1990s. Even today, the quality of the transplantation and emulation are compromised by the need to adapt them to local dynamics. Also, as noted so long ago by Yablonsky (1959), organizational sophistication is often lacking in youth gangs. We, therefore, should not expect for them to emulate parent gangs in the place of origin with great precision.

SUREÑOS IN THE BORDERLANDS

The saliency of gang migration has been debated in the street-gang literature for several decades (e.g., Hagedorn 1988; Maxson 1993). The most authoritative voices on the topic once found little support for its role in the spread of gangs over long distances (Maxson, Woods, and Klein 1996; Waldorf 1993). But others have since found that it *is* a significant cause of such proliferation, particularly in places with newly emerging gang problems (Knox et al. 1996; Moreno 2006; Tapia 2014; Yearwood and Rhyne 2007). Not surprisingly, the story of SUR-13's emergence in Las Cruces and the borderland region embodies this mixed set of findings on gang migration.

According to El Paso Police gang detectives, Sureño-affiliated gangs have been present in El Paso since the late 1980s or early 1990s (Borunda 2014a).

A recurrent theme echoed ad-nauseam by the borderland region's corrections and law enforcement communities is that California's three-strikes law, effected in 1994, was the most significant factor in the proliferation of California gang culture in southern New Mexico and west Texas. There is no credible research to substantiate the claim, but the plausibility of a deterrent "push factor" is clear. It is the most often provided reason for the growth of SUR-13-affiliated gangs in the borderlands region. However, as noted in chapter 1, there is a strong historic migration stream between El Paso and Los Angeles Chicanos for primarily normative (familial, work) reasons. Given that it is about one hour west of El Paso on Interstate 10, the same can be said of Las Cruces, which has numerous familial ties to the west. Many of the barrio gangs in both cities have attached 13 to their gang names for several decades, which coincides with the initial use of this signifier in LA (Valdez and Enriquez 2011; Morales 2008).[21]

SUREÑOS IN LAS CRUCES

Around the year 2000 appears to be when the presence of SUR-13 began to be felt in Las Cruces. Law enforcement interviewees in the current study noted that Sureños clashed with the city's established gangs in those years. LCPD gang detectives refer to SUR-13 as the dominant street-gang in Las Cruces today.[22] One theory is that the failure of the Sinaloa Cartel to dominate the plaza in Juárez–El Paso made Las Cruces the next most viable drug market by default (chapter 5 details the theorized link between SUR-13 and the Sinaloaenses). Eventually, most of the local gangs in Las Cruces became co-opted by SUR-13, as even the largest and formerly most powerful among them (ESL) began affiliating with 13 in its graffiti and tattoos, for example. But this appears to be driven more by the appeal of SUR-13 as a brand name than by force.

To evidence that SUR-13 is more of a brand name in the Chicano gang subculture than a coordinated, interstate network, there is an undercurrent of paternalism shown toward Sureños from southern New Mexico by "genuine" ones from California. It is interesting that it appears that this lack of respect applies less toward Sureños in Albuquerque and El Paso than those in Las Cruces. Perhaps the intensity of gang subculture in the larger cities is seen as more genuine to the "true-blues" and/or there are more of them in these larger cities involved in what are viewed as "real" sets.[23]

The distinction between true-blues and other homegrown sets of Sureños was first brought to light by gang-unit corrections officers in area lockup facilities (El Paso and Dona Ana County Jails and Southern Correctional Facility of New Mexico). When pushed on the issue, some were less convinced that the distinction was real, stating that it may have initially been this way but that those distinctions had faded over time. Others, namely the veteran officers, were clearer about these distinctions, fully aware that many wannabe gang youth native to El Paso and Las Cruces gravitate to the appeal of SUR-13, claiming allegiance to it without having real ties to proven sets of the gang.

COUNTING THE SUREÑOS

The number of active sets and active members of SUR-13 in Las Cruces is somewhat difficult to gauge due to the misinformation and guesswork that is inherent to the business of counting gangs and gang members. In early 2014, there were 342 documented members of SUR-13 in Doña Ana County. According to gang detectives in 2017, LCPD "does not keep a gang database"; however, the county jail classification process accounts for the confirmed members of various gangs that have been held there.[24] This is the number of members that generically claim SUR-13. In addition, there were about 20–25 members spread across several particular California-based Sureño subsets (e.g., Big Hazard, Maravilla, Florencia, etc.). Moreover, there are 48 confirmed members of the SSRN, a homegrown affiliate of the Sureños profiled earlier in this chapter. Finally, there are 38 members of a local gang LCPD has only referred to as "South Side." Information on a street gang with this name has not come to light in the current study, however.[25]

In El Paso, whose gang unit does keep a database, the number of members generically claiming SUR-13 was 685 as of 2018, making it the second largest gang in El Paso. As in Las Cruces, there are also various smaller groups that consider themselves Sureño affiliates. El Paso's is a more accurate count than that of Las Cruces because police gang databases are governed by a rather strict set of federal guidelines, and while not yielding a perfect count, they are a reasonable snapshot of the number of active members. With jail information, however—which is supposedly used to generate estimates in Las Cruces—unless a specific date range is offered, it is most likely a cumulative count of all members that have ever been held there. It does not get purged in the same systematic way as a police database.[26] Since El Paso's population is more than six times larger than that of Las Cruces, it doesn't make sense that Las Cruces has more than half the number of SUR-13 members as El Paso does, unless it was particularly inundated with gang members.

Of the authenticity of Sureños locally, a former gang officer with the Doña Ana County Sheriff's office commented:

> Mostly SUR-13 is not real here . . . at least their ties to La Eme are not real. We wouldn't want for that to happen. The few California guys we do have here are trying to organize them, but not doing too well. Our guys are too lazy, not truly committed to the lifestyle. (Jon)

Similarly, a former gang leader from Las Cruces discussed the intensity of gang activity there.

> In California, gang banging is real; it's a 24–7 thing over there. Over here, you have "weekend warriors" . . . guys sacking groceries or punching a clock throughout the week and gang banging with their homeboys on the weekends. (Serg)

Profiling a group like SUR-13 shows that the intensity of gang activity in Las Cruces is difficult to gauge. On one hand, it is a small city, so the expectations for the sophistication of its gang activity are not great. However, its position in the borderland region quickly complicates that issue. It is near the Texas and Mexico borders and has influences from California, west Texas, Albuquerque, and Juárez, primarily. Not surprisingly, members of the LCPD Gang Unit claim that they could easily justify a larger gang unit.

The Cruces Boys

The recent emergence of the Cruces Boys is among the most interesting developments in the modern gang landscape in Las Cruces. It was initially a main impetus for my research, due to the similarities this development shares with changes in gang structure in the central Texas locales I and others have written about elsewhere (Gundur 2018; Tapia 2017). Various professionals within law enforcement and corrections place the formation of the Cruces Boys between 5 and 15 years ago. This uncertainty is tied to the process of their formation as a gradual one. It comes by virtue of street gangs' general frustration with overbearing prison gangs inside incarceration facilities. The result is the natural, gradual formation of a street-to-prison hybrid that is organized around geography or, more specifically, the inmates' hometown.

Essentially, the Cruces Boys, like their counterparts from Albuquerque, the Burqueños, are "super gangs" that incorporate former street-gang members now incarcerated (Ferrante 2015). They even subsume members of rival gangs in the name of city-based unity to be able to resist the exploitative politics of the traditional prison gangs, Los Carnales and the Syndicato de Nuevo Mexico. Now, rather than fragmented street-gang members competing for the favor of the prison gangs, Chicano gangsters from New Mexico's two largest cities identify in lockup facilities as Cruces Boys in the south and Burqueños to the north-central part of the state.

Driving the formation of these city-based identifiers are intergenerational dynamics. A common theme identified by prison gang observers in New Mexico is that intergenerational conflict has been underway for the past decade among Latino gangs, an issue that possibly dates back to the year 2000. While these developments are slightly more recent than those in Texas, the rationale for their origins and structure are nearly identical. Throughout Texas, these city-based street-prison hybrid gangs are called "Tangos" (Gundur 2018; Tapia 2013; Tapia, Sparks, and Miller 2014; Tapia 2017). The latest one of these groups to formally develop (less than five years ago) is Chuco Tango in El Paso (Martinez 2016), formed to resist west Texas's dominant prison gang, Barrio Azteca (more on this in chapters 5 and 6).

THE CRUCES BOYS' BREAK FROM THE GANG HIERARCHY

Traditionally, leaders and core members of street gangs in New Mexico have climbed the ranks into one of two or three main prison gangs, which functioned as parent organizations to the local gangs like ESL in Las Cruces or Varrio San Jose in Albuquerque. In prison, a young inmate might choose to roll with or represent his hometown while serving out his sentence. This was done for protection, camaraderie, or as a natural extension of his street-gang affiliation. The deeper implication was that the inmate served as part of a reserve army for the prison gang and might be asked to perform illegal acts within the facility to benefit that parent group.

Historically, then, prominent street gang members were not only considered foot soldiers, but the fiercely loyal among them achieved a more distinguished level of recognition that could ultimately result in becoming a recruit of the prison gang. This carried both increased privileges and respect among Latino prison gangs and other inmates generally. It appears, however, that playing the role of foot soldier was not historically a rewarding experience for most inmates. Perhaps in New Mexico, as in Texas, too few of them were afforded the opportunity to become full-fledged recruits despite putting in ample "work" in the penitentiary to become worthy of consideration for membership. In short, the reward structure of the parent group failed to accommodate a large base of prison gang hopefuls over time. The widely heard claim among gang and nongang members alike is that too many young Chicanos were being used and filtered out by the existing hierarchical system, leading to the disillusionment of the next generation of would-be prison gang recruits.

Changing Structures

Whether to avoid the stigma of classification as a Security Threat Group in prison or for ideological or other functional reasons, the Cruces Boys and Burqueños have so far resisted the prison gang label. Members of these loosely affiliated groups claim they are a support network for inmates who want to do their time peacefully and avoid coercion from traditional Latino prison gangs. This reflects a changing mindset among the new generation toward a horizontal versus a hierarchical structure, and a new function for the Tango-type organization in New Mexico's jails and prisons. Some of the most relevant theoretical and policy questions include whether a transition from the defensive posturing of the Cruces Boys to one in which they assume the organizational characteristics of the traditional prison gangs is inevitable (Gundur 2018). Theoretical work on prison gang formation within the California state system offers some of the potential structural if not cultural dynamics driving this phenomenon.

Assuming that gangs in the correctional setting form for protection, as is the claim made by the Cruces Boys and Burqueños, Skarbeck (2012) discusses how a capable defense illustrates the power and ability to go on the offense. Inmates establish order among themselves on a level below that of official facility governance, giving rise to the inmate code and the development of convict norms. Issues such as overcrowding, scarce resources, and cultural or racial differences create the need for subgovernance. However, when a larger proportion of inmates have never served time, the norms associated with the inmate code are less effective where "new inmates misinterpret and disregard signaling mechanisms and disrupt the social system more frequently" (Skarbeck 2012, 23).

When new inmates are unfamiliar with the convict code, they are reprimanded or perhaps bullied by inmate leaders, who, in effect, are also the prison gang leaders (Davidson 1974; Jacobs 1974). The newer class of inmates eventually reaches some tipping point in terms of size or shared negative experiences, then seeks an alternate method of providing governance; hence, a new organization is born in the facility. Using prison data for California, Skarbeck (2012) illustrates that the rise of prison gangs in the 1950s and 1960s corresponded to a dramatic rise in the size of the prison population and a much younger age structure. This suggests that demographic changes made norms less effective and led to more inmate conflict, a thesis that is explored for Texas's Tango subclass elsewhere (see Tapia, Sparks, and Miller 2014).

In the context of this discussion, the elements affecting the collective conscience of the Tango-type groups in Texas and New Mexico have implications for theory regarding the organizational capacity of Chicano gang members. To note that a historically subservient group to the prison gangs, have, in such a short timeframe, evolved a collective mindset of rebellion, rejection of traditional gang norms, reformation, and resistance is additional evidence of the rationality of the Chicano gang population. If, in fact, these hybrid groupings, whose individual members supposedly lacked the wherewithal to become part of the elite group, are capable of this large-scale (statewide) reorganizing, it is noteworthy. It may even speak to the political consciousness of Chicano gang factions, which in this case somewhat resembles a form of Marxism. Given the high mortality rate among members of the elite groups, often murdered by their own organizations, these hybrid developments seem to represent an evolved form of rationality that resists the power-hungry model for which the ultimate goal is gang prestige.

THREE

Anthony, New Mexico
Influences and Network Linkages from All Directions

Introduction

The population of Anthony, New Mexico, is about 10,000 (City Data 2019a). It encompasses only four square miles and was an unincorporated town in southern Doña Ana County until 2010. It is 97.4 percent Latino, with a young age structure and large households, having more than one-third of its residents under age 18. By US standards, it is an extremely poor place with 40.2 percent of its residents living below the official poverty level. It is also unique in that a very high percentage of its residents (39 percent) were born in Mexico. Since becoming an incorporated city, it has generated enough of a tax base and other revenue to start a municipal police department, currently with 10 officers, which seems to have improved social control and public safety.

The town straddles the Texas–New Mexico border and is the larger portion of the city split by the state boundary. Anthony, Texas, has about 5,500 residents (City Data 2019b), and although it is a physical extension of Anthony, New Mexico, the Texas side is often considered to be different in terms of its crime and gang history.[1] Anthony is the midway point between Las Cruces and El Paso, situated about 20 miles from each. It therefore has network linkages to both places and is influenced by the cultural elements of each. Historically, its gang subculture and that of its neighboring communities are also largely influenced by the colonias west of Cd. Juárez, Chihuahua.

As I have done for the larger metro areas of El Paso and Las Cruces, I trace the history of gang activity in Anthony and its general vicinity in this chapter. Some of the most surprising findings in the broader study come from Anthony and its outlying areas, mainly because they are largely rural farming communities in the valley of a mountainous desert region. While the town of Anthony itself is quite small, a number of even smaller places with fairly well-defined boundaries surrounds it. The entire area comprises the southernmost portion of Doña Ana County, with Las Cruces to the north in the county's center (see fig. 3.3).

Early Delinquent Groups in the Anthony Area

Despite its small size, Anthony has seen quite a bit of gang activity, going back to the 1960s and escalating into its plateau in about 2010 (Day 2017). Its barrio gang origins appear to stem from Cd. Juárez, with the earliest known organized group, Los Papas, emerging as immigrants from the extremely impoverished colonias of Rancho Anapra, Colonia AltaVista, Buena Vista, and Bella Vista on the western outskirts of Cd. Juárez located about 10 miles from Anthony. One of their rivals were the Corner Pockets, one of the first homegrown gangs from Anthony per se. Other rivals of Los Papas were the Low Boys car club/clika, the group known today as Barrio Canuto Rifa of Canutillo, Texas, just across the state line, and the far west El Paso group, Barrio Sandoval of the Machuca Housing Projects. Future generations of Anthony-based gangs were more assimilated to US Chicano gang culture and came to be known as the Anthony Town Locos (ATL), the Dukes, and the Teners. Church festivals known as *kermézes* held at St. Anthony's and various other Catholic parishes in nearby communities were staging locations for area gangs, where fights often broke out.

The popular 1970s-era Doña Ana County sheriff Eddie DiMateo was frequently quoted in local newspapers discussing the problem spots between Anthony and Anapra and the adjacent riverside areas (Tessneer 1973). He noted that only a few deputies were on duty at a given time to patrol the communities of Vado, Chamberino, Anthony, La Union, and La Mesa, all of which were known to have delinquent territorial groups. He attributed some of the delinquency issues to clashes at Gadsden High School, which served the entire southern portion of the county. This was disputed by school officials who stated problems stemmed from dancehall parties in the community, attended by area-wide youth (several of these late 1960s melees are noted below). Gadsden High School has, however, historically had major issues with gangs, drugs, and delinquency, documented in newsprint (e.g., *Las Cruces Sun News* 1977), and commonly heard in firsthand accounts around the region.

THE TENERS

During the modern age of gang activity (late 1990s–2000s), some of the next several generations of area gang youth transformed into the Teners xv, a Norteño-affiliated group. In Juárez, the group was known as Los Tenebrosos, but in Anthony, they morphed into North Side Locos, Norte Side Rifa, and most recently as New Mexico Teners (NMT). As Norteños, they used the customary colors red and white. Many assume that the *Ten* in *Teners* refers to Nor*teño*, while others argue it more likely signifies *J* as the tenth letter of the alphabet (for their Juárez roots). Another quirk of this group is their adoption of 15 versus the 14 that Norteños on the US side traditionally use. This is also somehow attributed to their roots in Juárez, and possibly to the *ñ* as the fifteenth letter of the Spanish alphabet, but the exact origin of the 15 did not come to light in this study.[2] They are currently the dominant gang in Anthony and their main rival is Varrio Anthony Locos-13, who also descended from a particular branch of Los Papas.

VARRIO ANTHONY LOCOS (VAL-13)

Like their enemies, the VALs are also derived from Anthony's earliest gangs. However, in about 2003, VAL became affiliated with the Sureño nation and transformed into Treces (i.e., 13s). Since then, they have also been known as the South Side Locos, Anthony New Mexico x3 (ANM x3), or simply as SUR-13. Similar to processes occurring in nearby Las Cruces, the gang's affiliation to the Sureños was driven by several factors. First, urban lore in this area dictates there had to be a real link to one or more California-based Sureño sets in order for the group to establish a local set. Also, and perhaps as important, the decision to become Sureños was likely in response to the emergence of the Teners as Norteños.[3]

Reputed gang members Claudio Castañeda, Joseph Lucero, and Lorenzo Larrea helped to transform the VALs from a local, homegrown group to a legitimate set of the Sureño nation. As a result, the gang's status was elevated, but it was short-lived. Castañeda caused the vehicular deaths of several people in 2004 and fled to Mexico to avoid prosecution. He then returned to Anthony in 2005, and after a confrontation with rivals at a children's birthday party, he and Lucero drove by and shot up the party, injuring several children and adults. Castañeda was captured and convicted of both crimes (*Albuquerque Journal* 2008), disrupting the momentum that VAL-13 had gained. Their enemies, the Teners xv, quickly became the dominant gang in Anthony, but they have been met with resistance from the 13s ever since.

WEST SIDE DUKES-13 (WSD-13)

The West Side Dukes are said to have originated in Sunland Park, New Mexico, just across the border from Anapra (see fig. 3.3). They eventually migrated to the low-income subdivision Tierra Del Sol in Anthony, now referred to as "Duketown" (shown in the center of fig. 3.4). Initially, they were met with resistance from the resident gang, TDS-13, but they reportedly co-opted them or at least coexisted after some time. The Dukes were once considered to be among the fiercest gangs in town but were eventually overshadowed by the dominance of the Teners. Like the Valley Cartel Crew in Las Cruces, the Dukes were one of the few borderland street gangs with reputed ties to a drug cartel in Juárez. In fact, the gang's roots in Sunland Park suggests they migrated there from Juárez's westernmost colonia, Anapra. However, when it crossed the border, the name switched to English, going from Los Duques, an old Juárez gang (*Proceso* 2006) to the Dukes.[4] One of its core members, Jesus Flores, who helped to form the Anthony set in the 1990s, was arrested in May 2017 in a multiagency effort targeting about 30 drug trafficking subjects throughout the borderland region (Lopez 2017).

Proximate Locations in the Anthony Area

Anthony is surrounded by many smaller towns and rural communities that developed gangs of their own over time. In focus group discussions with elders from these areas, I discovered that these seemingly quiet areas once had a spirited weekend nightlife and a history of gang activity. For example, the small community of San Miguel regularly saw fights and other disturbances tied to the bars, clubs, and dancehalls in town. An incident between local gangs and "a gang from El Paso" in the summer of 1969 was large enough to make the sheriff request that the Riverside Dance Hall be shut down for repeated violence and disruptions. This incident reportedly involved 25–30 people brawling, using bricks and rocks as weapons, and firing a gun at police after an event at the popular *salón* (*Las Cruces Sun News* 1969b).

Elders mentioned several other places that were prone to rowdy incidents or violence throughout the valley (i.e., the smaller rural areas). These

FIGURE 3.1 | Riverside Dance
Hall. Credit: Author's photo.

included the Malibu Club in Vado, the Montezuma Club in Mesquite, and the Country Tavern and La Copita, both in San Miguel near Anthony. In the 1950s and 1960s, Anapra, New Mexico (later renamed Sunland Park, New Mexico), hosted the Sunland Night Club, which attracted young crowds from both sides of the US–Mexico border. In this particular area, the international boundary was practically nonexistent, and it remained so until about the late 1990s when a chain link fence separating Anapra, Juárez, from Sunland Park, New Mexico, went up. It was followed by a 15-foot steel fence erected as part of the 2006 Secure Fence Act (Flores 2017).

Figure 3.3 shows Mesquite to the far northwest of Anthony along I-10. Among the small towns in the region, it has one of the oldest gang traditions. Since at least the 1960s, its area youth, and especially its delinquent groups, were known as Mesquiteros. By the mid-1990s the area's gang was known as Varrio Mesquite Locos (VML 13). This group was particularly active in the late 1990s, and its influence extended to the neighboring communities of San Miguel and La Mesa (farming communities not pictured in fig. 3.3).

Also shown in figure 3.3 is Berino, neighboring Anthony to the north-

FIGURE 3.2 | The border fence at Anapra and Sunland Park. *Top* (a) The original chain-link fence stretching across the terrain; *bottom left* (b) the author standing by the 15-ft. steel beam replacement fence; *right middle and bottom* (c) and (d) the homes in Anapra, Juarez, seen by peering through the border fence, both old and new, respectively. Credit: (a) Photo courtesy of Molly Molloy; (b, c, and d) Author's photos.

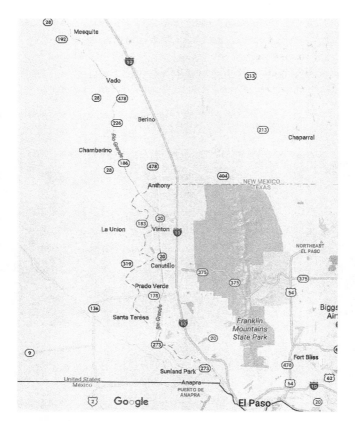

FIGURE 3.3 Map of the Anthony region and surrounding areas.
Credit: Map data © 2018 Google.

west. The gang from this area came to be known as Varrio Berino Heights (VBH-13).[5] It has never had more than 20 members and mainly competed with Varrio Anthony Locos-13 for turf and reputation. According to several former gang members from the area, VBH was not authorized to claim itself as a set of Sureño-13, and it was therefore said to be in violation of rules set by California-based Sureños (see chapter 2 for details on True Blue Sureños). This issue created conflict with VAL-13, who supposedly were sanctioned as a genuine set and perhaps saw themselves as enforcers of the legitimacy of the claim to SUR-13.

SUREÑO SUBCULTURE IN THE ANTHONY AREA

Of the 18 modern gangs known to have formed in the vicinity of Anthony and its outlying areas in recent decades, over a dozen of them are Sureño-type gangs. That is, they place 13 behind their barrio's name, use the southern affiliation, and use blue or grey as their gang colors, all of which in combination are unmistakably Sureño related. In some cases, these are real Sureño sets while others are not so convincing. This variation in authenticity or intensity applies to sets across the southwest and to ones that have appeared in distant places like Indianapolis and other US regions (Tapia 2014). Essentially, the further from California, and the smaller and less organized the gang, the less likely it is to be recognized as a true set with membership ties to California. Rather, it is often a popular gang for young, street-oriented Latinos to emulate at the local level (supposedly as with VBH-13).

Gangs in the borderland region have used the number 13 for decades. Where it is done to exaggerate the gang's sophistication and dangerousness, it is usually a cognizant reference to California Sureños and, by extension, to the Mexican Mafia prison gang (a.k.a. la eMe). But some of its ubiquity is attributed to delinquent youths' ignorance of these affiliations. Many only knew that 13 represents *M* as the thirteenth letter of the English alphabet, a reference to *Mexican*, or in gang terms, *Mexican pride*. Furthermore, as the Barrio Azteca (BA) prison gang based in El Paso–Juárez began to dominate organized crime in the region (see chapter 5), they became enemies with the California-based eMe. When the BA were weakened with police stings, sweeps, injunctions, and RICO prosecutions from 2005 to 2010, the popularity of claiming 13 resumed in the streets.

Sureño-affiliated gangs have been present in El Paso since the late 1980s (Borunda 2014a), appearing in Las Cruces by about the year 2000. This is not surprising, given the normative, historic migration stream between Los Angeles and borderland Chicanos (Burciaga 1992; Lopez-Stafford 1996; Torres 2010). In terms of barrio-gang connections between the two regions, there is a sustained cross-migration of gang culture and shared networks between them since the 1940s (Braddy 1960; Coltharp 1965; Garcia 1995; Ornstein 1983).[6] An often-cited reason for the growth of SUR-13-affiliated gangs in the borderlands region is California's three-strikes law (Borunda 2014a), which mandates a life sentence with no parole on a third felony conviction. The suggestion is that criminals facing this peril migrated eastward to avoid it. However, as the law was effected in 1994 and may have exacerbated cross-state gang connections or transplantations since then, as depicted in chapter 1, these had been occurring for decades before the law went into effect.

The 2017 Texas Gang Threat Assessment report called SUR-13 one of the most significant gangs in the El Paso region. It is also the largest street-gang affiliation in Las Cruces (e.g., see LCPD gang officer testimony in *United*

States v. Archuleta 2013). Clearly, in the Anthony area communities located between El Paso and Las Cruces, the sur-13 influence still dominates. Aside from those profiled above, there is Vado 13, West Side 13 from Chaparral, the Chambe Town Locos from Chamberino (all shown in fig. 3.3), and Varrio Meadow Trece (vmt-13) in Sunland Park and Santa Teresa (bottom of fig. 3.3). The Meadow portion of their name, while linked to their neighborhood of Meadow Vista, is often mistaken for its phonetic equivalent *Mero*. It is a slang term in Spanish meaning *bigshot*, in this case suggesting they are real 13s, or they are the real deal in terms of gang intensity.[7]

The West Side Los Pelones (wslp-13) either originated in Anthony or Las Cruces, as there have been sets noted in both places. In Anthony, they are one of several groups that boast real ties to California. Anthony also has a set of Barrio la diez y ocho (a local version of California's 18th Street gang). This gang is also present in El Paso and Las Cruces and also in enough places throughout the United States that they are effectively a gang nation.

In Canutillo, Texas, Barrio Canuto Rifa (bcr 13) is still a well-established gang with 26 current members in El Paso pd's Gang Unit database. Los Borlas (a.k.a. Borla Boys) from Borderland Road are a longtime rival of Canuto. Another well-known gang, Barrio Los Compadres (blc 13) are from West Way, Texas, near Canutillo. Finally, Del Otero Side (dos-13), a.k.a. Chapa Town Locos, a.k.a. East Side 13 are from Chaparral, New Mexico, situated along the Anthony Gap (Highway 404) in isolation opposite I–10 from the Anthony area communities (see fig. 3.3). The gang name reflects that they are from the Otero County side of the town of Chaparral, which, at 20,000 people and growing, has now spread across the Doña Ana County line into Otero County, New Mexico.

It is worth noting that the common affiliation to 13 in no way unifies these groups. In fact, many of them were each other's enemies at one time or another. This suggests local emulation of the Sureño brand name versus orchestrated networking by a sophisticated parent group based in California. The few non-13 affiliated gangs in the Anthony area are Del Bosque Town Locos (dbl) in the neighborhood of Del Bosque, Las Palmeras (lp), a small group in Berino who, by one account, is engaged in minor forms of delinquency, and by another, is a serious subset of the Teners. Finally, there were the Crazy Mother Fuckers (cmf) from the small community of Del Cerro near Vado, the Monte Vista gang from Chaparral, and a small, now defunct group called the South West Gambinos from Mesquite who were allied with the val-13.

FIGURE 3.4 | Varrio Meadow Trece Gang Members.
Top (a) Meadow Trece O.G.s, 1990s; *bottom* (b) recent
members "throwing" VMT. Credit: Photos courtesy of
J. Franco, Sunland Park Police Department.

Gang Violence in the Borderland Region

One of the purposes of this research is to assess the scope and intensity
of the gang subculture in the borderland region by examining its various
geographic components in turn. It may appear that smaller communities
are more benign in this regard, but the seemingly unsophisticated structure
of the groups does not detract from gang violence. In fact, it may even con-
tribute to it. Vargas (2014), for example, found that when drug markets are

well organized and regulated into turf areas and other agreed-upon arrangements, it tends to minimize the violence associated with street gangs. Chapter 2 shows that in Las Cruces, for example, gang turf has never been very well defined, which leaves room for disputed areas and appears to elevate gang violence.

While it is less certain how clearly defined gang boundaries are in the smaller outlying communities profiled above, in Anthony, gang turf areas tend to be well defined (see fig. 3.5). Nonetheless, a former gang youth from Anthony commented that "whatever gang could be seen controlling the Park [in the town's center], it was a good indicator of who was the dominant gang at the time" (El Chuy). Durán and Posadas (2015) write about a police substation that was established in central Anthony to combat gang violence in a portion of town the police referred to as "the box." Newspaper archives suggest gang fighting and drag racing were common occurrences in "the box" dating back to the 1960s (*Las Cruces Sun News* 1969c). The final portion of this chapter shows that Anthony did experience serious episodes of violence, much of it based on archetypal Chicano gang rivalry elements such as turf battles involving graffiti and quid pro quo retaliatory violence.

In El Paso, which is the dominant city in the region and thus the driver of local trends, the topics of gangs and crime levels present a profound paradox. On one hand, it is known as the birthplace of the pachuco and most things Chicano-gang related. But this appears to be a cultural marker and not one that translates into high levels of violence. This paradox has been glaring for quite some time, where, for decades, El Paso has been referred to as one of the safest large cities in America, based on its official crime rate as reported by the FBI. The paradox persists to date; in August 2017, within the span of a few days, news outlets reported both that El Paso's gang activity was up over 2016 levels (Gonzales 2017) and that El Paso was named the second safest city in America by the website SafeWise (*El Paso Herald Post* 2017).

While the gang subculture and lifestyle on the US side of the borderland region (i.e., Anthony, El Paso, Las Cruces, and Sunland Park) is profound, it does not have high gang violence rates compared to other major southwestern cities. This was apparent even during the popular lowrider cholo era of gang formations, when, in 1983, of the 38 homicides in El Paso, only two were known to be gang related (Olvera 1984b). When we compare places with large Latino populations known to have gang violence problems, the borderland region comprising El Paso, Anthony, and Las Cruces has among the lowest. Its levels of gang violence do not come near that of places like

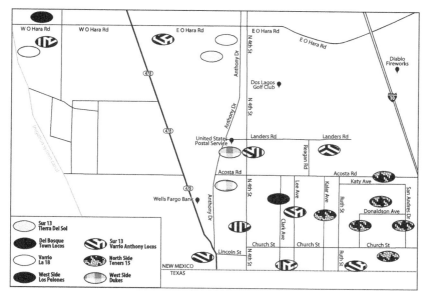

FIGURE 3.5 | Gang turf in Anthony, New Mexico, late 1990s–2010.
Credit: Graphic courtesy of J. D. Medrano, Anthony.

Albuquerque, Fresno, Houston, Las Vegas, San Antonio, and San Francisco–Oakland for example (see table 3.1). In fact, gang violence on the US side of the border region has never been very high.

Gang data is difficult to generate and hard for researchers to obtain. If police departments collect them at all, it is not a requirement to register them in FBI Uniform Crime Report data, for example. Therefore, it is at a department's discretion whether or not to collect it and when it is collected, it is usually well protected from the public or carefully (and often strategically) put out in press releases. Researchers must have good professional contacts or submit freedom of information requests to obtain crude or (where it exists) detailed gang data. Chapter 5 contains detailed gang data for El Paso, but for now, the violent crime rate is a reasonable proxy for a given city's level of gang violence (National Gang Center 2013). Although it is often conflated with "normative" or mundane (i.e., nongang) violent episodes, a considerable amount of violence in a given place tends to be gang related.[8]

Table 3.1 contains the violent crime rates per 100,000 population of various US cities in 2013. I chose a sample of cities with a high proportion of Latinos, and cities that are known to have Latino gang issues (in certain places, these overlap). I also include cities that are near the El Paso–Juárez

Borderland region and some in the Rio Grande Valley Borderland region of south Texas, also known for its drug cartel and Latino gang activity (Correa-Cabrera 2013). Finally, I include some cities with generally high violent crime and gang violence rates for comparison. These tend to have high proportions of black populations, or as with Boston, Houston, Dallas, and Miami, are high in both black and Latino populations.

Note that El Paso and Las Cruces are among the cities with the lowest levels of violent crime. Only Brownsville, Texas, and McAllen, Texas—both south Texas border cities—are significantly lower, with Dallas, Denver, and Riverside, California, at about the same levels as the borderland cities. All other cities have a higher, and in some cases, much higher level of violent crime than these borderland cities. Anthony's violent crime rate, while not very reliable given its small size, was 608 in 2013, but had dropped to 417 by 2014 (City Data 2019a). This is still higher than that of El Paso and Las Cruces, but the trend is normalizing into their combined range of about 340.

Gang Incidents

For the public and the press, the intensity of a local gang phenomenon is often gauged by some of its violent, memorable incidents, regardless of actual crime rates. This is especially true in a small community like Anthony where word travels fast and concerns about "gang problems" quickly set in. Robert Duran, an assistant professor at New Mexico State University in Las Cruces from 2006 to 2014, had his students venture out into the community to research gang issues for a class term project. Many students went back to their home communities of Anthony and Gadsden High School for information. One event some study group members found troubling was a widely attended town hall meeting in 2007 held by police and city leaders on the issue of gangs. The presenters "stereotyped youth of Mexican descent and blamed their parents for gang behavior and poor performance in school" (Southern New Mexico-Texas Gang Update 2008, 1). The meeting was held in response to a rash of gang-related deaths, the most recent at that time being the shooting death of 14-year-old Alberto "Betillo" Soto (Medina 2007), by a member of Barrio la diez y ocho (18th Street).

Just a few months prior, Gerardo Baltazar, age 17, of Barrio Canuto Rifa (BCR) was shot by Chito "Poyo" Longoria, age 20, of the Teners, allegedly over some crossed out tagging (*Albuquerque Journal* 2008). Longoria then spent the next few months on the run, hiding out in Juárez and other places

TABLE 3.1 | Violent crime rates per 100,000 population*
of various US cities in 2013

Albuquerque	742	Detroit	780	Miami	655
ANTHONY, NM	NA	EL PASO	347	NY/Jersey	456
Bakersfield	576	Fresno	510	Odessa	806
Baltimore	633	Houston	559	Philadelphia	937
Boston	503	Kansas City	468	Riverside, CA	333
Brownsville	240	Laredo	431	Sacramento	415
Corpus Christi	523	LAS CRUCES	333	San Antonio	460
Dallas	333	Las Vegas	678	San Diego	348
Farmington, NM	490	Los Angeles	375	San Fran–Oakland	570
Fort Worth	362	Lubbock	658	Tucson	433
Denver	328	McAllen, TX	283	Tulsa	516

* Rounded to nearest whole number.

USDoJ, FBI, CJ Info Service Div, "Crime in the US 2013" by MSA 2013. https://ucr.fbi.gov
/crime-in-the.u.s./2013/crime-in-the.u.s.-2013/tables/6tabledatadecpdf/table-6

in the region. According to officers with Doña Ana County, emboldened by
the shooting of Baltazar, he continued on a violent spree on both sides of
the border and was wanted by authorities in Juárez, too. He was suspected of
returning to Anthony where he carried out a series of drive-bys against the
VALS, earning himself and the gang a larger reputation for violence. At that
time, the VALS and Teners were at war, exchanging dozens of back and forth
drive-by shootings between them (Day 2017).

In February 2009, three Castillo siblings and two Orozco brothers (all
members of West Side Los Pelones) conducted a retaliatory drive-by shooting against a rival from the Teners in central Anthony. The younger Orozco
brother, Javier, 15, was one of three gang youth who victimized a traveler at
the highway rest stop in Anthony on I–10 several months later. His codefendants were Irvin "Shadow" Ramirez, age 16, of the Teners, and Jorge "Phat-
boy" Murillo, age 18, of Meadow Trece. They picked a victim at random, who
turned out to be a 20-year-old student from San Antonio traveling to California alone, and who had pulled into the rest stop to sleep. They accosted
him, shot him, took his car, stuffed him in the trunk of his own vehicle, and
burned it in a remote area nearby. Updates on the senseless rest stop murder made headlines for weeks with courtroom trials and prison sentencing
details continuing to run in the newspaper up to several years later.

Conclusion

By all accounts, gang activity in Anthony has diminished significantly since about 2010. But it is by no means dead, nor has related drug trafficking activity slowed in recent years. In fact, the areas described in this chapter are perhaps some of the most active areas of clandestine activity in the region, similar to the valley areas to the far east of El Paso–Juárez, a known stronghold of the Sinaloa Cartel (detailed further in chapter 4). As outlying, semirural areas with a high proportion of poor people with direct family and friendship networks to Juárez and Chihuahua, the outskirts of the Anthony area are a hotbed of drug and human smuggling activity. From 2007 to 2019, Doña Ana County accepted Department of Homeland Security funds to combat "border-related crimes." These funds are used to focus on the Sunland Park and Santa Teresa areas near Anapra (Soular 2017).[9]

The rural colonia quality of much of the area, with unpaved dirt roads, poor lighting, and shanty homes, often built with nonconstruction material, resembles those found in the colonias on the western outskirts of Juárez. It therefore serves as a good hideout location for many individuals wanted by law enforcement on either side of the border. The geographic position of Anthony, Chaparral, and Sunland Park between Las Cruces and El Paso, with its proximity to Anapra and other impoverished colonias to the far west of Juárez, makes these remote communities poorly policed areas ideal for the smuggling activity that has been characteristic of the borderland region for the past century.

The area's gang influences from and network links to these communities make it one of the most interesting places to study borderland gang activity. Upon occasion, the illegal activities of those operating in the area are apprehended by law enforcement and publicized in the media.[10] For example, in December 2016, three known gang members from Anthony, ages 19 and 20, were busted by the EPPD gang unit in El Paso for possession of drugs and firearms (*El Paso Times* 2016). In June 2017, a Juárez state police officer named Jose Rios Flores, age 33, was arrested in Vado, New Mexico, with 130 pounds of marijuana (KVIA 2017). A large operation headed by the DEA in April 2017 either charged or arrested some 30 drug dealers across the borderland region with alleged ties to the Sinaloa Cartel. While some of those named were in Las Cruces, El Paso, and Juárez, the largest proportion of individuals were from Anthony, Chaparral, or the smaller areas named in this chapter (Lopez 2017).

FOUR

Ciudad Juárez
The Epicenter Then and Now

Introduction

Previous chapters have detailed historical gang processes in far west Texas and southern New Mexico. One cannot, however, attempt to assess the gang landscape in the region without accounting for that of Ciudad Juárez and its influence on these communities. It has a symbiotic relationship in many respects with the US side of this border plex, and the gang histories on both sides of the border are profoundly connected in form and function. In fact, the extent to which this study shows that geography is important to the type of Chicano gang structure and culture that forms in the United States is largely a function of the Juárez influence. While some of these dynamics are also present in other places along the border with Mexico, no other pair of border cities comes close to the scope of cultural and practical exchange that exists between El Paso and Juárez. Although it is similar today, not even Tijuana–San Diego has the same level of proximity and historical connectedness, or the same compelling history of bandido and drug gang subcultures at the root of its modern Chicano gang developments.

This chapter begins by depicting some of the unique crime dynamics historically facilitated by the border context. El Paso and Juárez have always been connected in this regard, sharing their crime issues and, at times, jointly seeking solutions. Their level of collaboration has fluctuated and has seen a number of unanticipated problems over the years. One early example was the release of a notorious convict from south El Paso by Juárez officials in 1925. The release of Ysabel "Cara de Caballo" (Horse Face) Murillo was authorized by then mayor Fierro (*El Paso Herald Post* 1925b). "Horse Face" had escaped from Huntsville Prison in Texas where he was serving a 50-year sentence for robbery. He fled to Juárez and was let go despite an extradition request from justice officials in Texas. By contrast, in 1930 a Juárez police officer who shot and killed the notorious Juárez drug boss named El Pablote was allowed by the El Paso County Sheriff to carry a gun in El Paso and hide out from members of Pablote's gang who had avowed to avenge his death (Chessey 2016).

In recent decades, the death of us agents at the hands of Juárez-based drug organizations has occurred with some regularity on both sides of the border (Bowden 2002; Kolb 2013; Washington-Valdez 2006). The intelligence sharing function of the 2008 Merida Initiative increased cross-border efforts in the El Paso–Juárez sector in particular (Aguilar 2013), but not all results were positive. In 2010 joint efforts by Mexican and us officials to curb the flow of drugs to the United States resulted in the development of a large consumer base in Juárez and warfare among the gangs to control the market (Casey 2010b). Since then, once-hierarchical drug gangs have splintered into a critical mass of lower-level groups in constant conflict primarily over the distribution of methamphetamine (Borunda 2019; Castro and Vargas 2018; Esquivel 2018).

In 2017, there was a widely publicized agreement to improve collaboration between Mexican federal agents and the us Customs and Border Patrol (us Customs and Border Patrol 2017). Efforts to revive the sister-city image of shared governance and commerce between Juárez and El Paso (Guadian 2017) are frequent among city leaders today. A theoretical quandary in studying El Paso and Juárez is thus whether they truly have a shared sense of "place." On one hand, the cultural roots of their street subcultures are strikingly similar. But the "new" reality of Juárez as a critical plaza struggled over by Mexico's most powerful drug cartels draws an ever-clearer distinction between levels of public safety in the two places (Bowden 2010; Campbell 2009). According to Juárez drug violence writer Molly Molloy (2017), this reality is not new, as it has been occurring since the early 1990s. However, by 2010, Juárez's murder rate was the highest in the world (Puig 2013), which has had some effect, even if only psychological, on the El Paso side.

I argue that this setting has strongly influenced the emergence of specific segments of El Paso's Chicano gangs as some of the most intense forms in the United States due to their connection to Juárez drug gangs. All the while, a remarkable paradox is that El Paso is touted as one of the "safest cities in America," due to its low overall crime rate per FBI statistics (*El Paso Herald Post* 2017). Modern-day alarmism about the threat of Mexican crime to the public safety of us border cities thus appears to be misguided (Parker 2018). Alas, there is a saying among El Paso's nongang-, noncartel-involved

Chicanos that "what happens in Juárez, stays in Juárez." Perhaps it is true; or perhaps it is the widespread denial of the cross-pollination of drug-gang cultures that seems inevitable given the complicated, symbiotic relationship between the two cities (Vila 2000).

"Sin City" and the Juárez Legacy

The legacy of organized criminal activity in the borderland region is rooted in its reputation as a land of vice and opportunity for various forms of adult "recreation." Timmons (1990) writes about El Paso's national reputation as a "sin city" from the late 1800s through about 1918, known for its gambling, "tenderloin" red light district, numerous saloons, and Chinese opium dens. Bender (2012) argues that the regulation of El Paso's vice industries boosted those of Juárez, which had returned to relative normalcy following the revolution of 1910. The rise of the US Prohibition movement in 1918 and other local efforts to curb El Paso's vices propelled Juárez to develop these attractions to meet the demand (Nassif 2012). El Paso then served as the gateway to Juárez, but with its proximity to the new vice capital and its historical identity as such, these elements were residual and abundant on both sides of the border (Timmons 1990), especially after Prohibition ceased (Bender 2012). Moreover, it was a porous border at that time, which uniquely facilitated a varied set of organized crime practices scattered throughout the region.

Gun battles between smugglers and border patrol agents have been a constant feature in any known makeshift crossing of the Rio Grande in the El Paso–Juárez area for the past century (Campbell 2009; *El Paso Herald Post* 1934c; Timmons 1990).[1] There is also a long history of banditry in "Smeltertown," on the western outskirts of Juárez near the modern-day campus of the University of Texas at El Paso (*El Paso Herald Post* 1932b). The area surrounding the religious shrine at the top of Mount *Cristo Rey* in the small city of Sunland Park near Smeltertown has been the repeated site of robberies of devout worshippers by smuggling gangs (Timmons 1990). The most recent example of this practice was reported in 2016 (Lopez 2016).

Naturally, through the decades, organized illegal smuggling and hijacking of all types has been abundant in the region, including drugs (*El Paso Herald Post* 1935a), alcohol (*El Paso Herald Post* 1937), ammunition (*El Paso Herald Post* 1933d), counterfeit money (*El Paso Herald Post* 1933e), people in the sex trade (Bender 2012), train banditry, and stolen vehicles. A typical border crime example is the gangs of young boys known to rob El Paso pedestrians

FIGURE 4.1 | Mt. Cristo Rey in Anapra and Sunland Park.
Credit: Author's photo.

late at night as they returned from Juárez attractions (*El Paso Herald Post* 1932c).[2] Figure 4.2, provided by borderland crime historian Bob Chessey, is a group mugshot photo of several Juárez-based juvenile delinquents in the 1920s. It was given to him by the son of a former municipal police officer who kept his own scrapbook of local delinquents. The boys' names and street monikers appear above the photos, but no other information on them was provided.

While El Paso's rate of auto theft has never topped the nation, it has always been much higher than the US average (Thorsby 2016). In the 1920s and 1930s there was a very active Juárez-based auto theft ring operating in El Paso, keeping the topic in the news on a regular basis. A sample of headlines from the *El Paso Herald Post* from that era captures this.

"El Paso Police Battle Gang, Recovering Six Automobiles," March 6, 1920
"Sheriff Asks State Aid to Stop Theft of Cars by Juarez Gang," January 23, 1936
"Juarez Ring Working Again: 4 Cars Stolen This Month and Taken Over River," May 21, 1936
"[Sheriff] Fox Protests Mexican Gang Auto Thefts," October 24, 1936
"Group Operating on Border Changes Tactics: 37 Autos Unrecovered," November 20, 1936

FIGURE 4.2 | Credit: Photo courtesy of Bob Chessey, El Paso.

"104 Stolen Cars Recovered in 1936: Estimated 50 Missing Autos
Taken by Gang," January 1, 1937
"Wounded Car Thief Escapes: Man Shot at Bridge When He Tries to
Take Auto into Mexico," January 3, 1939
"Sheriff Estimates Stolen Cars Worth $36,000 Taken to Mexico in
Year," December 7, 1939

Early Drug-Gang Violence

Clashes between competing drug gangs in Juárez are not a new phenomenon. While El Paso's crime-fighting priorities in the early 1930s were booze bandits, auto theft rings, and to a lesser extent, youth gangs, Juárez was embroiled in a drug-gang war that often made headlines in El Paso newspapers. A series of stories chronicled the back-and-forth killings of major rivals in these rings. One noteworthy case was the murder of Jose "El Zapato Viejo" Yañez, who, at age 35, was the reputed leader of the Mexican Mafia in Juárez (*El Paso Herald Post* 1933f). His death came after a series of other homicides on both sides of the warring groups whose murdered members had street names such as "El Carnitas," "El Veracruz," and "El Consul Negro." A dumping ground for casualties of gang wars back then was the eastern valley of Juárez, still widely used for that purpose today (Arellano 2017; Washington-Valdez 2006).

Another significant capo murder was that of Simon Corral, a reputed Juárez drug dealer shot through the head and found near Tepeyac cemetery in south Juárez. The bodies of two others from his gang were found at La Piedrera, a rock quarry south of Juárez, another commonly used dumping location for gangland murders (*El Paso Herald Post* 1933g). The practice of abducting booze hijackers or other El Paso–based subjects who owed debts to drug gangs and disposing of them in Juárez was common in this era, and was euphemistically referred to as being "taken for a ride" (*El Paso Herald Post* 1935b). In one early case, the suspects in an abduction were Mexican federal agents (*El Paso Herald Post* 1928).

The fluidity of bandido gang networks across the border at this time was evident in a series of stories surfacing in the early 1930s. In one event, warring gangs of liquor bandits fought over hijacked cargo, resulting in the Juárez faction hunting down its enemies in broad daylight in downtown El Paso (*El Paso Herald Post* 1932d). A 45-year-old bandido named Augustin Avila of Juárez was part of a gang based in the far east El Paso lower valley communities of San Elizario and Fabens.[3] He was killed in a shootout with a border patrol agent upon crossing into San Eli "to contact members of his gang" (*El Paso Herald Post* 1932e). In another incident, a farmer from San Ignacio in the eastern valley of Juárez was robbed by a bandido gang based in Fabens (*El Paso Herald Post* 1931b). These adjacent valleys in far east El Paso and far east Juárez are still the site of much narco-related terrain (Borunda 2019; McKinley 2010a; US Dept. of Justice 2011; Washington-Valdez 2006).

A History of Violence and Lawlessness?

In thinking about whether Juárez is historically a violent or lawless place, one must consider its role in the Mexican Revolution of 1910 as a strategic location for both government and resistance forces. As such, it was the site of conflict between the Mexican army and revolutionaries, and a place of refuge for some of its most prominent figures on both sides of the struggle. Many northern Mexicans fleeing the revolution resettled in El Paso, initially creating a panic among the Anglos of Texas (*La Frontera* 2017). In many places along the border, this caused state-sanctioned aggression against Mexican refugees, led by the Texas Rangers, infamous for their lynching of Mexicans and other forms of brutality. El Paso seems to have suffered fewer of these indignities than other, more remote parts of the state,[4] but as Carrigan and Webb (2003) note, archives and literature on Mexican lynchings are sparse and incomplete. As noted in chapter 1, El Paso relegated its Mexican arrivals fleeing the revolution to the slums of Chihuahuita (Timmons 1990; Uhl and Meglorino 1993) near the modern-day downtown sector.

For a number of decades following the aftermath of the revolution, Juárez was not known to be a particularly violent place per se. As Mexico's fifth-largest city, Juárez's identity has been one of resistance and vice, and it is known to be a major thoroughfare in routine migration north. Indeed, Juárez's original folk name was El Paso del Norte or the pass to the north, changed to Juárez in 1888 (Timmons 1990). Still, some consider it to be less of a cosmopolitan city than Tijuana, the other major border city to the United States. Whereas both places host migrants from the deep south of Mexico, all over Latin America, and other parts of the world, the proportion of such migrants to Tijuana is supposedly higher. In official statistics, a full 80 to 85 percent of Juárez's inhabitants in 1990 and 2000 were from Chihuahua or other bordering states in northern Mexico (INEGI 2006; Vila 2000). However, others contend that the proportion rose far more than what was reflected in official statistics due to the rapid growth of maquiladora industries (a factory in Mexico run by a foreign company and exporting its products to the country of that company) (Molloy 2017; Washington-Valdez 2006; Zea 2012). The constant and massive migration caravans seeking asylum at the US–Mexico border from Central America in 2018 and 2019 have once again significantly altered the composition of recent arrivals to the region.

Because Mexico has not kept reliable crime data for most of its history (Persio 2017), it is difficult to say with much certainty how Juárez's violence has compared to violence in the rest of Mexico, in El Paso, or anywhere else. It wasn't until the mid-1990s that Mexico began tracking its homicide data (Linthicum 2017), allowing for about 20 years of trend data so far. Quiñonez (2016) dug up some quasi-official data for Juárez from 1990, when there were reportedly 45 murders, comparable to El Paso's 35 murders in that year (US Dept. of Justice 2017a). The Juárez murder rate rose in the mid-1990s and the number remained steady at about 220 per year until 2008 when things took a drastic turn for the worse.

Challenging the "Sister Cities" Metaphor

It is clearly overstated, but if Juárez and El Paso could once be characterized by local residents as essentially "the same city divided by a river" (Vila 2000), the drug cartel–fueled violence that broke out in Juárez from 2008 through

2012 may have killed the metaphor forever. The level of carnage was such that it earned Juárez the title of the world's murder capital when the violence peaked in 2010. The contrast in public safety between the two places was buttressed by El Paso's title as "The Safest Large U.S. City" in that same period (Eastaugh 2017). Juárez recorded about 1,600 murders in 2008, about 2,400 in 2009, and 2,766 in 2010 (Sierra 2014).[5] This astonishing level of violence seems to have changed the landscape, the local economy, the sentiment, and perhaps the social fabric of the place permanently (Nassif 2012). For several years it appeared that Juárez was on the rebound, making a strong comeback toward normalcy (Quiñonez 2016). Then the violence broke out again, making 2016 through 2018 record years for bloodshed (Chavez 2017; *El Diario* 2018), with 2019 currently on a comparable pace (*El Diario de Juárez* 2019).

Various sociologists who have studied the modern era of hyperviolence in Juárez attribute the deterioration of its public safety to structural forces such as changes in the economy and the neglect of the state. Nassif (2012) and Sierra (2014) both discuss the damage caused by the rise and rapid decline of the maquiladora industry, the resultant displacement of small businesses as traditional economic drivers, and the failure of the state to provide any meaningful support to the citizens of Juárez to compensate for these changes. Detailing a host of social problems in every aspect of public life, they argue the state has allowed things to fall apart in Juárez. This has created a critical mass of disillusioned Juárenses, who are desperate to create economic opportunities for themselves. The Mexican government estimates that 400,000 persons with the means to do so have fled to El Paso (Casey 2010c; Corchado 2016). The "opportunities" offered by the drug cartels appeal to certain youth of the lower classes, creating a surge in this type of activity in Juárez, a highly sought-after plaza by the cartels. These developments represent a stark contrast to the subculture of traditional Juárez barrio gangs, who resemble and arguably gave birth to the El Paso pachuco and the more contemporary cholo profiled in previous chapters.

Borderland Barrio Gangs: The Juárez Roots

On the US side, El Paso, Texas, lays claim to being the birthplace of the zoot-suit pachuco, hence the nickname "El Chuco" as it is widely known by many, including scholars and other authors (Burciaga 1992; Coltharp 1975; Garcia 1995; Torres 2010). However, given the cultural commonalities shared by Juárez and El Paso historically, Juárez also has a legitimate claim to being the birthplace of the pachuco subculture. Valenzuela (2013) splits its genesis between barrio Chaveña in Juárez and Segundo Barrio in El Paso. As noted in chapter 1, the zoot-suit style was made popular in the early 1940s by Mexican actor and Juárez resident German Valdez with the character Tin-Tan. The monument dedicated to this figure in Juárez's downtown market-square is a testament to the importance of the pachuco as a salient border-dweller identity. After all, the pachuco style represents a form of countercultural resistance among lower-class Mexican American boys in reaction to discrimination by US whites (Bogardus 1943). It is also clear that the style is heavily influenced by Mexico's urban barrio subculture.

Whatever side of the border represents the true anthropological origin, the zoot-suit pachuco subculture was thriving in both cities in the 1930s and 1940s. And both sides were cognizant of the groups and related street issues on either side. For example, the El Paso newspaper reported on a large group of Juárez teens identified as pachucos and their confrontation with Juárez police officer Jose Garcia, who held the group at gunpoint until reinforcements could arrive to arrest them (*El Paso Herald Post* 1944). In another incident at the downtown Juárez movie theater Cine Eden, rival pachuco gangs fought each other with knives, ice picks, and broken tequila bottles, killing one and injuring several before police arrived (*El Paso Herald Post* 1958c). As seen in chapter 1, these activities resembled those of El Paso's pachuco gangs at the time. In fact, it is my contention that for many years, pachuco and, later, cholo subcultures that existed in El Paso and Juárez essentially mirrored each other in style, purpose, and intensity.

A central thesis of the current work is not only that Juárez–El Paso gang subcultures are symbiotic in terms of their influence on each other but also that there are numerous network connections among groups from both sides of the border and throughout the region. My study documents the following barrio gangs with a presence on both sides of the border throughout the years.

19th Street	Los Duques a.k.a.	Los Papas
Anapra	the Dukes	Los Pelones
Barrio/Varrio	Los Gatos	Los Tirilones
Chico Trece[6]	Los Home Boys	Meadow Trece
Buena Vista	Los Nazis	Tenebrosos
(a.k.a. El Rojo)	Los Ortiz	Trojans/Los
El Puente Negro	Brothers	Troyanos

FIGURE 4.3 | Juarez
pachucos and *cholos*
of different eras.

Top to bottom
(a) A group of young
Juarez *pachucos*, ca. 1945;
(b) a group of young
Juarez *cholos*, ca. 1985;
(c) modern-era Juarez
youth street gang, ca. 2010.
Credit: Photos courtesy
of Edmundo Lopez,
El Paso.

There are lesser-known others with roots in the Juárez colonias of Rancho Anapra, AltaVista, and Chaveña that were reestablished at some point in Anthony, Sunland Park, and other communities between El Paso and Las Cruces. Not coincidentally, these Juárez barrios were among those known to produce the largest and most serious gangs. The colonia known as Cuauhtemoc alone once had at least 20 gangs (Morales 2017).

The following is a list of some of Juárez's older, most reputable gangs.

72-Anapra	K-13	Los Gatos
Angeles 30	La Botella	Los Harpis 15
Barrio Alto	La Mosca	Los Harpis 20
Barrio Chico	La San Pedro	Los Harpis 30
Trece	Las Pink Ladies	Los Muertos
Barrio Muerto-55	Los Ahorcados	Los Pinguinos
Bella Vista PA	Los Apaches	Los Rebeldes[7]
Buena Vista	Los Chonillos	Los Rojas
Cakos-90	Los Dandys	Los Yenkas
Calaveras	Los Demonios	Papalotes
Calecia-13	Los Diablos	Play Boys
El Sky	Los Diamantes	Rancho Anapra
Fresas	Los Duques	Refuego

The Modern Gang Landscape in Juárez

In 2005, the municipal police gang unit, Grupo Delta, reported there were 492 gangs operating in Juárez (*Proceso* 2006), an increase from 320 in 2004 (Villalpando 2004). However, the Delta unit's commander stated, "The youth street gangs are nearly a thing of the past" (*Proceso* 2006, 1). This did not mean that the active gangs didn't involve youth, but to suggest that a different sort of gang had emerged from the old-fashioned cholo gangs such as those listed above. He further noted that the traditional gangs had nearly disappeared, naming several that were now extinct, the few that still existed, and the few that had been significantly weakened over time. By 2009, the number of gangs in Juárez had not changed, equating to about 12,000 members on the city's gang unit list (Sierra 2014, 632). More than 75 percent of these members were said to be between 12 and 17 years of age. Moreover, most if not all of these gangs were loyal to one of about 10 or 12 adult gangs with cartel ties. The most prominent of these were Mexicles, los Artistas

Asesinos, los Doblados, los Aztecas, los Pura Raza Mexicana, los Linces, and los Troyanos.

By 2011, the number of gangs and gang members in Juárez had doubled to an estimated 25,000 members across 950 gangs, according to a city official (Villalpando 2011). These gangs were said to operate in about 100 of Juárez's 800 neighborhoods. With a total population of about 1.3 million, some 30 percent (360,000) of Juárez's residents were 13 to 20 years old. Of these, an estimated 20,000 of them (5 percent) belonged to a gang. Assuming that the vast majority of these youth are male, the gender-specific gang prevalence rate would be at least double, or about 10 percent of all young men in the city. It is worth noting that this is comparable to the proportion found in San Antonio, Texas, in 2007 with about 9 percent of all young black and Chicano males involved in gang activity (Tapia 2017). In El Paso, the comparable figure was about 5 percent in 2011.[8]

Nassif (2012) adds more detail to this bleak picture, noting that 30 percent of all Juárez kids ages 12–15 are not in school. Of the 13–24 age group, about 120,000 (50 percent) are not in school or working (244). Ainsle (2013) referred to this as one of Juarez's most serious social problems. In 2008, 30 percent of murder victims in Juárez were under 20 years old and all of the youth centers appeared to be run by gangs. The gang prevalence estimate Nassif (2014) cites is 15,000–20,000 members across 500 gangs. About 30 gangs are considered to be extremely dangerous, tied in deep with cartels and, in some cases, with US gangs (247). Public trust in the police is alarmingly low, with about three-fourths of the populace skeptical about police effectiveness and integrity.

Research subjects in Sierra's (2014) study of former gang youth explained that organized crime all but dissolved the old barrio territories that were prominent in the 1990s and early 2000s. The barrio gangs' street-corner function was far more innocuous before the cartels moved in. The cartels began recruiting and training the most desperate, daring, and ruthless members of Juárez's youth street gangs to become *halcones* and sicarios (lookouts and hit men). There was a clear difference in character between those that sought out or allowed themselves to be recruited and those who refrained. According to Sierra's interviewees, the cartel recruits are the deepest into drugs and are already preying on nongang residents in the barrio before joining the adult gangs. They are now being socialized by the cartel to become "true psychopaths," said his respondents.[9] Since Mexico's headway with the arrests of high-level cartel members (Agren 2017; Parker 2018), once-dominant groups appear to be splintering and diversifying their crimes to gasoline theft, human smuggling, kidnapping, and extortion. In keeping with a prediction about the proliferation of street-level gangs in Juárez made several years ago (Corcoran 2012), this is changing the structure of the gang landscape yet again, as most recently reported by Esquivel (2018).

Comparing Juárez's and El Paso's Gang Prevalence

In 2002, the famed El Paso–Juárez underworld author Charles Bowden wrote, "El Paso has more gangs per capita than any city in Texas" (27). While this was either speculation or a repeating of something police in every major city claim to journalists or writers, it happens to be plausible.[10] The number of gangs in the El Paso Police Department's gang database for 2006 showed 472 active gangs and other gang-like delinquent groups (Borunda 2006). This is almost identical to the number reported in Juárez at that time, and yet El Paso's population is about half a million less than that of Juárez. This means that per capita, gangs are more prevalent in El Paso, and depending on the number of actual gang members it has, it could have a higher rate of gang membership. There is no reason to assume that the gangs in Juárez are larger than those in El Paso; that is, that the average number of members per gang is higher. The paradox, however, is that in 2006, El Paso experienced only 15 homicides (US Dept. of Justice 2017a) versus 250 in Juárez (Quiñonez 2016).

By 2009, the number of gangs in El Paso had risen to 539 (Borunda 2011), while the number in Juárez remained the same at about 500 (Sierra 2014). The number of gang members in their respective databases, however, was far different. There were double the number of persons in Juárez's gang database at about 12,000 (Sierra 2014) compared to El Paso's at around 6,000 (Borunda 2011). When the number of members in the El Paso gang database suddenly dropped to under 4,000 in 2011, a local gang intervention activist was publicly critical of the police practice of counting members, calling it a flawed system. The police's public response raises a key methodological point that could account for the drastic difference in the number of members reported for Juárez and El Paso, despite having the same number of gangs. The EPPD spokesman stated the drop in gang membership was due to the expiration of the set period of years that one can stay in the gang database if not involved in gang activity per US federal code 28 CFR, Part 23, which governs the removal of a person from the active gang database. As Mexico is not known to have a similar statute, those numbers more likely reflect a cumulative total of known gang members minus attrition by death. Recall from chapter 2, this is similar to the estimates used in Las Cruces as well.

Discussion

This chapter shows the similarities and differences in the gang activity of the sister cities to analyze trends over time and to understand more about gang etiology in this unique borderland setting. While the historical roots of the pachuco subculture, and resultant barrio and cholo gangs, are common to the entire region, there is a clear divergence with the appearance of the youth-adult hybrid gangs in Juárez in recent years. The manner in which powerful drug cartels seemed to "come in like nothing" (Nassif 2012, 238), disrupting the traditional barrio-gang order and co-opting many of its street youth, changed the landscape in Juárez, perhaps permanently. For Juárez and El Paso to report the same number of gangs in the recent era is quite remarkable, suggesting that they may share some common structural causes of gang membership. Yet, the stark difference in these cities' murder rates at the same time shows a radical difference in the intensity of the modern gangs in Juárez.[11] This was created by an almost undecipherable set of macrolevel forces to include the social ills of poverty and inequality, police and state corruption, and the insatiable demand for illegal drugs in the United States.

Ciudad Juárez, Chihuahua, has always been a vibrant Mexican metropolis, rich in culture, commerce, and innovation. One of the nation's largest cities, it is widely recognized for its dynamism, due, in major part, to its proximity to another large city on the us side, providing ready access to first-world amenities and cultural experiences (Vila 2000). The shared history of these adjacent places as vice-ridden "sin cities" has seemingly conditioned the modern criminal subcultures we see there today. Nassif (2012) is one of several Mexican sociologists writing on the state of modern Juárez who attributes its current condition to this history, in addition to a host of contemporary social ills brought on by the neglect of the state toward its citizens.

In terms of gang violence, Juárez's current woeful condition is truly a new and unprecedented circumstance. While Juárez's violent crime rates began to surpass those in El Paso in the early 1990s (Quiñonez 2016), it became an epidemic by 2008. Given the shared history of bandido subculture, and the facilitation of a unique form of outlaw behaviors on the border, what can account for such a radical departure of Juárez's violence from those levels thought to be normative in the region? (See, e.g., the low violent crime rates of El Paso, Las Cruces, and Anthony offered in chapter 3.) Equally puzzling is that the gang subcultures of each of those places is strongly conditioned by and, in many cases, connected to those of Juárez, even in recent times. Washington-Valdez (2006) attributes the horrific violence subculture that came over Juárez to the influence of Colombian-style tactics introduced by the Carrillo-Fuentes Cartel in their effort to destabilize the region for control of the Chihuahua drug corridor.

While Juárez's gangs date back to the post-revolution era, we do not know much about early social service efforts by the state to intervene in, for example, pachuco era delinquent groups. We do know, however, that its more recent cholo manifestations were met with goodwill intervention by city-sponsored programs and agencies in the community. In the early 1980s, the city formed the Concilio de Pandillas (Council of Gangs) and ran a program called Barrios Unidos. Its components were job training, sports, substance abuse therapy, and community service (Copeland 1983). Twenty years later, Juárez still had such an agency called El Centro de Asistencia a Jóvenes Pandilleros (Center for Youth Gang Assistance), in addition to the state's Unidad de Atención a Pandillas (Unified Response to Gangs), which performed mediation between gangs and the communities where they thrived (Villalpando 2004). At last check, Juárez's stubborn conscientious-ness to alleviating social problems continues to produce groups devoted to addressing gang issues (Nassif 2012).

In thinking about the stark contrast in the behavior of Juárez gangs versus those on the US side of the border region, it is worth noting that well-funded gang intervention programs are currently nearly absent on the US side of the region. In fact, while it never hurts to have such programs, they are simply not as needed at this time as they have been in others. Delinquency levels in the borderland, and in the United States as a whole, are historically low currently (Males 2017).[12] Although no cogent evidence has been forthcoming, many suspect this is tied to demographic trends like the birthrate, primarily, in addition (perhaps) to techniques used in schools and the juvenile justice system to curb delinquency. If part of what Juárez—and the rest of Mexico—is experiencing is tied to (1) demographic trends, (2) economic recession, and (3) widespread corruption in the public sector and law enforcement (Bowden 2002, 2010; Molloy and Bowden 2012; Nassif 2012; Washington-Valdez 2006), these structural and cultural issues will not be easily overcome.

Finally, with regard to spill-over contamination of US communities by Mexico's drug violence epidemic, alarmist claims are regularly made by police spokesmen and politicians like former Texas attorney general Greg Abbott (Llorente 2011). Some of these were made after a series of random incidents occurring at the height of the epidemic. One involved stray bullets, thought to be fired from over a mile away in Juárez, hitting El Paso city hall. Reports of other isolated incidents involving border patrol agents being fired upon or assaulted with objects from the Juárez side sporadically surface, yet, recall from chapter 1, this has been happening along the river since the 1930s. In 2017, former US Attorney General Jeff Sessions' claim that El Paso is "ground zero" in the fight to secure the border from cartel spillover came at a press conference held there, which angered local politicians and business leaders (Borunda 2017a). Then Mayor Oscar Leeser and others reinforced the sister-cities metaphor primarily in terms of commerce. His successor, Dee Margo, and Juárez Mayor Armando Cabada continued to promote the sister-city ideal in a joint council meeting in October 2017 (Guadian 2017).

While cartel operatives and associates are no doubt present in many US communities, aspects of their business, namely the violent ones, seldom come to light. It appears that when they are discovered by police they are well publicized in the press, as it serves to support the "spillover" narrative that is popular with law enforcement. For example, when a federal informant was shot outside his home in east El Paso in 2009, killed by an 18-year-old Ft. Bliss soldier supposedly working for the cartel, it made headlines (Borunda 2009). Then there was the abduction of a cartel operative in far east El Paso, whose corpse was later found in Juárez (Farmer 2016).

There may a good reason why we don't hear more about cartel or drug gang spillover. Law enforcement's need to support the spillover narrative is often at odds with its need to keep certain investigations secret so as not to ruin them. Note, however, that the 2017 National Drug Threat Assessment listed a single example of targeted cartel violence spillover into the United States in 2013 for which prosecution took place in 2016 (US Dept. of Justice 2017b). After conducting intensive fieldwork on drug gangs in El Paso–Juárez, Gundur (2017) concluded that drug trafficking organization (DTO)–related effects on the El Paso side were virtually absent.

To be fair, on the nexus of cartel and Mexican state-level operations, far more clandestine cross-border connections, murders, and other maneuvers are said to occur than what becomes public (Bowden 2002; Bowden 2010; Campbell 2009; Washington-Valdez 2006). In terms of more normative gang implications, a cross-border development involving El Paso's primary prison gang, the Barrio Azteca, has dominated the discussion about bi-national organized crime for the past dozen years or so. Portions of chapter 5 profile the roots and evolution of this traditional south El Paso barrio group, which is now held out as the epitome of a violent cross-border crime syndicate.

F IVE

El Paso's Modern Gangs and the Barrio Azteca

Introduction

The case for El Paso–Juárez as the origin of the pachuco and cholo subcultures, two distinct stylistic periods in the US Chicano gang timeline, was made in previous chapters and supported in prior research (e.g., Cummings 2003; Obregon-Pagan 2003). This is not for bragging rights over Tucson, San Diego–Tijuana, or Los Angeles but to establish the rich history of the subculture in the region to now examine its modern manifestations. Valenzuela (2013) is the most specific with naming the origin, placing pachuco genesis between Barrio Chaveña in north-central Juárez and the adjacent Segundo Barrio in south El Paso in 1939. I now analyze the modern forms of this genuine borderland subculture, once thought to be a more innocuous, if not normative, type of street corner society. Having offered the gang histories of each of the other population centers and communities that comprise the borderland region in turn (Las Cruces, Anthony, Santa Teresa, Sunland Park–Anapra, Chaparral, and Cd. Juárez), this chapter returns to El Paso's modern gang landscape, picking up the timeline in the 1970s and 1980s where chapter 2 left off.

Having spent my first 18 years of life in El Paso (1974–1992), growing up in a high poverty Chicano part of town (the lower valley shown in fig. 5.1), this author was all too familiar with the region's cholo-era subculture in particular. Per the photos and other descriptions in previous chapters, it was replete with a certain style of dress, attitude, and setting. It contained a specific slang vernacular, the use of lowrider vehicles blasting soul and R&B music from the 1950s and 1960s (i.e., "oldies"), a macho-bravado demeanor, and an anti-authority attitude. It was not a widespread subculture but reserved only for a certain type of street-oriented individual; although this part of my recollection is in conflict with other scholars' ideas of cholos as a gentler, often misunderstood group (Cummings 2003; Olvera 1984a). Typically, in the lower- and working-class Chicano communities of El Paso, cholos had a strong Mexican orientation, many with thick accents and an alternate jargon and, presumably, more recent or current links to Juárez or East LA in terms of family origin. Generally, it is a stigmatized, deviant identity by the larger society in all southwestern locales.

Borderland Gang Intensity and Violence

In mid-December 1981, *El Paso Herald Post* reporter Frank Ahlgren wrote a four-part series on gangs in El Paso. He characterized them as being involved in hard-core crime by that point in their evolution. While the city's violent crime rate back then was higher than it is today, it still was among the lowest in the southwestern region and in the nation. Of the 12 cities listed in table 5.1, only Austin, San Antonio, and Las Cruces had lower overall violent crime rates at that time. But El Paso had the very lowest rates of homicide and was second lowest in armed robbery—two crimes thought to be elevated by a serious local gang problem in a given place (National Gang Center 2013).[1] While Austin, San Antonio, and El Paso are similar in size, Las Cruces is much smaller, with about one-sixth the population of any of these three cities.

Whereas barrio gangs are reputed to be violent, it is peculiar to find that a region with such a robust history of these formations is among the safest places in the United States. Recall that chapter 3 discusses this paradox, hypothesizing that the abundance of Chicano gang formations in the border region is primarily a cultural marker, versus one that has the consequence of elevated violence. This paradox has been glaring for decades, wherein El Paso has been rated one of the safest large cities in America, per the crime rate. The contradiction continues today, where on one hand, it is stated that El Paso's gang activity increased from 2016 to 2017 (Gonzales 2017), and on the other, it is found to be the second safest large city in the United States (*El Paso Herald Post* 2017). As shown in chapter 4, even more puzzling is the stark contrast between El Paso's and Juárez's violence levels, both thought to be driven, to a considerable degree, by gang activity (Nassif 2012).

Durán (2018) has written about the unjust villainization of barrio gangs in the border region by the authorities, the press, and, thus, by the general public. From its inception as a barrio identity, scholars of the pachuco subculture likened it to a mere countercultural style among lower-class Mexican

City	Violent Crime	Armed Robbery	Homicide
Albuquerque	1,150	349	12
Austin	581	265	13
Denver	829	374	14
El Paso	771	209	4
Fresno	840	448	17
Ft. Worth	1,496	617	30
Houston	924	549	26
Las Cruces	505	132	12
Los Angeles	1,658	877	24
Phoenix	844	272	10
San Antonio	625	311	21
Tucson	973	275	8

* Rates per 100,000 population, rounded to nearest whole number

Source: US Department of Justice 2017a

American boys, who were not well accepted by white America (Bogardus 1943). My profile of El Paso gang history in chapter 1 vacillates on this point, presenting evidence that the delinquency of early borderland street gangs contained both benign mischief and serious delinquency, to include extreme violence. Characterizations of El Paso's gangs as a serious social problem from the 1950s (e.g., Rahm 1958) to the present day (e.g., Gonzales 2017) suggest that the subculture has retained its high intensity level over time.

In thinking about the structural and cultural mechanisms creating these violence nuances in the borderland region's gangs, there is no doubt that some of it is rooted in the fact that the US side is highly saturated with Latinos, who are 83 percent of El Paso's inhabitants (US Census Bureau 2019b). Numerous criminological studies show that violence levels in US Latino communities (namely immigrant communities) are far lower than those of blacks, even approximating those of whites (e.g., Desmond and Kubrin 2009; Martinez 2002; Morenoff 2005; Xie and Baumer 2018). Prominent research on this topic shows that Mexican American communities in particular are less violent than black ones (Bradshaw et al. 1998; Martinez 2014), and in some studies, even less violent than white communities (Sampson, Morenoff, and Raudenbush 2005). To the extent that gangs are a reflection of the broader ethnic community, this helps to explain low levels of violence in El Paso, despite the abundance of gangs there.

Even older research on Latino enclaves in larger cities and in other, smaller border cities have seen these protective effects as well. Nestor Rodriguez (1993) writes that the constant influx of Mexican migrants to large southwestern cities like Houston in the 1980s made the poverty experience in Latino areas different from that of its black areas, and that of poor populations in other US regions. He notes that Latino immigrants tended to harmoniously mix into established Chicano communities in the Southwest, which we now know dilutes the effects of violence and other negative outcomes usually associated with concentrated poverty (Martinez 2014; Sampson et al. 2005). Valdez (1993) made a similar assessment for the border town of Laredo, Texas.

BORDERLAND LATINOS AND THE UNDERGROUND ECONOMY

In Texas border areas such as Laredo and the Rio Grande Valley, poor Latinos adjusted to high community-level rates of poverty by relying more on the informal economy, namely on the drug trade, which is abundant in those regions (Richardson 2012; Valdez 1993), as it is in El Paso. Although the drug addiction, sex work, criminal activity, and welfare dependency that is normally associated with underclass subculture among gangs is present in all US regions, drug trafficking and its availability are more abundant in the Southwest, especially in border cities. This remains an important distinction from the midwestern and southern underclass scenario that disproportionately affects black communities.

Countless contemporary writers have noted the ubiquity of drugs in El Paso–Juárez (e.g., Bowden 2002; Campbell 2009; Cartwright 1998). Whereas the drug trade can be a main cause of violence where the demand is high and supply is relatively low, as in nonborder regions with larger black populations, El Paso does not experience this. The cost of drugs is relatively low, and the products are readily available, seemingly reducing the need for gang conflicts over the street markets. Furthermore, street-level drug sales are governed by a taxing system referred to as the *cuota* whereby the dominant prison gang will tax 10 percent of all the drug sales it is aware of and decides that it can enforce. This tends to organize drug market activities that would otherwise lead to violence between drug dealers and drug gangs for control of the market.

For the past few decades, the Barrio Azteca (BA) has enforced the tax in most El Paso barrios and the city's other areas of drug sales activity. Once discovered, the failure of an independent drug dealer or gang to pay the tax may result in violence. Gundur (2017) notes that the BA maintained a monopoly on the cuota in El Paso for several decades. Few Chicano dealers are known to challenge the edict, but there are certain gangs from which it is not always enforceable, and these tend to lead to isolated cases of serious gang violence. There has been resistance from the BA's rivals, the Sureño Trece, and some of the black gangs in northeast El Paso that are discussed below are considered exempt. Other gangs have also been known to resist paying the cuota at times, but usually not for long, or not without confrontation, such as the case with several Lower Valley gangs. These included the Nasty Boys in Fabens and a small, tight-knit group from Ysleta called Varrio La Mora who became part of the larger federation called Chuco Tango (Borunda 2018a; Martinez 2014).[2]

GANGS, GEOGRAPHY, AND RACE-ETHNIC HYBRIDS

For more context on the topic of gangs, race, and violence, consider the case of San Antonio, which is often likened to El Paso due to its similar size and socioeconomic makeup. Its gang patterns and Latino gang culture, while similar to El Paso's to start, experienced a cultural shift away from traditional barrio gang norms in the 1980s and 1990s (Tapia 2017). Although it is along I–35, a major drug corridor from Laredo, it is a full 2.5 hours from the Mexican border, thus the drug economy and local gang culture are not that of a border town.[3]

As a matter of demographics and gang migration, eventually many Latino street gangs in San Antonio began to mimic black gangster subculture. This was due to the strong influence of gang subcultures migrating in from Chicago, Houston, Dallas, and even San Antonio's own black gangs, who are historically more violent than its Latino youth gangs (Bradshaw et al. 1998; Martinez 2014). The violent crime rate in San Antonio, while often lower than El Paso's and Las Cruces's from 1980 to 2000, far surpassed them thereafter. Perhaps El Paso's proximity to Mexico (i.e., as a perpetually Latino-saturated place) keeps its Latino gang subculture more traditional (ethnocentric) as compared to the ethnically hybridized ones in Texas cities of other regions. If so, it is possible that this relative insulation from black gang cultural influences has implications for its violence rates.[4,5]

Whatever other structural characteristics create low violence rates in Latino immigrant communities (for details, see Feldmeyer 2009; Nielsen, Lee, and Martinez 2005; Sampson et al. 2005; Xie and Baumer 2018), it is clearly a US phenomenon that does not extend into Mexico's border communities. This is evidenced by Juárez's astronomical violence levels, even though its ethnic composition is similar to that of El Paso. The two cities experience radically different levels of violence despite being part of the same urban sprawl separated by a political boundary. This precludes any essentialist notions that "Latinos [or whites] are simply less violent than blacks by nature" that underlie most biological approaches to understanding criminal behavior. If it were true, Juárez's violence levels—and now that of many places in Mexico—would be as docile as El Paso's. There is thus much to be said for the combination of socioeconomic conditions, governance, cultural norms, and other macrostructural factors in the production of violence in a society.

The discussion about El Paso's low crime rates and radical departure from Juárez's modern violence is not meant to suggest that El Paso's gang member population as a whole is tame and nonviolent. On the contrary, it is *because* of its unique geographical positioning that several menacing and otherwise serious Chicano gang formations have emerged in El Paso over time. The next section begins to profile several of these gangs from the 1970s forward, discussing related elements of local gang dynamics in the process. While many of these are traditional territorial barrio gangs, some formed cross-border links to Juárez's drug cartels, making them among the most potentially dangerous Chicano gangs in the United States.

Growth of the Gang Landscape

South and central El Paso continued to host the bulk of pachuco and cholo subcultures into the 1960s and beyond. But the number of delinquent youth groups exploded soon after, expanding into other parts of the city. El Paso's lower valley to the far southeast of the city, for example, became a potent context for Chicano gangs from the 1960s through the 1980s (Ahlgren 1981; Chiechi 1984; *El Paso Herald Post* 1960, 1961, 1965a, 1965b, 1967; Thompson 1984). In Ysleta, for example, there was Barraca and Varrio Calavera near the Tigua Indian Reservation, Los Lotes on North Loop and Dale Drive, and the Comancheros and the Royal Knights near Riverside High School. In the mid-1970s large gangs called Heaven and Hell and Chicano Pride formed and their clashes dominated much of the lower valley gang scene until cholo groups like Los Ortiz Brothers, Los Home Boys, Varrio Los Kennedys, White Fence, and Gran Varrio Pachuco emerged later that decade. Figure 5.1 contains the turf areas for these and other lower valley gangs in the areas of Ysleta and Socorro, primarily.

Meanwhile, in El Paso's more traditional gang areas in the central and

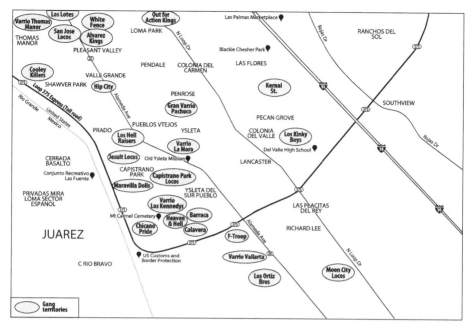

FIGURE 5.1 | Lower Valley gang turf areas, 1970s–early 1990s.
Credit: Isabelle Burke.

south sides, warfare among the x-14s, Segundo Barrio, the T-Birds, Sherman, the Wanderers, and Del Diablo were dominating headlines (Olvera 1983, 1984b; Tinsley 1982). Also gaining notoriety were the Mestizos, Los Santanas, and Varrio Grandview (VGV). While Del Diablo and the T-Birds were the largest gangs in El Paso in the late 1970s and early 1980s, a smaller but fierce group was emerging. This group, Los Fatherless (LFL), from the Alameda-Paisano intersection in the south central area, would soon become the most notorious modern barrio gang in town. Even in the press, the larger, older gangs expressed concern for the Fatherless's rapid growth and intensity (Olvera 1984b).

Several of the 1960s groups profiled in chapter 1 became stronger in the 1980s. These included the central city gangs Varrio Glenwood Street (VGS), Barrio Lincoln, and Varrio San Juan (VSJ). In the Lower Valley were Varrio Hacienda Heights, Thomas Manor, Alvarez Kings, *Capistrano Locos*, and the *Marmolejos*. In the West Side's projects were *Puro Barrio Sandoval*, *Barrio Machuca*, and *Los Compadres* in Canutillo (far west El Paso). Several California-based satellite gangs were also setting up shop in El Paso.

These were Florencia-13, Lopez-Maravilla (LMV), Varrio Big Hazard, and the previously mentioned White Fence, all reputable East LA gangs. Two well-known Chicano gangs in northeast El Paso at that time were Los Midnite Locos (LML) and Logan Heights near the Ft. Bliss Army Base, an area historically notorious for its crime and disorder (turf areas in fig. 5.2).

Northeast El Paso

The tenderloin red-light district in central El Paso, widely written about (e.g., Bender 2012; Campbell 2009; Nassif 2012), was not the city's only area of historical vice. Due to the placement of Ft. Bliss Army Base in the northeastern part of the city, the surrounding neighborhoods developed their own adult attractions to cater to military enlistees from throughout the United States (Timmons 1990). As early as 1916, a small red-light district developed in an area called Lynchville, which hosted a number of brothels and speakeasies (*El Paso Herald Post* 1932f). Naturally, this conditioned the area's future environment, a historically low-income area, to become one of the most problematic parts of the city for police. Similarly, families from Logan Heights, a World War I–era neighborhood for military personnel, complained of neglect by the city of El Paso not long after its annexation (*El Paso Herald Post* 1948).

In 1998, an El Paso Police Department research assistant named Kimberly Forsythe wrote a brief report called "The Angel's Triangle." It offered a profile of the crime problems and efforts in community policing in the northeast area El Pasoans have known for so long as the "Devil's Triangle." Its neighborhood watch group worked with community policing officer Raul Prieto to effect socioeconomic changes and combat the crime issue. They strategically began calling the area the "Angel's Triangle" as a first step in the transformation plan. Here is an excerpt from page 1 of the report.

> A triangular shaped tract bordered by three major streets: the Patriot Freeway, Dyer, and Hondo Pass, the area was home to 7,705 individuals (according to 1990 and 1992 census data) . . . Largely composed of young families receiving public assistance, and families of lower ranking military retirees. Nearly one third of the population was under the age of 12 . . . According to a 1994 report . . . Wainwright [elementary] student enrollment was 100% economically disadvantaged. The unemployment rate in the area approached 15%, significantly higher than the city-wide average of 10% . . . covered

with low income rental housing units, many of which were poorly maintained and marked with graffiti by neighborhood gang members. Drug deals were openly conducted in the apartment common areas and the neighborhood park. By 1994, the crime rate in the area had reached an all-time high.

The report stated that since traditional methods of policing had not worked in the area, a community policing strategy was attempted in 1995. Officer Prieto worked with the 25-member Angel's Triangle Neighborhood Association to essentially implement a "broken windows" style of policing (see Kelling and Wilson 1982). Like other spurious claims of crime reduction made by proponents of the broken windows strategy nationwide, the Police Department reported significant drops in crime in the targeted area. The report credited the intervention for the crime drops, but neglected to note that crime was dropping precipitously in the broader city, the state, and the nation at the time. Successes would be short-lived, however, as the northeast area returned to being one of the most gang-ridden parts of the city, and it remains so today.

Per social disorganization theory, "bad" parts of town tend to retain their character over time due to the delinquent subculture historically entrenched there with stubborn gang traditions (Bursik and Grasmick 1993; Kornhauser 1978). The northeast was similar to areas right along the border in terms of its criminogenic intensity. For example, it had the same types of disorder involving shootouts between liquor bandits and hijackers in the Devil's Triangle in the early 1930s (*El Paso Herald Post* 1932g). Recall from chapter 1 that in northeast El Paso, the Dukes were well established by 1950. The Logan Heights area, established in 1909, also gave birth to one of El Paso's longstanding gangs, still known today as Barrio Logan Heights. The neighborhood was originally built for World War I–era military families, but was annexed and left to deteriorate into a low-income area by the early 1950s (*El Paso Herald Post* 1948).

The Barrio Logan Heights gang have continued to thrive as a multigenerational group, currently with 76 members in the EPPD gang database.[6] Another longstanding northeast area gang is the Los Midnight Locos (LML) with 81 members currently, and the Bishops, a mixed-race gang who became Bloods in recent decades. Both of these gangs claimed turf near Andress High School (fig. 5.2). Eisenhower Crazy Hood (ECH), with only five current members documented by EPPD, came out of the Eisenhower housing proj-

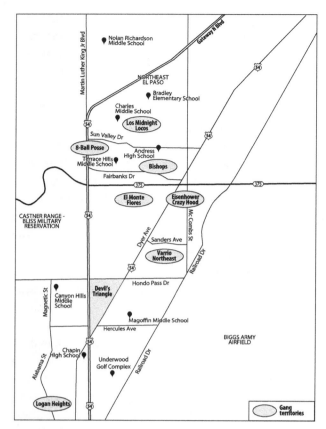

FIGURE. 5.2 | Northeast El Paso gang turf, 1970s–early 1990s.
Credit: Isabelle Burke.

ects, adjacent to a smaller group named El Monte Flores (EMF), now with only three documented members. Below them is Varrio Northeast (VNE-13), which has remained the dominant gang in that part of the city and is currently El Paso's sixth largest gang with 158 members. The One Nation Locos, Hated by Many, 3-6 Mafia, and the Straight Mother Fuckin' Thugs are some of the newer groups that are prevalent there today. Many black and racially mixed sets of the Bloods and Crips also exist in the northeast area.

In 2007, a rivalry broke out between LML and members of the Lopez Maravilla (LMV) gang. LMV is a California transplant that had been in Central El Paso since the 1970s. El Paso Police Department Gang Lieutenant Miguel Zamora of the Northeast Substation said families with ties to the LMV moved to the northeast after being displaced by the floods that struck El Paso in 2006. "The gang is not native to the Northeast and as its numbers grew, so did the rivalry," he said. (Borunda 2010). LMV, who have since relocated their base back to central El Paso and other locations throughout the city, have 62 members in the gang database.

BLACK GANGS IN NORTHEAST EL PASO

El Paso is one of the largest metropolitan hubs for US Latinos, who comprise 83 percent of the county's 850,000 inhabitants (US Census Bureau 2019b). Only 4 percent of its population is black, and this population is noticeably clustered in the northeastern portion of the city, stemming from Ft. Bliss (Statistical Atlas 2017).[7] Although they are a small proportion of the population, "modern" black gangs have been present in the city for nearly 40 years. According to veteran officer Andy Sanchez of the El Paso Police Gang Unit, the Bloods gang dates back to the early 1980s in the northeast section (Borunda 2009). This predates the actual arrival of Bloods sets per se in El Paso by a few years, but it was probably not long after the Bloods and Crips became notorious in LA in the 1980s that their influence was also felt in El Paso.[8] These groups became so popular with ghetto and barrio youth of the era that in the late 1980s and 1990s "sets," if not locally grown copycats, of both gangs began to spring up across the nation (Decker and Van Winkle 1996).

Some of El Paso's Crips sets are also formidable, but the northeast's two predominant black gangs in the modern era have been the Bloods and their rivals, the Gangster Disciples (GDs). The GDs are also commonly known as "Folks" or Folk Nation, originally formed in the 1960s in the midwestern United States. However, the EPPD gang database currently has them listed as separate groups with 55 GDs and 334 Folk members, making Folks the third largest gang behind Sureño Trece and Barrio Azteca. The Bishops, from Irvin High School, were a homegrown predecessor to the various Blood sets that became highly active in the early 2000s at both Andress and Irvin High Schools.[9] By then, there were mixed-race gangs at both schools, such as the Piru Bloods, comprised mostly of black members, but also some Latinos (Borunda 2010). Other prominent sets included the Red Dog Pirus, the Bounty Hunters, One-Trey-Five (135) Pirus with New Jersey roots, and 109 Pirus with St. Louis roots. Except for the Piru Bloods, none of these gangs appear to be currently active per the EPPD gang database (see appendix A for details).

In March 2009, El Paso County District Attorney Jose Rodriguez filed a civil gang injunction request against 27 members of the Bloods gang, who dominated drug sales and other illegal activities in the Devil's Triangle (Bracamontes 2009). Gang injunctions restrict the civil rights of those named in the suit as a means of restoring order to the targeted neighborhood. They are issued by the state attorney general's office and are justified by police records, police intelligence, and the sworn testimony or written affidavits of gang officers and citizens affected by the disorder caused by the gang. About half of the defendants challenged the suit and were dropped from it, ultimately resulting in the issuance of an injunction against 13 members of the Bloods (Dominguez, 2009). At least 3 of these members had Latino surnames, indicating that Latinos are indeed core members of El Paso's most serious black gangs. As of 2015, Bloods members named in the 2010 injunction were still involved in lethal violence against the Gangster Disciples (Borunda 2015).

The dominant narrative regarding black gangs in El Paso is that they stem from gang-involved soldiers or army families from other places, who are stationed at Ft. Bliss (Barajas 2002; Borunda 2008a; Gerstein 2006). In 2006, Jeremy Francis of the FBI stated on local television news that law enforcement had identified at least 80 members of the military who had committed gang-related crimes in El Paso. Reginald Moton, who commanded the EPPD Gang Unit during the years that black gangs became highly active (2005–2010), regularly confirmed to the press that Ft. Bliss was a big part of the dynamic, as did one of El Paso's most well-known gang officers turned federal agent, Mary Lou Carrillo (Gerstein 2006). As evidence of the black gangs' influence, in 2015 a former Ft. Bliss soldier who became an El Paso County Juvenile Probation officer, Timothy McCullough, was tried as an associate of the GDs involved in a local teen prostitution ring (US Dept. of Justice 2015).

In 2005 the Gangster Disciples clashed with members of Barrio Azteca at a nightclub, leading to a shootout at a fast food restaurant later that evening (Roberts 2008). This was one of the first major incidents signaling the intensity of Ft. Bliss soldiers' local gang involvement. Indeed, they were now clashing with the region's most powerful street-to-prison hybrid gang. The Georgia Boys was a particularly active set of GDs who had conflicts with other servicemen and gangs native to El Paso (Borunda 2008a). The Crips also experienced clashes with the Barrio Azteca (Chavez 2010), which shows the intensity of the former in recent years. Northeast El Paso remains a hotspot for gang activity today, and while the traditional problem areas are still salient, areas on the fringe of the northeast section such as Harrison Avenue are now reportedly affected, too (Fertig 2017).

As of 2017, the El Paso Police Department's gang database showed 325 gangs in the city. The criterion for inclusion in this query was any group with three or more persons currently listed in the member database (Gibson 2017). It includes self-proclaimed street and prison gangs, car clubs, tagging crews, party crews, and motorcycle gangs that meet the standard definition of a group of three or more persons engaged in illegal activities and who use a common name, sign, symbol, or color (National Gang Intelligence Center 2016, 4; Texas Department of Public Safety 2018). A street gang intervention specialist named Rob Gallardo was a longtime critic of local law enforcement's method and practice of counting gangs, calling the count flawed at best (Borunda 2011). This has been an issue in crime and justice studies for some time. The counting of gangs and gang members is not a futile practice, but Rob Gallardo was correct to question its validity.

The counting of gangs is known to be notoriously unreliable (Ball and Curry 1995; Curry and Decker 1997; Jacobs 2009). Recall from chapter 1 the divergent estimates of El Paso's youth gang prevalence reported by the press, the police, and intervention specialists from the 1930s–1950s. This illustrates that the scope of "the gang problem" has been a poorly understood and politicized issue for decades. As secretive, dynamic groups, gang existence, their structure, and their activities are elusive and, therefore, prevalence estimates are prone to vary widely. It does not appear that this process has gotten much better in recent decades either (Greene and Pranis 2007). Figure 5.3 shows the number of El Paso gangs from official police estimates reported in various newspaper articles and official police reports over time.

One curious finding is the height of gang proliferation in 2009 with nearly 100 more gangs than in 1993, which was often considered to be the peak of gang activity in El Paso (Kirk 1993) and in all places across the nation (Howell 1999). Then, by 2011, the number of gangs was less than half of what it was at its height in 2009. This was the drastic drop that Rob Gallardo was most critical of in the press. One of the reasons for such fluctuations may lie with the rules that govern inclusion of individuals in the gang member database. Federal statute (28 CFR, part 23) and Texas Code of Criminal Procedure Chapter 61 require removal of a person from the active gang database if he or she does not re-offend within a two-year timeframe for juveniles and five years for adults. Most large agencies (likely including EPPD) will place these cases in an inactive file unless or until a new offense is recorded. Often, when

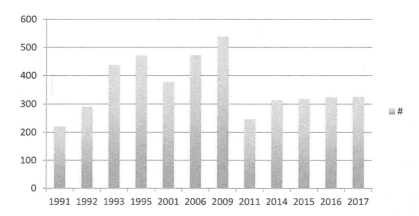

FIGURE. 5.3 | Number of gangs in El Paso over time.

a known individual is about to expire from the database, officers will make contact, check for traffic or other bench warrants, and so forth in an effort to avoid the expiration. Thus, depending on whether three or more members of a particular gang are in or out of the database at a given time, their entire gang could be added or removed accordingly from a separate database containing only gang names, not individuals.

Given this limitation it is questionable whether police gang databases offer a reasonable estimate of the number of active gangs. For example, out of the 325 active gangs in El Paso in 2017, a full 40 percent (n = 129) of them had only three or four members. An additional 21 gangs only had five members, leaving about 175 gangs in El Paso with six or more members, which might be considered a fairly organized gang with a core group of loyal members. In thinking about whether gang prevalence rates may be used for political purposes, consider that in February 2017, 10 additional officers were assigned to assist with gang unit functions after reports that gang activity was up over 40 percent from 2016 (Gonzales 2017). With some 20 officers now on the unit, the coverage ratio is about 1 officer for every 11 serious gangs (i.e., with six or more members). The number of members is a reasonable gauge of gang seriousness, in terms of its network size, organization (i.e., hierarchy), resources, reputation, and influence. Thus table 5.2 contains a list of El Paso's current largest and, presumably, most serious gangs.

To note that only 35 gangs have at least 40 members in them offers a unique perspective of the gang problem in El Paso. If these are in fact the city's most serious gangs, this amounts to a ratio of less than two groups to

Gangs	Members	Gangs	Members
Barrio Azteca	989	Moon City Locos	68
Sureño Trece	685	19th Street	67
Folk Nation	334	Sunset Territory	65
Bloods	297	3-6 Mafia	64
Crips	201	Lopez Maravilla	62
Varrio Northeast	158	Gangster Disciples	55
Chuco Tango	151	Hacienda Heights	55
Varrio Glenwood Street	98	Mexican Crazy Krew	49
Latin Kings	97	The Brown Dawgs	49
Los Fatherless	93	Straight Mother Fuckin Thugs	48
Varrio San Juan	85	Tango Blast	44
Los Midnight Locos	81	Segundo Barrio Kings	43
Northside Locos	77	Thug Life Crips	43
Varrio Logan Heights	76	Westside Nation	43
Segundo Barrio	75	Varrio Gatos Locos	43
Florencia Trece	74	Lower Valley Hoodlums	40
Los Skunx	70	True Nation Society	40
Hated by Many	68	One Nation Alone	38

El Paso County Sheriff's Gang Task Force

monitor per officer in the gang unit. While it is reasonable to assume the amount of attention each requires by law enforcement is proportional to its size, there are sure to be lots of exceptions. Some smaller gangs may be particularly intense in terms of solidarity, organization, and crime involvement, for example. Therefore, in reality, monitoring and managing gang dynamics from a police standpoint is more complicated than considering their size alone. Nonetheless, the sheer volume of groups and members with a track record for being antisocial, delinquent, and criminal is an important indicator of the scope of an area's gang problem.

In describing the changing structure of modern Chicano youth gangs in San Antonio, Valdez (2005) makes an important observation that also seems to hold true of El Paso's gangs. He notes that during the height of the gang epidemic in the 1990s, Chicano youth gangs had less "staying power" (i.e., turf, tradition, and lifespan) than those of prior generations. Of the 36 gangs listed in table 5.2, about one-third are new gangs without a deep, multigenerational history in El Paso.[10] An examination of the complete set of 325 current gangs, however, would yield a dramatically higher proportion of first generation or new age gangs. The current street-gang landscape in El Paso, then, is a mix of old and new, Chicano and black gangs, seven of them being very large (150 + members), and a large proportion (over two-thirds) of them as small gangs with 10 members or less. Important is that neither this current snapshot nor the historical view in chapter 1 account for the numerous reputable gangs that have existed in El Paso from the 1970s through the 2000s. Appendix A, therefore, contains an inventory of all reputable gangs made known to the author in this research project, assembled by decade.

The Barrio Azteca

The single largest gang listed in table 5.2 is by far the Barrio Azteca (BA). This is not its only distinction, however. It stands apart from all other groups in El Paso gang history in a number of ways noted here and in other sections of the book. The history of El Paso's borderland crime context presented thus far, including the Juárez dynamic in chapter 4, illustrates the region's potential for producing a modern supergang. The BA, as it has come to be known by law enforcement and the region's public, is in a small class of Chicano prison gangs that can only be described as the elite among the ignoble. Like most others in this class (e.g., La Eme, Nuestra Familia, the Texas Syndicate, Mexikanemi, Hermandad de Pistoleros Latinos [HPL], and Sindicato de Nuevo Mexico [SNM]), it was born in a Texas prison facility under the mantra of "protection" and self-preservation from regional tribalism and race conflicts (Gundur 2018; Rivera n.d.).

Like other Chicano prison gangs, the BA is governed by a constitution and paramilitary structure and rationalized by the recognition of the US Chicana/o as an oppressed people. In their early stages of formation, Chicano prison gangs tend to espouse a philosophy that they are soldiers for La Raza (i.e., Latinos), on the front lines against a corrupt system of social control (the US Justice system). As they grow in size and power, this message tends to get diluted or lost as they strategize and maneuver for dominance inside the prison system, and establish a highly capable criminal and often lucrative organization in the "free world." Thus, in many ways, from its inception and early evolution, the BA was not much different than other groups of its ilk, even emerging at about the same time as most Texas-based prison gangs in the 1980s (Fong 1990; Gundur 2018).

The BA's main distinction among prison gangs is its geographic home base of West Texas and Juárez. Generally, regionalism governs the formation of such factions (e.g., Mexikanemi in San Antonio, Texas Syndicate in Austin, SNM in Albuquerque). As a large metroplex, there are enough Chicano inmates from the El Paso–Juárez borderland region to form a critical mass in the Texas prison system. With a high poverty rate and a population exceeding 1.2 million in the region in the 1980s (Peach and Williams 1994), a significant number of Texas prison inmates originated from the area at the time the BA was formed.

The abundance of El Paso's barrio gang activity provides a large base of potential recruits into the BA gang over time, and it is able to be selective from among a mass of "hopefuls" who aspire to become part of the primary criminal group from their region. It operates the same for all prison gangs throughout the southwestern United States. But what has distinguished the BA from most other prison gangs historically is its uniquely favorable geographic placement with Juárez as its neighbor. This allowed the gang to flourish in the underworld very quickly, and in a way that perhaps no other US Chicano gang ever has.[11, 12]

THE BA'S BARRIO ROOTS

Like all Chicano prison gangs, the BA is a conglomeration of the most capable and criminally embedded from its home region. By this point in its 30-year history, this extends to Las Cruces to the northwest, Odessa and Midland, Texas, 280 miles to the east, and into the state of Chihuahua to the south. It is well known that prison gangs inevitably branch their operations out into the community, but their barrio roots are less often considered by gang scholars. One noteworthy exception was sociologist Alfredo Mirandé (1987) who wrote that the hierarchy from street to prison gang was a poorly understood topic. He went on to describe the decades-old East Los Angeles barrio gang Hoyo Maravilla as a feeder group to la Eme in California. Others have since updated this issue for that region (Morales 2008; Valdez and Enriquez 2011), but few have illustrated this with groups outside of greater LA County.

In the Texas prison system, inmates from certain parts of the state are reputed to be the fiercest in terms of their demeanor and comportment inside lockup facilities. El Paso is among these places and is perhaps the most often stereotyped in this regard—although San Antonio inmates would take issue with this characterization. Lurline Coltharp (1965) makes this claim about El Paso inmates in her linguistic study of pachuco slang in the Southwest.

As she notes, this is something that is often heard by word of mouth among Texas inmates. In his unpublished memoir on being a founder of the BA in a Texas prison, Rivera (n.d.) also reinforces this view. My own historical work on San Antonio's barrio gangs (2017) captures some of this sentiment about El Paso as well. The two cities have a longstanding rivalry in the penitentiary, and although it is currently dormant due to the negotiation of several peace treaties, El Paso's reputation among San Antonio *pintos* (ex-cons) is *firme* (upstanding; tough). Here, I offer that the intensity level reached by the BA stems, in large part, from that of its street gang predecessors in Segundo Barrio and south-central El Paso.

While some speculate that the 1950s gang X-14 are the predecessors to the BA (Barker 2012; Chavez 2019; *Proceso* 2006), the primary modern feeder groups to their formation are Del Diablo (DDT), the T-Birds, Los Sherman, and perhaps more than any other gang, Los Fatherless. Of course, this is not an exhaustive list; those known or perceived by BA leadership to be the most capable (mentally and/or physically) and loyal from any other El Paso barrio gang is also approached for recruitment. Some of Los Fatherless's core members of the 1980s and 1990s, when the gang was particularly aggressive, would go on to rise in the ranks of the BA in the early 2000s. One former Fatherless member, Juan "Conejo" Michelletti, became the scourge of the BA when he turned state's witness in the 2008 RICO case against the gang (Borunda 2008b). Although supposedly only a *soldado* for the BA, he testified that he had been working as an FBI informant for three years prior to the filing of these federal charges.

Another former Fatherless member who rose to the rank of lieutenant in the BA was Ricardo "Chino" Valles de la Rosa. Born in Juárez, Chino owned a body shop in El Paso's Lower Valley before going to prison on a drug charge in 1995 (McKinley 2010b). He was reportedly central in ordering the murder of El Paso County Jail officer Arthur Redelfs and his wife in Juárez in 2010.

An interesting controversy surrounding the case was tied to the motive. Despite early adamant statements from gang leaders that the officer was targeted for having "disrespected" the BA, local justice officials would not accept this possibility and seemingly orchestrated an alternate story about "mistaken identity." While some gang leaders eventually acquiesced to this new official version, no definitive conclusion has ever been reached, or at least not publicized. Perhaps officials felt it would be conceding too much power to the BA, or perhaps there was a backstory involving Redelfs and/ or his wife, a US Mexican Consulate employee, that never fully surfaced.[13] Bowden (2002) once noted that members of the Mexican Consulate in Juárez had a track record of cartel involvement. That another consulate employee's vehicle was attacked simultaneously, resulting in the death of her husband, was an indication there was far more to the story (for detailed treatments of this case, see Ainsle 2013 and Casey 2010a).

The BA was subject to a gang injunction in 2003. It is an interesting application of this widely used antigang tool, because it is typically reserved for street gangs (O'Deane 2011). Accordingly, injunctions are accompanied by the designation of a small geographic area as an "off-limits" zone for those individuals named in it. EPPD's gang intelligence at that time noted that the gang's turf was Segundo Barrio, where they extorted small businesses for *renta* (rent) and sold drugs on the streets and in area establishments. El Paso's County Attorney at the time, Jose Rodríguez, was granted the injunction, restricting the movement and activities of 32 specific members of the BA in Segundo. This part of the gang's history is also a testament to its barrio roots. Considering that the BA existed for more than 15 years by 2003, the injunction indicates that it was still a street-prison hybrid of sorts at that time. The members named in the injunction, no doubt, were still very much tied into their old street-gang networks.

The BA and the Juárez Cartel

Even though the modern brand of drug gang (cartel) activities have been salient in Juárez since the 1980s (Bowden 2002; Campbell 2009; Washington-Valdez 2006) police accounts of El Paso's gang dynamics in the early 1990s note that formal ties to them were rare among area gangs (Barajas 2002). Due to the cross-border social histories of its members, many either born in Juárez or with other family links there, the BA appears to be one of the rare groups of border dwellers that has always had ties to Juárez drug gangs (Gundur 2019; Ortiz Uribe 2014). In the years immediately following the gang injunction, that arrangement seemingly became more formal. One hypothesis is that the 2003 injunction, the subsequent investigations, sweeps, and resultant RICO prosecution that took shape around 2007 drove the BA to forge its ties much more closely to Juárez.

The BA has a Juárez counterpart known simply as the Aztecas that supposedly formed in 1990 in the Bella Vista colonia (*Proceso* 2006), a longtime barrio gang area (see chapter 4). Note this is only about four years after the BA is said to have formed in the Texas prison system (Barker 2012; Chavez 2019; Gundur 2019). Thus, it might be argued that the BA has been tied to Juárez since its inception. As an example of this group's historical binational nature, the BA uses the term *tirilon* to refer to the rank of lieutenant in its organization. Recall from chapter 1, this was the term referring to Juárez's earliest pachuco zoot suiters (1930s), who were also active in El Paso in the slum tenements in Chihuahuita and Segundo Barrio (Morales 2017). While the modern group's formal organizational ties to Juárez are now more complex, clearly the BA has a strong sense of its historical roots as a cross-border phenomenon.

The Juárez faction, Los Aztecas, has had its own leadership structure since at least 2001, and likely earlier. While "T-Top" Alvarez, "Shotgun" Perea, "Chicho" Meraz, "Tolon" Cardoza, and "Gino" Mona were some of the recent gang leaders constantly in the news in El Paso, lesser known capos "Baby" and "El Diablo" were more quietly running the Juárez sect (*Proceso* 2006). Former EPPD gang unit commander Javier Sambrano estimated that Los Aztecas were tapped by the Juárez cartel for formal cooperation in 2003. In poring over news items, intelligence reports, and similar literature on the gang's operations, it is clear that the Juárez and El Paso factions were once more independent of each other but cooperated closely (e.g., Campbell 2009; Chavez 2009; Gundur 2017; US Dept of Justice 2011).

In time, it became more accurate to consider the Juárez and El Paso factions of the BA as one large, unified entity, whose members are either based on one side of the border or the other, with frequent movement between the two places (Chavez 2019; Sanchez 2009; Serrano 2017). When a member was wanted by Mexican authorities, he might hide out on the El Paso side, and vice versa. It is clear, however, that as pressure was placed on the BA by various segments of the US justice system, the two factions became more unified and fluid. As is common in US investigations of Mexican-based drug gangs, there are unforeseen and unintended consequences of creating other, often, worse problems (Epstein 2015). It appears that clamping down on the BA with the best suppression tools in the US law enforcement toolkit resulted in pushing its operations further into Juárez, where they are not well monitored, and, thus, have a strategic advantage for conducting their business in El Paso. Moreover, the more directly they operated with the Juárez cartel, the higher the gang's level of criminal embeddedness became.

The BA and the Battle for the Plaza

In about 2007, the Juárez and Sinaloa Cartels began a battle for control of the Juárez–El Paso "plaza" or drug corridor (Campbell 2009; US Dept. of Justice

Texas Department of Public Safety (DPS), claims that when the Juárez Cartel's stronghold on the plaza was weakened by competition from Sinaloa, it effected shifts throughout the hierarchy, down to the street level. The BA, who is allied with the Juárez Cartel, was also weakened in turn. The group was simultaneously hit by a series of RICO prosecutions after significant targeting of the group by the FBI and local gang taskforces for more than a decade (Borunda 2014b; Sanchez 2009). This placed the gang in its most vulnerable position since its rise to power. Its threat level was even downgraded in the 2015 DPS report, which noted its capacity on both sides of the border had been diminished, placing it on a more even playing field with other Texas gangs. It remained at this downgraded level in the 2017 DPS report, but then reemerged as a Tier 1 threat in the 2018 report (Texas Department of Public Safety 2018).

Table 5.2 shows that the second largest gang in El Paso, behind the BA, is the Sureño Trece (SUR-13). The 2015 Texas DPS report claims the SUR-13 was tapped by the Sinaloa Cartel to assist in challenging the Juárez Cartel/BA for control of the plaza, emboldening and empowering SUR-13 in the region. The underlying assumption is that the California Eme prison gang, as the "parent" organization of the SUR-13, was now involved in the struggle for dominance over the drug trade in the borderland (more on this in chapter 6). However, while the BA, the Juárez Cartel, and its Juárez-based enforcement arm, La Linea, were weakened, the setback only proved to be temporary, as these groups have shown high levels of resilience (Borunda 2014b; Texas Department of Public Safety 2018).

The sophistication of the BA gang's network required a series of RICO prosecutions against a large number of operatives, stretching the trials out significantly. Lieutenants Manny Minjares and Chino Valles took guilty pleas in 2016 and 2017, respectively, while the top BA-Azteca capo remained at large for more than 10 years before being caught by the Mexican army in June 2018. Eduardo "Tablas" Ravelo had been on the FBI's top 10 most wanted list for more than a decade. He was considered critical in cross-border operations and deeply embedded with the Carrillo-Fuentes drug trafficking organization in Chihuahua. Before his capture, his elusiveness had FBI agents speculating that he may have even undergone plastic surgery to disguise his appearance (Einhorn 2011; Sanchez 2009).

As documented in chapter 4, gang-related violence in Juárez, while elevated since the 1990s, began to escalate dramatically in 2007, reaching its peak in 2010, and gradually diminishing thereafter. To specify the primary

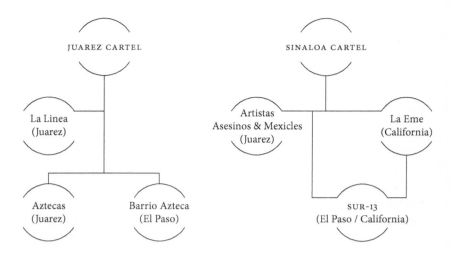

FIGURE 5.4 | Rival drug gang hierarchies in the borderland ca. 2005–2017.

groups and their hierarchies at that time, figure 5.4 shows the Juárez Cartel's primary "muscle" or hit squad was La Linea, supported by Los Aztecas and the BA both in roles of violence and in the smuggling and dissemination of drugs to the street level.[14] Rival Sinaloa Cartel's muscle were the Artistas Asesinos (AA) and Los Mexicles. Like the BA, these gangs were empowered from being barrio-prison hybrid gangs to cartel operatives.

The supposed role of SUR-13 within the Sinaloa hierarchy thus comes with a caveat. It is important to recall from previous chapters that the SUR-13 is perhaps the most widespread brand name in Latino street gang proliferation across the United States, with most of its membership as US-born teenagers starting up sets in various cities and neighborhoods at their own discretion. Thus, it is not a unified gang per se, but a "nation" or a loose federation of gangsters spread about the United States who operate by roughly the same codes and use the same colors and mantras. Their level of sophistication as a whole then, is not comparable to that of the other gangs in figure 5.4, who are strictly regional and hierarchical within themselves.

As noted in chapters 2 and 3, there is an important distinction to be made between the true blue or real adult Sureños with direct ties to the California Eme and those locally formed, homegrown sets comprised mostly of youth. There are enough serious adult sets in the borderland region, to include those in Las Cruces and Anthony, that a specific caliber of Sureño likely did begin to assume this role for the Sinaloenses. Some of these true blue

Sureño sets in the region include Big Hazard, Maravilla, Florencia, White Fence, and Playboy.[15] As far back as 2009, law enforcement reported serious clashes between the Sureños and the BA (Borunda 2014a).[16] However, this is at least partly, and perhaps entirely, due to the Eme and the BA being natural enemies, and the SUR-13 is an extension of la Eme. If these clashes are inherently over turf, then their respective connections to rival Mexican drug trafficking organizations (MDTO) only reinforced this tension.

While they have reportedly been in El Paso for decades (Borunda 2014a), the Sureños' presence became most evident in the past five years or so. A series of high-profile drug busts and sweeps from 2014 to 2017 by the FBI, DEA, and local police gives credence to the purported link to Sinaloa. Most of these were seizures of large amounts of methamphetamine, which the Sinaloenses were known to produce and smuggle into the United States more than any other cartel at the time (US Department of Justice 2011). It is interesting that despite their supposed ties to the Sinaloa Cartel and the California Eme, the SUR-13 has never been given a Tier-1 classification by the Texas Department of Public Safety. This is the highest threat level in its biannual assessment of gang activity in the state. Similarly, for two consecutive reports (2015 and 2017) the BA was classified as a Tier 2 threat along with a large grouping of street and prison gangs. These "threat" levels cannot be taken at face value, however. For example, that Tango Blast, MS-13, and Latin Kings are three of the four groups classified as Tier 1 gangs in the 2017 report is problematic and misleading.

First, members of Tango Blast and other Tango groups are numerous across Texas, but they are not a Security Threat Group in the prison system, nor are they considered to be highly organized on the street. By design, they are simply a support group for its members to "do their time peacefully" (Tapia 2013, 5) and return to normal life once back in their communities (see Gundur 2018; Tapia 2017). With isolated exceptions, they do not aggressively organize as a proactive criminogenic group. Moreover, like the SUR-13, they are a loose federation of groups, each claiming a "hometown" or Tango while incarcerated in county or state facilities. It is not known why they pose such a high risk in the DPS report.

MS-13 may have a growing presence in Dallas and Houston, but it is not formidable in other parts of Texas. Even in Dallas and Houston, they are not dominant or even considered a major competitor by and among other gangs. Similarly, the Latin Kings are not indigenous to Texas. Their traditional strongholds are in Chicago and New York, primarily (Brotherton and Barrios 2004). Like the SUR-13, they have a presence in most major cities but are not strongest in Texas or in other parts of the Southwest. Some report Latin King links to Sinaloenses, and if so, it has clear implications for the dissemination of drugs on the streets of Chicago. But of the drug trafficking activity between El Paso and Chicago (see Borunda 2017b), the role of the Latin Kings is not likely to be very great. These issues not only detract from the credibility of the DPS reports, but even worse, the agency appears to be propagandizing the issue of gangs, ranking these three groups high on the threat list for political purposes. In his coverage of the capture of the Barrio Azteca leader, Asmann (2018) echoes these concerns about the Trump administration's needless creation of a moral panic with false rhetoric on cartel spillover effects.

SIX

The Role of History and Geography on Criminal Subcultures

Introduction

In such a vast and diverse metroplex like El Paso–Juárez, barrio gangs may seem to some like just an obscure subculture among many others in the big city. Yet, gangs are as important a part of the community's fabric as any other, as their existence reflects some significant part of the city's values among gang and nongang members alike. Gangs thrive in the underground economy, a universal phenomenon that serves all social classes. Moreover, by virtue of the less than ideal social contexts most gang members were born into, they do not always choose the gang lifestyle; rather it "selects" them for being marginalized members of society in some way.

Unlike much of the academic work on gangs, this book does not delve too deeply into the fundamental causes and interpersonal consequences of gang membership.[1] Rather, it is a broad overview of the historical, organizational, and subcultural elements that unraveled in a region that represents the epicenter of the 100-year Chicano gang phenomenon in the United States. Over the better part of this period, barrio gangs were a staple of social life in poor and working-class Chicano communities across the Southwest. Street gangs as we once knew them may be headed for extinction in the face of rapid societal and technological change and, as seen here, other shifts in social relations. Thus, from an anthropological standpoint, writing about them now is perhaps more important than ever.

One of the study's goals was to understand more about gangs as a long-standing feature of social life in Chicano communities. Nowhere was such an examination more warranted than El Paso for being the birthplace of the pachuco versus other places that have been the focus of many such studies (e.g. LA, Chicago, San Antonio). An important question addressed by examining gangs historically is the extent to which the subculture has spread and changed over time. On the US side of the border, anchored by El Paso, the roughly century-long history of gangs was shown to influence those in surrounding areas and those in distant places, including a migration of the pachuco style from El Paso to Los Angeles.

Despite the abundance of research on Chicano gangs generally, there is only sparse information about the various forms these groups took over time. Their unique histories, longevity, economic opportunities, conflicts, and other politics are seldom the focus of extended works. By tracing the structural evolution of such groups, the different forms they take in the major population locales in the borderland region, and their network ties across the region, my aim was to more comprehensively help fill this gap in the literature.

In describing the nuances of gang history and organization, one risks alienating the "law and order" oriented reader, who might suspect some glorification of the gang lifestyle has occurred. On the contrary, such an undertaking reminds one that gangs often emerge from some of the worst social conditions, mostly brought on by socioeconomic inequality. Aside from the obvious—violent clashes that occur among gangs—there are other ugly facets of that atmosphere, most of which were barely addressed here. Yet, all gang researchers are fully aware of how strongly negative contexts and behaviors correlate with the gang lifestyle. Some qualitative and ethnographic gang researchers even purposely position themselves to see this up close.

For many of us, these contexts represent some part of the human condition that is difficult to grasp, and thus it keeps us intrigued. That illicit, underground societies would form among those on the margins of society and continue to adapt to social change is an interesting notion to many. That most of these are comprised of poorly educated misfit youth, who effectively organize their groups despite formal, legal efforts to deter and disband them is equally fascinating.

The interpersonal struggles that many gang members experience with drug addiction, family dysfunction, cycles of violence and abuse, blocked opportunities, anger, frustration, depression, and other social ills that disproportionately plague the underclass were not the focus of this work. But in collecting stories of the reputable persons and occurrences in the barrios studied here, the murders, suicides, lengthy incarcerations, and other misfortunes of many gang-involved individuals were recounted by interviewees, in newsprint, and other sources. There is still much more to unearth in this regard—perhaps in future work on these topics in the region. My colleagues

Howard Campbell (2009) and Rob Durán (2018) are among those that have illuminated more of these elements in their work on the region than I have, but there is still more to explore there.

The Role of Geography

In the world of science, idiosyncrasy is typically problematic. This is especially so for the structuralists, for whom the order of things, even in the social spheres governing human interaction, is expected to be formulaic. Such positivism is not likely to give much weight to the role of place in shaping sociological outcomes. Given the same or a similar set of conditions, what is observed in one place should also occur in another. I myself have argued elsewhere (2017) that historical forays into the gangs of large Chicano urban centers will yield insights on the structural contours of gang life in other such places. The problem is that the position is too theoretical, as no two places are ever truly the same. That is, no two places experience equal structural or cultural conditions. In short, the local histories of all places, their city and neighborhood politics, and so forth are idiosyncratic.

Conducting a case study of street gangs in the El Paso–Juárez borderland region demonstrates that place and history matter greatly to the particular type of criminal subculture that emerges in a locale (see Gundur's 2018 comparison of El Paso and Phoenix as more evidence of this). While the structural perspective is still useful to compare gang developments in various places, I continue to argue that no other place in the world is quite like the El Paso–Juárez border region, a position that others who wrote on its crime subcultures have also taken (Bender 2012; Bowden 2002; Campbell 2009; Cartwright 1998; Quiñonez 2016). And yet, the criminogenic implications of this place appearing to be optimally positioned to be crime ridden falls flat on the US side. Despite the richness of its pachuquismo and cholismo, high poverty rates, and a long list of barrio gangs spread throughout the region over time (see appendix A), violence on the US side of this region is astonishingly low. Indeed, Durán's (2018) work on gangs and delinquency in the borderland region refers to this fact as a "miracle" so profound, he titled his book accordingly.

As seen in chapters 4 and 5, the first-meets-third-world contrast can be striking along parts of the Juárez–El Paso border. In other instances, it is difficult to distinguish which side is which (see, e.g., the findings of Vila 2000). In this regard, *place* and its boundaries are often difficult to define. This has been a problem for sociological studies of neighborhoods and crime for nearly a century (Bursik and Grasmick 1993), and for treatments of "place" more generally (Gieryn 2000). In the current study, the "sister cities" metaphor versus the "totally different places" narrative is so problematic precisely *because* of the proximity the cities share and the cultural, familial, and economic ties that such closeness fosters. I must echo that Juárez and El Paso and, residually, its entire region is wrought with contradictions that are difficult to analyze and make sense of in this regard.

Ethnically, culturally, and, to some extent, socioeconomically, the population base of Juárez and El Paso are arguably quite similar, but for the past few decades, the levels of gang violence between them are dramatically divergent. Immigration and citizenship status tends to be a major moderator of any similarities they might otherwise share in population composition, but if the political boundary was not as salient, there would likely be even less of a distinction between the two populations. Again, the complexity of the region's contradictions reinforces that social conditions, style of governance, levels of state corruption, the drug war as its own beast, and other macrostructural factors matter a great deal in the production of violence in a society. Any essentialist notions about the "types of people" prone to engaging in the worst forms of gang violence are therefore mitigated by this case study.

Chapter 5 argues that the Barrio Azteca (BA) is the quintessential cross-border gang, uniquely produced by the culmination of historical forces in the region. The demand for drugs in the United States and changes in the patterns of production and distribution in the Western Hemisphere made El Paso–Juárez one of if not *the* most important of plazas on the US–Mexico border for some time. As in the days of Pancho Villa and the Mexican Revolution, this border continues to be a strategic context for hegemonic forces, now having much to do with the economics and politics of the behemoth illegal drug industry and human migration flows in North America. The justification for the federal antidrug intelligence resources that are focused on this border region thus appears to be to maintain a strategic advantage over drug cartels by controlling the plaza.

As a genuine barrio-prison-hybrid gang at one time, the El Paso–based BA was uniquely positioned to capitalize on this circumstance. When the gang formed in the mid-1980s, it was not seemingly with this goal in mind. It simply was another prison gang comprised of incarcerated barrio gang members, formed under the same conditions and for the same reasons as all the other major Chicano prison gangs in the Southwest—as a combative force against other predatory groups and other prison politics (Gundur 2019).

While many US barrio gangs, if not individual members within those gangs, now have developed ties to Mexican drug cartels, none has become so embedded in their operations over time as the BA. Yet, the only truly distinguishing characteristic of the BA among other barrio-prison gangs was its geographic origin. To be fair to the structural perspective, there are other examples of US gang–Mexican cartel connections in other areas of the border, but the symbiotic nature and longevity of their ties to Mexican groups do not yet compare to that of the BA and the Juárez cartel.

Due to its positioning in the San Diego–Tijuana border region, a group similar to the BA, called Barrio Logan, developed a working relationship with the Arellano-Felix Cartel in the early 1990s. But these ties proved superficial, having weakened soon after the arrests of several key Logan members (Sullivan 1999). However, the renewal of bloody struggles between various cartels and lower-level gangs for the Tijuana plaza (Dibble 2018; Lira, Orozco, Ferreira, and Shirk 2018) is surely making use of such US-based groups again. In Laredo, Texas, such links between the Zetas Cartel and a decades-old prison gang called the Hermandad de Pistoleros Latinos (HPL-45) recently came to light (Buch 2013; Santana and Morales 2014) and continue to take shape. Finally, in the Rio Grande Valley of south Texas, the Tri City Bombers (TCB), a longtime barrio gang, were recently busted trafficking drugs for the Gulf Cartel (US Dept. of Justice 2017b). There is also reportedly a heavy presence of the prison-cartel-hybrid gangs el Partido Revolucionario Mexicano (PRM), Los Paisas, and their various city-based crews operating in that region (Martinez and Montilla 2018; Santana and Morales 2014). There may be other, less significant examples of such collaborations on other parts of the border, but these are some of the few major, publicized cases to date.

Geographic placement has clearly facilitated the formation of these ties and will continue to do so with factional splintering now occurring among the major Mexican DTOS (Agren 2017; Castro and Vargas 2018; Esquivel 2018; Lira, Orozco, Ferreira, and Shirk 2018). While Mexican drug gangs have been involved with US barrio and prison gangs for decades, more research is needed on the southwestern border for a better sense of how extensive these gangs' dealings with Mexican drug suppliers are. For example, until research on the PRM, Los Paisas, HPL, and the TCBS is conducted in the way I have done for the BA and Juárez Cartel in chapter 5, we'll not know the level of sophistication there.[2] Furthermore, gang threat assessment reports put out by both federal and state agencies tend to create more public alarm about these topics than is warranted. The propagandizing of the border crime threat by justice agencies involves the branding of such elements as *narcoterrorism*. But sociological analyses are needed to help to determine the depth and sophistication of US barrio gang and cartel links as a particular issue in border security. Unfortunately, to date, we have mostly hyperbolized law enforcement and military perspectives on the matter (e.g., McCaffrey and Scales 2011).[3]

Levels of Violence, Intensity, and Spillover

In evaluating the knowledge about US–Mexico border crime threats, the El Paso–Juárez region has been the most studied so far by academics, the media, and other writers. The profound irony in their findings is the utter lack of spillover activity into the United States from Mexico. Despite the BA serving as a poignant example of a cross-border crime network, the implications for the US side of the region are surprisingly mundane. They simply reflect the typical southwestern big-city issues with gangs and drugs with little apparent infiltration or cultural norm changes being effected in El Paso by these cross-border connections. Moreover, compared to other such southwestern cities similar in size, like Albuquerque, Las Vegas, San Antonio, and several southern California cities, the violence levels brought about by gang activity are much lower in El Paso. As proposed by El Paso natives in chapter 4, perhaps "what happens in Juárez, *does* stay in Juárez."

The lack of spillover on the US side of this borderland region is so remarkable that it cannot be overemphasized. Yet, the opposite happens; politicians and justice officials regularly warn of some looming threat of drug-gang infiltration from Mexico, and the phrase "the sky is falling" does not seem to ever lose its foreboding effect (Gundur 2017). Vila (2000), a perceptive Argentina-born sociologist studying El Paso–Juárez from UTEP in the 1990s, noted that an "us versus them," if not "us *apart* from them" narrative dominates the region when it comes to comparisons between Juárez and El Paso. I will leave it to those more philosophical voices to gauge whether such a powerful trope is capable of helping to create the containment of violence on the Juárez side, perhaps as a byproduct of first-meets-third-world neglect of the former toward the latter. Others might more simply sum it up as a lawless state meets a law-and-order state.

Regional Networks and Social Intricacies

In examining the contours of the borderland's street gangs, this work seeks to evaluate the extent to which gang-based network links exist across the region. This serves to inform notions about the meaning of *place* in criminology, namely its scope. It began by describing the similarities in the streetwise pachuco subcultural elements in both Juárez and El Paso. Indeed, it is difficult to pin the origin either in Juárez or El Paso (Valenzuela 2013), and that is because of the symbiotic nature of these places. This book is replete with examples of cross-region connections within the gang subculture. Thus, not only are Juárez and El Paso gangs symbiotic in terms of their cultural influence on each other, but there are a multitude of network connections among individuals and groups across the border and throughout the region. Just a cursory analysis of gangs that exist(ed) in both Juárez and on the US side or which migrated to one side from the other yielded about 20 examples (chapter 4). In terms of individual criminal links, this number would easily get into the thousands at any given point in time.

To be effective, drug trafficking requires a great deal of camouflage. In a dense population center located on the US–Mexico border where drugs are abundant, this seems to take place with relative ease and frequency. It is only when some dispute or settling of a score from a debt owed and so forth occurs that the insidious elements with a normative façade are discovered. For example, in February 2017, *El Diario* newspaper reported on a triple homicide in an upscale bar in Juárez. Two of the victims were university students in Juárez and the other at UTEP. The Juárez District Attorney called it "part of a dispute over the control of the retail crystal meth market" and "a new generation of gangs [that involve] university students, people with a lot of education from the upper middle class who dress well and pass unnoticed" (*El Diario* 2017b). It is worth noting that the same description of middle-class kids joining drug gangs was offered by the Juárez municipal police more than ten years earlier (*Proceso* 2006). Similarly, in January 2018, a student at Ysleta High School in El Paso's lower valley was shot dead in a makeshift auto mechanic shop in Juárez as part of a dispute between drug gangs (Borunda 2018b).

These few anecdotes reflect the fluidity of cross-border drug networks that incorporate the most inconspicuous of actors. As Campbell (2009) notes about the region, these networks are so endemic that "everyone is affected by drugs in the El Paso–Cd. Juárez region. If it's not the person himself . . . then it's a friend or relative . . . everyone knows someone, or is related to someone who is a drug trafficker or consumer" (180). If this is accurate, and it is entirely plausible given the lengthy history of contraband smuggling in the region (as per chapter 4), then one might even refer to it as "normative." The accessibility of profitable opportunities from the drug- or human-smuggling trades might be seen as a form of capital and Campbell's (2009) notion is all the more cogent when we consider the strong familial connections that crisscross the region's urban centers and smaller communities studied here (Vila 2000).

My fieldwork for this book focused sharply on the gang topic, and it was always presented to research subjects as such. But inevitably, with time, rapport, and trust, many subjects intimated about other "things" either they, their family, and/or friends witnessed or were involved in, and may have even gotten busted for or hurt by. In studying criminal subcultures in the borderland, one always gets the sense that there are many untold secrets of criminal involvement embedded within a patchwork of relative normalcy or mundane poverty conditions within the family. This might include the death of a loved one via drug overdose or through deeper levels of involvement than what might be expected from interacting with a seemingly "average" Chicano or Mexican working-class family. As I found in San Antonio (2017), the nexus of social class and criminality in the Chicano community is one of the more sensitive and complex subjects to unravel, bordering on the taboo in terms of data collection. Even police families have black sheep and other personal relationships to ex-felons, and it is surely more common with black and Latino officers.

Probing the topic of regional gang networks with members of law enforcement in my research yielded many contradictions. In 2018, an officer from a specialized unit in El Paso told me about a case involving a very active set of Sureños from Anthony who regularly cooperated with groups in El Paso for robberies, theft, and drug deals. This complemented my own findings about the crisscrossing of networks in the region evident in historical records and interviews with nonlaw enforcement border dwellers. However, when asked about any gang connections between Las Cruces and El Paso, a veteran gang officer in Las Cruces commented that there were not many to speak of, both in terms of rivalries and alliances. While in some cases, special units officers can be evasive with a curious civilian researcher like me, this scenario of conflicting information played out often enough with various officers interviewed that it is a salient theme in my findings.

Having interviewed agents or corrections officers (a mix of active and retired) from across some 10 different departments including city, county, state, and federal agencies in the region, I often asked them if they knew each other. There were some veteran officers that everybody knew, or at least knew of. But there were other seasoned gang officers that did essentially the same job for different jurisdictions only 20 to 50 miles apart, and who did not seem to know each other, much less cooperate on cases. Despite the friction known to exist among agencies of varying levels, this was surprising, given the cross-agency gang intelligence meetings that are supposedly held regularly. The geographic areas I studied on the US side contained two counties located in different states (technically), easily comprising more than 500 square miles in landmass. Therefore, the region may be just large enough that info sharing across the various law enforcement agencies is not as regular or efficient as one might imagine. Perhaps also the nature of communication and interaction in the criminal underworld is such that much of it goes under the law enforcement radar—not easily detectable. These are difficult things to gauge, even for those inside law enforcement who work assignments that include gangs.[4]

Such topics also raise the issue of how criminal networking occurs. And it remains somewhat theoretical, despite knowing that officers monitor phone communication and social media pages and use other types of physical surveillance, both traditional and high-tech. Still, it is difficult to see the forest from the trees where the network structure of street gangs, prison gangs, drug crews, prostitutes, auto-theft rings, and so on and their potential links to Mexican cartels or other higher-order crime groups is elusive. Given what Campbell (2009) and others claim about the ubiquity of drug-related activity that may qualify as normative, the network possibilities appear to be so numerous it is bewildering. Matched with the high levels of corruption thought to exist within law enforcement on both sides of the border, it is clear why many assert the war on drugs is a farce.

Given the historically low violence rate and the lack of any significant cartel violence spillover to the US side, the high priority the Department of Justice and local law enforcement give to fighting the "drug war" is interesting. The El Paso Intelligence Center (EPIC), headed by the DEA, leads this effort for the entire Western Hemisphere, and while it is uncertain exactly how it utilizes the information, the agency collects much data on criminal networks on both sides of the border. Seemingly without a cogent justification, construction of the latest multimillion-dollar Texas Anti-Gang (TAG) center was completed in September 2017 in El Paso (City of El Paso 2017; El Paso County Government 2016).[5] Hence, the criminological paradoxes in the El Paso–Juárez border region continue to abound.

Nuances in the Region's Street Gang Structures

As noted throughout the book, contemporary Chicano gangs in the El Paso–Juárez borderland are most influenced by those in California. Moving eastward, El Paso represents the last major city in this portion of the Southwest. The next major cities in the Sunbelt (Austin and San Antonio) are nearly 600 miles to the east, placing them in a whole other region comprising central and east Texas, to include Dallas-Ft. Worth to the north and Houston to the far east. The Chicano gang subculture in that region is different from that of the El Paso region in important ways.

Similar to how the gang subculture emanating from Los Angeles influences the western region, that of Houston dominates most of Texas. A hybridized street-to-prison federation now organizes (however loosely) Texas Chicano gangs under the Tango structure in all major cities. Houston's Tango Blast is the largest of these groups, having the most influence over gang subculture in most of Texas in general.[6] As noted in chapter 5, El Paso's Chuco Tango, the seventh largest gang in the city, is the latest addition to this movement in Texas.[7]

To assert that the El Paso–Juárez region's Chicano gangs are primarily influenced by California essentially means that Sureño is the most common affiliation (per southern California), with a considerable presence of Norteño affiliation stemming from northern California. While the nuances of Sureños and Norteños relative to their emulation groups in the borderland were discussed at length in earlier chapters, much less has been presented about the alternative Chicano gang structures in the landscape. The Chicago influence is formidable in the numerous Folk and People (Kings) sets in the city, but this is characteristic of every major US city. The more salient structural gang issue in El Paso for the most recent period (2015–2020) involves the Chuco Tango as an extension of the Houston-based and, more generally, Texas-based federation of street-prison hybrids.

First presented in chapter 5, Chuco Tango is El Paso's newest significant gang, and it has been every bit as disruptive as its youthful, rebellious counterparts in the rest of Texas are reputed to be (see Tapia 2013). For the past 15 to 20 years, Tango federations in major Texas cities (except El Paso) have dominated young adult Latino gang structures in jails, prisons, and streets. Its late arrival to El Paso is likely conditioned by several factors. First, Tangos are known for rebelling against their parent groups, which are the dominant prison gangs in each major Texas city (Mexikanemi in San Antonio, Raza

Unida in Corpus Christi, Texas Syndicate in Austin and Houston, etc.). In El Paso, this would amount to rebelling against the Barrio Azteca (BA) and, by extension, the Juárez-based Aztecas, La Linea, and the Juárez Cartel. As menacing and untouchable of a group the BA was from the 1990s to about 2010, a rebellion by their foot soldiers, Chuco Tango, was not a realistic possibility nor was it in their interest.

The second possible factor keeping Chuco Tango from taking the rebellious stance that its counterparts in the rest of Texas did ties back to the El Paso–Juárez borderland region's larger culture. To begin, chapter 5 argues that the high density of Latinos in El Paso keeps violence down since Latino population density is a significant negative correlate of violence (Desmond and Kubrin 2009; Martinez 2002; Morenoff 2005; Sampson et al. 2005). El Paso's high Latino density is of course attributable to its proximity to Juárez. Among the other major cities in Texas, it is unique in this regard. It is the only large Texas city (more than 300,000 population) on the Mexican border and, therefore, its Chicano gangs are influenced more by Mexican gang norms and structure than those in any other large Texas city. Juxtaposing its Chicano gang norms to those of the rest of Texas, it is much less racially hybridized and less gangsta-oriented than it is barrio-oriented. This subculture is not readily conducive to Tango gang norms.

I sought to test this notion in the current study. In my interviews with corrections officers in El Paso, I probed the theme of Chuco Tangos as racially and ethnically hybridized gangs. My questions to these officers on this matter were, in many cases, ultimately asked in a very direct, slang vernacular that they must understand to be effective gang officers. Especially where I felt officers (and other insiders closer to the gang milieu) were not fully grasping the essence of my inquiry, I simply asked whether and to what extent Chuco Tango members were *enmayatados*. This is a slightly derogatory slang term in the Chicano working-class and gang contexts to ask "how black" a non-black person is/acts, and whether they regularly associate with blacks. The equivalent in relation to the white race is how *agringado* one is.

When it was clear to subjects what I was asking about, the responses were surprising to me. With very few exceptions, the answer to this question was resoundingly that the Chuco Tangos are not in the least bit hybridized in this way. Jail and prison officers stated that Spanish and Chicano slang was their primary vernacular and that they clashed with blacks in jail and on the streets. Furthermore, their gang norms were still very much characteristic of the region and not like those of Houston, Dallas, and so forth. In these places, young Chicano gang members do, to a large extent, adopt the speech, customs, norms, and other subcultural elements of black gangsters. Part of this is a demographic matter, as there is a much higher proportion of blacks in Houston and Dallas, therefore leading to more cross-racial interaction in the underclass and apparently more racial harmony in terms of the ethnic hybridization of gangs.

The subcultural gang orientation of many modern-day Chicano gang members, even in San Antonio as one of the heavily Houston-influenced Tango cities, is decidedly gangsta (Tapia 2017). These Tango groups are also somewhat post-racial in that they accept white and black members to keep their membership numbers high to maintain the edge over the oppressive traditional Latino prison gangs whom they rebel against. It therefore remains to be seen what will become of Chuco Tango, who appear to be taking advantage of the vacuum of power on the street brought on by the weakening of the Barrio Azteca, their former parent group. Given their traditional barrio orientation, their historical underlying ties to the BA (which, despite their newfound rebellious stance towards the BA, never fully dissolves), and their willingness to engage in criminal enterprises out in the streets (Gundur 2018; Martinez 2016; Rivera 2016), they may become the next major cross-border gang in the region.

A Final Assessment

After a 23-year hiatus, I returned to live in the El Paso–Juárez borderland in fall 2015. Upon exploring the gang landscape in Las Cruces, I quickly learned of a street-prison hybrid called the Cruces Boys (CBS). This was a conglomeration of former street-gang members from Las Cruces, currently or formerly incarcerated. Like the Tangos of Texas, the CBS subsume even members of rival gangs in the name of city-based unity to be able to resist the exploitative politics of the traditional prison gangs in New Mexico.[8] Now, rather than having smaller fragmented groups of street-gang members competing for the favor of the prison gangs, Las Cruces-based gangsters have unified in lockup facilities as the Cruces Boys. The exact same phenomenon occurs in the north-central part of the state among the Burqueños of Albuquerque, New Mexico's largest city.

Like the Tangos of Texas, at the heart of the formation of these city-based groups are intergenerational dynamics. As in Texas, such conflict between this younger generation and the older prison gangs has been underway for the past decade in New Mexico, possibly even as far back as 2005.[9] While these developments are slightly more recent than those in Texas, the rationale for their origins and structure are nearly identical. Learning of the recent emergence of the Cruces Boys and Burqueños was a primary impetus for my research, due to the similarities this development shares with changes in gang structure in the central Texas locales I previously studied (Tapia 2017). In my estimation, we are witnessing the widespread emulation of the modern, Houston-based Chicano gang structure throughout the Southwest and it has various organizational implications.

Whether to avoid the stigma of classification as a Security Threat Group in prison or for ideological or other functional reasons, Tango-type groups have so far resisted the prison gang label. Members of these loosely affiliated groups claim they are a support network for inmates who want to do their time peacefully and avoid coercion from traditional Latino prison gangs. This reflects a changing mindset among the new generation toward a horizontal versus a hierarchical structure, and a new function for the Tango-type organization in jails, prisons, and streets across the Southwest. The key theoretical and policy question for the borderland is whether the Cruces Boys or the Chuco Tangos will eventually assume the organizational characteristics of the traditional prison gangs (Gundur 2018). From recent news media reports, this already appears to be occurring in terms of criminal enterprise outside of prison (Martinez 2016; Rivera 2016; US Dept. of Justice 2017c). Since police and corrections gang intelligence is not readily shared with the public, there is sure to be much more offensive maneuvering occurring with these groups in the streets than what has come to light.

If the trend toward Tango-type empowerment continues to spread westward, it is possible that it would affect Chicano gang structures in the "mecca" of southwestern gang locales, LA. The current southern California Chicano gang hierarchy is the Mexican Mafia prison gang la Eme on top, and the Sureños as their foot soldiers (Morales 2008; Valdez and Enriquez 2011). This decades-long arrangement is thought to be so well organized that most think it won't be affected by widespread changes in regions further east. However, the origin of developments occurring from Houston to Albuquerque over the past 20 years is driven by a fundamental sense of injustice among inmates and street criminals themselves. If the rewards of a group's position in the hierarchy are perceived to be inadequate to a critical mass of inmates, they may organize a revolt among themselves. If resentment toward prison gangs' methods of profit sharing or other manners of doing business grows, the discontent could create an eventual shift, as seen in Texas. Due to the forces of migration, interactions in federal prison, and the like, enough LA Sureños will come into contact with members of Tango Blast, Chuco Tango, and the Burqueños that mere exposure to their plight might motivate them to put up similar forms of resistance against their parent group.

These developments in Texas and New Mexico reflect the collective conscience of once-subservient groups in the hierarchy and therefore speak to the organizational capacity of younger Chicano gang members. To note that the Tangos have, in such a short timeframe, evolved a collective mindset of rebellion, rejection of traditional gang norms, reformation, and resistance is evidence of the rationality of the Chicano gang population. If, in fact, these hybrid groupings, whose individual members supposedly lacked the wherewithal to become part of the elite groups, are capable of this large-scale reorganizing, it is theoretically important and could possibly have implications for California structures. This political consciousness among Chicano gang factions might even be said to fit within a Marxist framework. Given the high mortality rate among members of the elite groups (prison gangs), often murdered by their own organizations, these hybrid developments seem to represent an evolved form of rationality that resists the power-hungry model for which the ultimate goal is gang prestige.

Nonetheless, information gathered from correctional officers in the borderlands' prisons and jails on this topic suggests that Sureños already enjoy a high rank within their hierarchy. In a way, true-blue Sureños in the borderlands are effectively representatives of the California Eme, replete with the *mano-negra* (black hand) symbol tattoos on their bodies and the ability to tax street gangs for drug profits. Therefore, some argue that LA-based Sureños have already been empowered by la Eme to the point that Sureños are content with the status-quo and do not feel the need to stop taking orders or attempt to rebel and take over. Some gang savvy observers speculate that such a Tango-type shift is already underway within the Eme-Sureño hierarchy, but nothing of the sort is evident as of yet. In northern California, the Nuestra Familia-Norteño hierarchy is nearly identical to that in the south, and whether shifts might occur there remain to be seen as well.

THE DECLINE OF STREET GANGS?

The modern era has ushered in drastic changes in the way street gangs in particular conduct themselves. Los Angeles-based journalist Sam Quiñones (2014) recently wrote a piece for the *Pacific Standard* called "The End of

Gangs," in which he compellingly argues that street gangs have disappeared from public view in southern California. If place matters, as I have asserted in this work, the importance of studying the borderland's Chicano street gangs apart from those in California is underscored. But one must admit that Quiñones' observation that old barrio gang hangouts are now clear of open congregating is becoming more of the norm across the Southwest. He notes that gentrification of inner-city street-corner gang hangouts and nongang families again enjoying public parks without fear of infringing on gang turf represents the end of gangs as we once knew them.

Gundur (2017) makes the same observation for public spaces in El Paso and Phoenix after conducting drug gang–related fieldwork there. Indeed, implied in these claims is that we are in a post-street-gang era that is largely driven by the use of communication technology, making it less necessary to engage in public loitering to conduct gang business. As a result, the "turf" component that is emblematic of Chicano gangs more than any other type of ethnic gang has become less important as an organizational feature.

I began my study in 2016, conducting the initial networking and exploratory fieldwork to gain a sense of the nature and scope of gang issues in the borderland. Having started out in Las Cruces, the response I often got from former gang members, juvenile probation officers, and school officials was essentially that gang banging is sort of a thing of the past. That is, while it is not completely gone from the landscape, it has drastically toned down in the past eight to ten years. Subjects went on to say that if gang activity is still prevalent, it is far less obvious in recent years. Gilbert Cabrera, a former alternative school teacher in Las Cruces and author of *Gangs in Our Schools, an Educator's Guide*, stated that in 2005, some 70 to 80 percent of his pupils were gang involved. Today, for him, the issue of gangs in schools is barely even there.

In public presentations, Las Cruces's gang officers note that today's gang members do not look the part. Rather, their appearance is designed to blend into the normal population to be as inconspicuous as possible. Moreover, there are unlikely alliances between gangs that are traditional enemies and who were in a state of war only a few years prior. Of the numerous gang insiders I have spoken to for various studies conducted over the past ten years or so, the refrain on this topic has been that "colors, turf, etc. do not matter much anymore . . . all that matters is making money." Some of the popular phrases among today's barrio and ghetto youth are "Money Over Bitches" and "Money Over Everything."[10] For example, members of the Harris

County (Houston) Jail Gang Unit report seeing these tattoos on a number of inmates, who are now known to associate with former rival gang members (Tapia 2013). Part of these dynamics also includes far more racial intermingling among gang members than was seen in past generations. In the end, the practices of gangs of the millennial generation seem more practical than those of past generations, reinforcing the notion of an evolved form of rationality among modern Chicano gangsters.

APPENDIX A

Historical Street Gangs Inventory, El Paso

1930S–1950S

2-N. Documented in the *El Paso Herald Post* (1951b) as warring with Lucky 13s and 7-X.

2-X. A reputable east El Paso gang in the early 1950s suspected of stealing grenades from Ft. Bliss Army Base and being involved in a series of shootings (*El Paso Herald Post* 1951a). Their turf was on Raynor and Copia Streets per historian Fred Morales.

4-F. Turf was at Fourth and Florence Streets (Birge 1962). Gang formation details in chapter 1. Several members still living.

7-X. Toughest El Paso gang in the 1950s (Moore 1976). Turf: Virginia Street by the Alamito Housing projects (Birge 1962). In 1946, members killed a Ft. Bliss soldier when he asked them to apologize for lewd comments toward his wife. The gang also attacked Patrol Officer J. McAlpin by the Santa Fe Bridge in 1949 (Finley 1950). Three members committed suicide in 1949, two by hanging and one by gunshot (*El Paso Herald Post* 1951b).

Aces. Wore jackets with their gang name in El Paso High School (*El Paso Herald Post* 1956).

Alamito. Resident gang from the Alamito Housing Projects, St. Vrain to Park Street and Third to Fifth Street in Segundo Barrio. See figure 1.9. Now a gentrified area called Alamito Terrace.

Baby Dolls. A female gang from Hacienda Heights (Bel Air). One 15-year-old member was badly slashed by a member of the Little Darlings (*El Paso Herald Post* 1957a), also from Hacienda Heights. See chapter 1 for details.

Barrio La Roca. Across from Jefferson High School on Alberta Street, behind Thomason Hospital (Ahlgren 1981; Campbell 2009). See figure 1.7.

Barrio Sobaco. A conexión among 12–15 adobe homes near the San Juan barrio in central El Paso (Campbell 2009). Chelsea Street, by old Coors Brewery (now a limo service, per Fred Morales). See figure 1.7.

Beeboppers. Near Zavala Elementary on Hammett and Pera Street in south-central El Paso (see Campbell 2009). Members wore a black jacket. Several members still living. See figure 1.7.

Boggies. Documented in the *El Paso Herald Post* 1956. Wore the color blue.

Campbell Street Gang. On Fifth and Campbell, mid- to late 1940s. (UTEP 1978).

Canal Street. a.k.a. *La Canal,* a.k.a. Canal Kids (CKs) in Rahm (1958). Canal Street in Chihuahuita. See figure 1.9.

Charles Gang. Mid- to late 1940s (UTEP 1978). Charles Street in Chihuahuita.

Charms. Began in 1956 by former members of 4-Fs, Lucky 13s, and Little 9s at Stanton and S. Kansas (Birge 1962.) See figure 1.9.

Chihuahuita. Los Pinochos hung around *La Tienda de Bucha* at 911 S. Chihuahua in the 1930s (Morales 2017). *Los Tirilones,* 1930s, were from the same area. *Los Tigres de* Oregon Street in the 1930s and the Roadblockers in the 1950s were from Chihuahuita. In the 1960s the Oregon Eagles, Cougars, Sinners, Night Hawks, M'Ja, La Canal, and the Puente Negro gangs were all from Chihuahuita.

Clovers. A 1940s gang in the tenements at the corner of Eighth and El Paso Streets (Morales 2017).

Cobras. a.k.a. King Cobras from La Chaveña in Juárez, across from Segundo Barrio (Rahm 1958). Another source puts them in Barrio San Juan in Central El Paso (Delgado 1997).

Del Diablo. a.k.a. X-9, southeastern side of the inner city on the US border with Juárez. See figure 1.7. Listed as DDTs in Rahm (1958). Del Diablo Territory (DDT) is still listed in the current EPPD gang database with 12 members.

Dominos. Named in Rojas (2007) in or near Diablo turf. Started out as a social club.

Ducks. On Stanton and Seventh between the Oregon Eagles and the Alley Cats.

Dukes. Northeast side; one of El Paso's oldest gangs. Enemies of 2-X and Lucky 13s (*El Paso Herald Post* 1951b). The Dukes badly assaulted a youth after an Ysleta High School graduation in 1949 (Finley 1950). The Dukes were the largest gang in El Paso at the time.

Durango St. a.k.a. Los Durangos or Duranguito. Overland and Durango Streets.

Duchesses. Female auxiliary to the Dukes. (*El Paso Herald Post* 1950).

Florence St. Mid- to late 1940s gang (UTEP 1978). Predecessors to 4-Fs and the All-Stars.

Gamblers. a.k.a King Gamblers (Rahm 1958). Burgess High School. Wore black jackets with old English letters; firebombed the principal's home (*El Paso Herald Post* 1956).

Happy Wanderers. From Rahm (1958). Sacred Heart Youth Center.

Knights. Wore jackets with their gang name on it in Austin and Bowie High Schools (*El Paso Herald Post,* 1956).

Lads & Mads. From Rahm (1958). Sacred Heart Youth Center.

Lincoln. Lincoln Park area. Copia to Paisano north of Alameda. El Calvario Church (demolished) was a landmark. There are different sets within the Lincoln areas (per Jessie). See figure 1.7.

Little 9s. From Rahm (1958), the pee-wee group to the ok *Nines.* Many Little 9s joined the Charms in 1956 (Birge 1962).

Little 10s. From Rahm (1958). Sacred Heart Youth Center.

Little Angels. El Paso Herald Post (1965c) "Police Probe Shooting, Fight Link." Names an old rivalry between the Little Angels, Seven-Elevens, and Lucky 14s.

Little Darlings. Girl gang badly slashed a 15-year-old member of the Baby Dolls (*El Paso Herald Post* 1957a). Both gangs from Hacienda Heights. See chapter 1 for details.

Lucky 13s. Enemies were the Dukes and 2-x (*El Paso Herald* Post 1951b). See chapter 1 for other gang details.

Lucky 14s. See "Gang Clashes over Girl; Murder Charges Filed." (*El Paso Herald Post* 1959a). "Youth Chases His Enemy, Knifes Him" (*El Paso Herald Post* 1959b).

Lucky Lords. Varrio San Juan's old barrio gang. Paisano east to North Loop. Landmarks: San Juan Boxing Gym, San Juan Catholic Church. See figure 1.7.

Mesa St. Gang. Mid- to late 1940s (utep 1978). Predecessor to Shamrocks (1960s).

Midway Gang. Early 1930s according to Lee Shamaley, between Downtown and Five Points (Ahlgren 1981). Turf between Cotton and Yandell Streets (Morales 2017).

Missouri Dillingers. In central ep per Louie Burrus (2017). See figure 1.9.

ok 7. Turf was on Seventh Street in Segundo Barrio (utep 1974). ok refers to the area between Oregon and Kansas Streets (Morales 2017).

ok *Nines.* a.k.a. Ninth St. Gang. Controlled a big area of Ninth Street between Oregon and Kansas (Birge 1962).

Old Ft. Bliss. a.k.a. El Fuerte per Morales (2017). Also see Finley (1950). This is one of the earliest cross-border gangs as this Ft. Bliss installment was on the border near UTEP.

Oregon St. In 1930s (utep 1978). a.k.a. Tigres de Oregon, predecessor to Oregon Eagles of the 1960s.

Pachuco Hops. Not a prominent gang, but named in a 1957 newspaper article about youth caught stealing hubcaps at Eucalyptus & Magoffin Streets. (*El Paso Herald Post* 1957c).

Panthers. Paisano projects per Tony Valenzuela (2017). See figure 1.7.

Parkers. From Rahm (1958), a.k.a. Park Street. Mid- to late 1940s. Also utep (1978). See figure 1.9.

Rebels. From Rahm (1958). Possibly the Dolan Rebels of the 1960s in south-central (Campbell 2009). See figure 1.7.

Red Devils. See *El Paso Herald Post*, 1956.

Red Eagles. Copia to Hammett near Zavala Elementary. Hangout was El Luga corner store. Several members still living. a.k.a. Luga Losers in 1960s. Los Stones de Lugas in 1990s.

Road Blockers. From Rahm (1958). Santa Fe and Ninth in Chihuahuita. See figure 1.9.

Roadrunners. Wore jackets with gang name in Austin High School (*El Paso Herald Post* 1956).

Saints. Bowie High School (*El Paso Herald Post* 1956). There were the Ochoa Saints and El Pujido Saints; both groups attended Bowie and are depicted in figure 1.9.

Scorpions. Estrella and San Antonio streets, by Paisano. a.k.a Cypress Street Scorpions, claiming Barrio Park on Finley Street. Serious rivalry with X-14 involving several attacks and retaliations, some lethal (*El Paso Herald Post* 1958a).

Seven-Elevens. Enemies of Lucky 14s and Little Angels (*El Paso Herald Post* 1965c).

Sherman. Sherman Place housing projects, est. 1953. a.k.a. Del Sherman Territory (DST). See figure 1.7. Sherman Park Locos are listed in the current EPPD gang database with 3 members. DST listed with 24 current members.

Sinners. From Rahm (1958). Chihuahuita area, Santa Fe Street and Seventh. See figure 1.9.

South Mesa. 1930s–1940s (UTEP 1974). Predecessors to Los Tecatos and Shamrocks.

Tirilones. Appeared in several UTEP oral histories as being a synonym for "Zoot Suiters." However, see *Chihuahuita.*

Tortilla Flat. In 1940s south El Paso, may have migrated to Los Angeles (UTEP 1974). See details in chapter 1.

TPM. From Rahm (1958). Sacred Heart Youth Center.

Valverde Frogs. Valverde Street in south-central by Our Lady of the Light Church. See figure 1.7. One of Campbell's (2009, 86) interviewees claimed they eventually merged with Clardy Fox.

Wyoming St. Gang. In 1930s–1940s (UTEP 1979).

X-9. See *Del Diablo.* Also see figure 1.7.

X-14. a.k.a. Los del Catorce. On Olive Street (Ahlgren 1981). Tays Projects. See figure 1.7.

1960S–1970S

Alley Cats. The Alley at Oregon and El Paso Street to Fifth and Oregon (Salazar 1972). See figure 1.9.

All-Stars. Florence and Fourth (Salazar 1972). See figure 1.9. Also see Kansas All Stars on Kansas Street.

Ascarate Copperheads. Henderson Elementary (Campbell 2009). See figure 1.7.

Blue Stars. El Paso and Fifth (Salazar 1972). 600 Block of S. El Paso (Ahlgren 1981). See figure 1.9.

Chicanos In Action (CIA). Salazar Housing Projects on 311 S. Eucalyptus near Paisano Drive (Sotomayor, 1976).

Clardy Fox. Southeast inner city. From Delta to the Border Freeway. Modesto Gomez Park on the west, Glenwood Street on the east. See figure 1.7. One of Campbell's (2009, 86) interviewees claimed they eventually merged with Valverde Frogs.

Comancheros. Listed in Campbell (2009) as being near south-central EP, presumably tied to the street name Comanchero in that area. However, their turf was in Lakeside in the lower valley per several interviewees.

Cougars. Tenements at 900 block of S. Chihuahua (i.e., Los Presidios). See figure 1.9.

Dare Devils. Virginia and Eighth (Salazar 1972). See figure 1.9.

Destroyers. In the Paisano Street projects near the Coliseum. Diablo territory. Hangout S. El Paso Street and La Placita. See figure 1.7.

Devil or Angels. Paisano Projects per Tony Valenzuela of Jefferson High School. See figure 1.7.

Dolan Rebels. See Rebels in Rahm (1958) and in Campbell (2009). Dolan Street between Paisano and Delta. See figure 1.7.

Flaming Angels. Salazar Housing Projects on 311 S. Eucalyptus near Paisano Drive (Sotomayor 1976). Armijo Center (Ahlgren 1981).

Fonzies. Salazar Housing Projects. (Sotomayor 1976).

Individuals. Small click in the Lower Valley's Loma Vista Neighborhood (Bel Air High School). Very disruptive at the school. Members became Brown Berets.

Jokers. Park Street behind Bowie Bakery. See figure 1.9. An offshoot group were the Olders.

Kansas St. All Stars. See *All Stars.*

La Sana. From the Salazar Housing Projects, 311 S. Eucalyptus (Sotomayor 1976). Known hangouts were on San Antonio and Rivera Streets, and Wyoming Street.

Los Tanques. Near the silver refinery tanks on Trowbridge Avenue (Campbell 2009).

Myrtle St. Muertos. Magoffin area north of Segundo Barrio. See figure 1.9.

Nazis. Paisano Projects (Campbell 2009, 86). See figure 1.7.

Newman Raiders. Myrtle and Newman Streets in the Magoffin area. See figure 1.9.

Noble Lords. Tornillo and Paisano (Salazar 1972). See figure 1.9.

Ochoa Kreeps. Named on a blog about known El Paso gangs and documented in Campbell (2009, 136) as an offshoot of the *T-birds.*

Ochoa Saints. Ochoa and Seventh (Salazar 1972). See figure 1.9.

Oregon Eagles. In 1960s, on the 1000 block of S. Oregon Seventh (Salazar 1972). See figure 1.9.

Psychos. Listed in Campbell (2009) and mapped in figure 1.7.

Puente Negro. Participated in drug and human smuggling across the river in Chihuahuita. Rivals with other gangs from the area over this hustle (Campbell 2009). El Paso faction known as the River Boys (Morales 2017).

Rio Linda. Park Street by the river (by Peyton's Meat Packing Plant along Eleventh Street). Fred Morales (2017) notes that Rio Linda was once a larger area, but its southern section was granted to Juárez in the Chamizal dispute.

Royal Knights. Conflicting info on their location in the newspaper. Park and Sixth

(Salazar 1972) versus Lakeside (Ahlgren 1981). Other insiders recall the gang name as Royal Dukes in Lakeside (Tommy, Ben). There was also a 1980s gang in Las Cruces called the Royal Chicanos, and in the 1990s, the South Side Royal Knights.

Saints. Ochoa Saints were near the T-birds' turf on Fifth Street. El Pujido Saints were in the northeast corner of Segundo Barrio across Delta Avenue (both mapped in fig. 1.9). Ahlgren (1981) listed the Saints' turf on "San Antonio Avenue near the Salazar Housing Projects" on Eucalyptus.

Santanas. Fifth and Campbell (Ahlgren 1981). See UTEP (1978) for Campbell St. Gang in 1930s.

Scavengers. In the five points area. See figure 1.7.

Shamrocks. Mesa and Fourth (Salazar 1972). See figure 1.9.

T-birds. Ochoa and Seventh. See figure 1.9. Controlled the Armijo Recreation Center. Listed in the current EPPD gang database with 14 members.

Tecatos. A group of ex-cons who used dope at the rebote (handball) courts behind the Armijo Center that the T-Birds ran. They had serious, fatal clashes with the T-Birds in 1972 over this turf (*Las Cruces Sun News* 1972; Moore 1976).

Texas Addition. Central El Paso near San Juan barrio (Campbell 2009).

Trampas. St. Vrain and Fifth (Salazar 1972). See figure 1.9.

Trojans. Turf by the El Paso Coliseum in south-central EP (Campbell 2009).

Los Vagos. Stanton and Ninth. See figure 1.9.

Varrio Glenwood Street (VGS). Glenwood Street in Central El Paso (*El Paso Herald Post* 1965). In 1996, three died in a shootout on Glenwood Street after a gang party (McArthur 1996). There are 98 current members of VGS in the EPPD Database in central, the eastside, and other areas.

Varrio Grand-View (VGV). North of Five Points by Austin High on South Cotton/Idaho near Cordova Middle School to the west and Wiggs Middle School to the east. Currently 13 members in EPPD Gang list.

Wanderers. Clardy Fox (*El Paso Times* 1982). See *Happy Wanderers* in "1930s–1950s."

LATE 1970S–1980S

8-Ball Posse. 1980s–1990s Ysleta in the lower valley; Capistrano/Varrio Los Kennedys. No longer in the EPPD Database. The northeast also had a set of 8-Ball in the Sun Valley West neighborhood. See figure 5.2.

13th & 14th street gangs. Dyer and Hercules (Ahlgren 1981).

Barraca. Near the Ysleta Tigua Indian Reservation. See figure 5.1. Currently 7 members in the EPPD database.

Barrio Gang. Hondo Pass in the northeast (Ahlgren 1981).

Blue Diamonds. Salazar Apartments. Also listed (perhaps erroneously) in the newspaper as Armijo Center Pee-wees (Ahlgren 1981).

Capistrano Locos. a.k.a. La Capi. Ysleta, Border Freeway. See figure 5.1.

Calavera. In Ysleta, turf borders with Barraca. See figure 5.1.

Cedar Grove. Riverside by border freeway. Four current members in EPPD Database.

Chicano Pride. One of the largest Lower Valley gangs in the late 1970s and 1980s. See figure 5.1 for turf area near the Kennedy projects. Wore black jackets (Ahlgren 1981).

Cooley Killers. Shawver Park/Pasodale in the Lower Valley (Yarbrough and Border Freeway). See figure 5.1.

East Valley Locas. Girls gang in Eastwood and Hanks High Schools (Alghren 1981).

Gran Varrio Pachuco (GVP). Lower Valley (Ysleta) by Roseway Park/Pendale Road and railroad tracks. See figure 5.1.

Hacienda Heights. Lower Valley (Bel-Air High School) area. Yarbrough and Lomaland by Hacienda Heights Elementary. Currently 55 members in the EPPD Database.

The Heads. Irvin High School in the northeast (Ahlgren 1981).

Heaven n Hell. Ysleta. See figure 5.1 for turf area in and around the Kennedy Projects. Possibly "once known as Los Sapos" (Ahlgren 1981).[1]

Hip-City. Finita Apartments in the Lower Valley between Pasodale and Ysleta. See figure 5.1 for turf area.

Huercos del Diablo. Possibly pee-wees to DDT in the Paisano projects (Ahlgren 1981).

Invaders. A small group of about 10 members from Anapra, a.k.a. De Anapra Territory (DAT). Used a tattoo resembling Mt. Cristo Rey (see chapter 4 for info on this location in Anapra/Sunland Park).

Kernal Street Gang. Kernal Street in Lower Valley off Zaragoza and Betel. Currently has thirteen members in the EPPD gang list. See figure 5.1.

Kinky Boys. Ysleta/Del Valle in the Lower Valley (fig. 5.1). New Waver/Car Club/ Dance Group turned gang.

Limas y Octubre. Eastwood and Hanks (Ahlgren 1981).

Logan Heights. VLH. Northeast neighborhood gang near the Ft. Bliss Army Base. See figure 5.2. VLH has 76 members listed in EPPD's gang database currently.

Lopez Maravilla. From East LA but arrived in Central El Paso (Colfax Street) in the 1970s. Moved to the northeast after being displaced by the floods in 2006.

Los FatherLess (LFL). Central El Paso. See figure 1.7. Listed in the current EPPD gang database with 93 members.

Los Hell Raisers (LHR). Phillipy Street by Ysleta High School. See figure 5.1. Rocker gang predecessors to Compton Varrio Largo (CVL).

Los Home Boys (LHB). Ysleta-based gang. EPPD gang list currently shows 6 members. Gangs with this name were also present in Anthony, Juárez, and Las Cruces.

Los Lotes. Dale Street and N. Loop (Lower Valley). See figure 5.1 in chapter 5.

Los Midnight Locos (LML). Decades old northeast side gang by Andress High
School. See figure 5.2. There are currently 81 Members in EPPD's gang list.

Los Ortiz Brothers (LOB). Originally from Colonia Hidalgo in Juárez. Their El Paso
turf was on the border between Ysleta and Socorro (see fig. 5.1) but ties to Juárez
remained. Currently 31 members in EPPD database. In 1994 Miguel "Cricket"
Ortiz, age 21, was wanted for five gang murders in Juárez and three aggravated
robberies in El Paso (Fonce 1994).

Low Boys. A car club/clika from Anthony, New Mexico.

Maravilla Dolls. Girl gang from Maravilla Street by Ysleta Middle School. See
figure 5.1.

Mesa Vista. Lower Valley (Bel-Air) Hillcrest Middle School (Ahlgren 1981).

Mestizos. From Fifth and Tays Streets in Segundo Barrio. Rivals of the
Thunderbirds (Ahlgren 1981).

Paddlefoot. Small Ysleta gang (Lower Valley). Mentioned by a jail gang officer.

Parkdale Latin Kings. Most likely from the Parkdale neighborhood near Ascarate
Park (Clark Street and Alameda Avenue), but current EPPD Gang Officers are
unsure. They are no longer in the gang database.

Satisfaction. Car club/gang from the Lower Valley.

Sunland Park. a.k.a. Sunloco (see Renteria 1979). The more recent gangs from
Sunland Park are Anapra and Meadow Trece.

Thomas Manor (Locos). Riverside area in the Lower Valley. See figure 5.1. There are
5 current members in the EPPD Database. A gang officer stated they evolved
from the Wanderers.

Varrio Los Kennedys. By the old Ysleta Boys Club and Mt. Carmel Cemetery. There
are 5 current members in the EPPD Database.

Varrio Northeast. See figure 5.2 for gang turf. Still a very large gang with 158
members in EPPD database. Now it is the "parent" group to many smaller
northeast gangs, both black and Latino.

Varrio San Juan. Central El Paso. See figure 1.7. Currently 95 members in EPPD
gang database.

The Virgins. Renfrew Drive in the upper East Side (Ahlgren 1981).

White Fence. LA roots but have been in El Paso's Lower Valley for decades. See
figure 5.1 for turf location. There are 10 current members in EPPD database.

1990S–2000S

3–6 Mafia. Located in south-central (Finley Street). Currently have 64 members in
EPPD gang database.

18th St. California copycat/transplant. Currently 33 members in EPPD database.
Also present in Las Cruces, Anthony, Berino, La Mesa, and Vado, where they go
by Varrio La diezyocho (VL18).

19th St. Juárez-based transplant. Gundur (2017) states, "They go back four generations in Juárez." There are 67 current members. Rivals to Glenwood Street.

Against the System (ATS). Lower valley Tag-bangers. Three members in EPPD gang list.

Alvarez Kings. The AKs from the Alvarez Housing Project on Lomaland and North Loop Avenue (Lower Valley), see figure 5.1. AKs have 25 current members in the EPPD gang list. Now have spread to the Montana Vista area.

Barrio Fabens (Locos). Far eastern Lower Valley. Adjacent to El Valle de Juárez. Nine current members in the EPPD gang database.

Barrio Nuevo. Far eastern Lower Valley. San Elizario, Clint, Socorro, and the Tiguas. Eight current members in the EPPD gang database.

Barrio San Angel (BSA). From the Sparks colonia near Horizon in far east El Paso. Currently, 13 members in the EPPD gang database. Attended Socorro and Montwood High Schools.

Big Hazzard. Central El Paso. Originally LA-based. Currently has three members in the EPPD gang database. In 2017, one member, age 53, was arrested with a Mexicles (Juárez gang) member, age 38, in El Paso for weapons and drugs possession.

Blythe Street. Possibly present in Chaparral and Horizon, but not in the EPPD database. LA-based; violent (Morales 2008).

Borla Gang. a.k.a. Borla Boys. Borderland Road near the Texas–New Mexico border. Longtime enemies of Barrio Canutillo.

Broadway Kings. Riverside area in the lower valley. Three current members in the EPPD gang database.

Brown Dawgs-13. Well-known northeast side gang. Currently 49 members in the EPPD gang database.

Brown Pride (Krew). Has 32 members in the EPPD gang database. Possibly linked to BP Locos, with four members in the database and Brown City Gangsters (BCG) with 33 members in EPPD list.

Carnales over Bitches. See Money over Bitches (MOB); in EPPD database with four members. Folk Nation affiliates. Men of Business (MOB) is also a new crew of violent youngsters in Las Cruces.

Centro Side Locos. Central-northeast side gang involved in a murder clash with Varrio Logan Heights (Merritz 2009).

Compton Varrio Largo (CVL). Influenced by Compton, California, transplants in Ysleta (Lower Valley). Eventually joined a larger federation called the Crazy Rascal Gang (CRG).

Crazy Rascal Gang. LA-based gang. Currently 13 members in the EPPD gang database. Once had clicks in San Elizario, Clint, and Socorro in the far eastern

Lower Valley. Also see *Barrio Nuevo*. Their proximity to the Valle de Juárez border enabled drug and human smuggling in the 1990s–2000s until the border fence was reinforced.

Dead at Birth (DAB). a.k.a. DABers from the Lower Valley. Not listed in EPPD database.

Del Meadow Side. Turf is in central-northeast El Paso (Fort Boulevard) to the mountain on west side. There is some confusion about whether it is linked to Meadowside-13 or Meadow-13 or even "Middleside" [*sic*], all of which are in the EPPD gang database.

Eisenhower Crazy Hood (ECH). Eisenhower Projects in the northeast. See figure 5.2. Five current members in EPPD gang database.

El Monte Flores. Northeast side gang. See figure 5.2. Three members in EPPD database.

Female Body Inspectors (FBI). Montwood High School area tag-banger crew, year 2000. Involved in 2001 homicide against the Young Ones (TYO). Neither is in the EPPD database. See *Garcia v. El Paso Limited Partnership* (Sonic Drive In), 2006, Texas Court of Appeals.

Five Points Kings. Pershing and Piedras Streets in the Five Points area. Has 21 current members in the EPPD gang database.

Florencia Trece. Known as one of three California supergangs with sets throughout the United States (Schovolle 2008). Currently has 74 members in the EPPD gang database, present in south-central El Paso, Juárez, and Santa Teresa, New Mexico.

F-Troop. Socorro/Ysleta based gang. South Loop area by current Loop 375 and Walmart. See figure 5.1. Roots in Santa Ana–Anaheim, California. Five current members in EPPD gang database.

Gangster Disciples. Northeast side. Has 55 members in the EPPD gang database. Mixed-race gang representing the Chicago influence on El Paso.

Goon Mafia. Possibly a.k.a. East Side Goons listed in EPPD gang database with four members. See also Goon Squad (n = 5) in the database.

Happy Valley Gang. LA transplant. Currently 11 members in the EPPD gang list, and reportedly in the Roosevelt Projects in the Devil's Triangle (northeast side).

Hated By Many. Northeast side. Has 68 members in the EPPD gang database.

Hollywood Knights. A 1990s Austin High School area gang. Not in EPPD gang database.

Hoover St. Crips. One of five Crips sets in El Paso. Has 29 members in the EPPD gang database.

Immortal Empire. West Side gang. Currently has 19 members in the EPPD gang database.

Latin Kings. Help to represent the Chicago influence on El Paso. Has 97 members in the EPPD gang database.

Lopez Maravilla. By Thomason Hospital in central El Paso. It has 62 members listed in the EPPD gang database.

Los Compadres (BLC). West Side El Paso and West Way, Texas (by Canutillo). Old-school pachuco gang. Main rival is Barrio Canuto Rifa (BCR-13).

Los Polvos. Montana Vista area in the upper east side. No longer in EPPD database.

Machuca Housing Projects. West El Paso near Sunland Park. The original families forming this barrio were from Smeltertown, the community surrounding the American Smelter and Refinery Company (ASARCO) plant in the coal mines west of El Paso.

Mafia Real Killers. Northeast (Logan Heights area). Has three members in the EPPD gang list.

Marmolejos. Varrio Marmolejo Apartments (VMA-13). North Loop and Carolina in the lower valley. Has seven members in the EPPD Gang database. Also listed in the Chucotown Streetlife Facebook page.

Mexican Crazy Killers (MCK). Listed in the Chucotown Streetlife Facebook page. Also see Mexican Crazy Krew (n = 11) and Mexican Crazy Klica (n = 49), both in the EPPD gang database.

Meadowside. Nine members in the EPPD gang database but likely mislabeled as "Middleside."

Moon City Locos (MCL). Moon City area in Lower Valley (Socorro). Has 68 members in the EPPD gang database. In 1994, numerous members of the gang were arrested for the brutal beating of a 17-year-old member of the Socoloco gang (McDonnell 1994b).

Nasty Boys Gang (NBG-13). a.k.a. South Side NB-13 in the Lower Valley (Fabens). In 1997 they were El Paso's second largest gang (*Jasso v. State of Texas* 8th District Court 2001). Known for having resisted Barrio Azteca's extortion attempts at one time. There are now 29 members in the EPPD gang database. Possible offshoot: West Side Nasty Boys set in Las Cruces, mid- to late 1990s.

Northeast 13. Northeast El Paso (n = 3) in the EPPD gang database.

Northside Locos. Northeast El Paso (n = 3) in the EPPD gang database. The gang started around 2005.

One Nation Alone (ONA). Northeast El Paso. Currently with 38 members in EPPD gang database.

One Nation Locos (ONL). Northeast El Paso, currently with 15 members in the EPPD gang database.

Out For Action (OFA) Krew/Kings. Lee Trevino and Castner Street by White Fence's old turf. Six OFA Krew members are currently listed in the EPPD gang list. Also likely mislabeled as "One-Action Kings" in EPPD database (n= 3).

Piru Bloods. Date back to 2004 in the northeast (Andress High School area). Spinoff from the Bishops (see fig. 5.2). The Piru Gang has 14 members in the EPPD gang database, and Blood Hound Piru has three members. Borunda

(2009) notes the following northeast side gangs, none of which are in the EPPD Database: Red Dog Pirus, Bounty Hunters, One-Trey-Five Piru (135) from New Jersey, and 109 Piru from St. Louis.

Puro Barrio Sandoval (PBS). West Side El Paso's Housing Projects with 20 members currently in the EPPD gang database.

Reyes del Varrio. Northeast but spread out citywide. Has 21 current members in the EPPD gang database. They are a branch of *Sureños*.

Salazar Gang. Salazar projects on Eucalyptus Street by Bowie High School in Segundo Barrio. There are three members currently in the EPPD gang database. The 9th St. & Salazar street gang also has three members in the database.

Socoloco. Socorro-based gang (Lower Valley) across Socorro High School. One member was killed at a party by the Nasty Boys Gang in 1997 (see *Jasso v. State of Texas*, 8th District Court 2001).

Skunx. An East Side gang according to the El Paso County jail gang unit. They have 70 members in the EPPD gang list. A recent shooting at Barfly (bar) in East El Paso (February 2017) is thought to be Skunx gang–related.

Straight Motherfuckin' Thugs (SMT). A central-northeast area gang in the 2000–2010 era. One member was murdered by the Barrio Logan Heights gang in 2007 (Merritz 2009).

True Nation Society (TNS). City of Horizon (far east El Paso). Has 40 members in the EPPD gang database.

Valley Side Mafia/Mob (VSM). Four members in the EPPD gang database, but no turf information.

Varrio Campestre (Locos). Originally (1980s) from Alameda Avenue and Vineyard Street in Socorro. Later moved to east-central Juárez. Two members, "Froggy" and "Caveman" (brothers), were killed by BA Ricardo "Enano" Zuniga in 2015 over drugs (Martinez 2016).

Varrio Chico Trece (VCT). Memorial Park area in north central El Paso, approximately Montana Street to Fort Boulevard. They are no longer in the EPPD gang database. *Barrio Chico Trece* (BCT) emerged from *Colonia Anahuac* in Juárez in the 1980s. VCT is also present in Phoenix, Arizona and in San Clemente, California (Morales 2008).

Varrio Chiquis-13. Roots in Ventura County, California. Not in the EPPD gang list, but see Chifton Chiqueros with four members. They are also named in the Chucotown Streetlife Facebook page.

Varrio La Mora (VLM). Lower Valley (Ysleta). See figure 5.1 for turf area. Had two competing drug factions and several raids by the EPPD CRASH (gang) unit 1990s–early 2000s. Recently resisted the Barrio Azteca's cuota ending in a murder near their turf (see Martinez 2014).

Varrio Meadow Trece (VMT). a.k.a. Mero 13, Merote Trece, Mero Sur 13. Sunland

Park and Santa Teresa, New Mexico. Enemies include Varrio Anapra 14 and
Barrio Canuto Rifa (BCR-13).

Varrio Northeast (VNE). Currently has 158 members in the EPPD gang database. See
also NE Locos and NE Trece. According to insiders, there was a split between
NE-13 and Varrio NE, the Gomez versus Mynes factions respectively.

Varrio San Miguel (VSM). Ysleta gang by Paddlefoot Street. Their tagging is still
seen on dumpsters in the area.

Zaragoza Mafia. East siders. They date back to the early 2000s.

APPENDIX B

Historical Street Gangs Inventory, Juárez

1960s–1970s

Barrio Alto Colonia
Bella Vista Colonia
El Refuego
El Sky
La Botella
La Chaveña

La Mosca
La San Pedro
Los Ahorcados
Los Chonillos
Los Diablos
Los Diamantes

Los Muertos
Los Tabachines
Los Yenkas
Papalotes
Puente Negro
Puente Rojo

1980s–2000s

72-Anapra
Barrio Alto
Barrio Chico Trece
Barrio Negro
Barrio Noveno
Barrio Retiro 13
Bella Vista
Cacos 30
Calaveras
Calecia-13
Compas 13
DDT
El Refugio

El Rey
K-13
La 21
La Piedra
La Pradera
La Quinta Loma
Labio Seco
Las Pink Ladies
Los Big Boy
Los Carmelos
Los Demonios
Los Fresas
Los Gatos

Los Harpis 15, 20, 30
Los Home Boys
Los Jodidos
Los Leones
Los Moreros
Los Nazis
Los Ortiz Bros.
Los Teipiados
Los Tenebrosos
Mero Trece
Muertos 13
PlayBoys
West Side

MODERN JUÁREZ STREET-JAIL HYBRID GANGS

19th Street
Angeles 30
Artistas Asesinos
Azteca 13
Barrio Muerto 55
Cacos 90
Ceresos 13

El Rebote
El Triste
Juaritos
La Empresa
Locos 23
Los More 13
Los Pinguinos
Mexicles

Rebeldes
Retiro
Rodeo
Santana
SMK
Vagos 15
Zapata

NOTES

INTRODUCTION

1. The Mexican Census Bureau reports 2,500 residents in Praxedis in both 2005 and 2010. http://www.beta.inegi.org.mx/app/buscador/default. html?q=praxedis+guerrero. See Borunda (2019) for details of the most recent struggle for control of the region.

CHAPTER ONE

1. The El Paso-based club 915 Pachucos y Pachucas Unidos and Juárez-based Grupo 656 are both Chicano culture enthusiasts who participate in competitions across the southwest showcasing their zoot suit outfits, typically at lowrider car-shows.

2. A US vicinity inhabited by impoverished Latinos and typically isolated from other, more affluent parts of the settlement.

3. Duran (2018) has written about the unjust villainization of barrio gangs in the border region by law enforcement, the press, and the general public. From its inception as a barrio identity, scholars of the pachuco subculture likened it merely to a countercultural style among lower-class Mexican American boys, who were not well accepted by white America (Bogardus 1943). The extent of the delinquent character of early gangs in El Paso and elsewhere is thus an issue for debate by scholars of this subfield. For so many others, including police, street interventionists, and other practitioners like Father Rahm, this is their most apparent characteristic. My own work (on the 1930s and 1940s especially) vacillates on this point, containing ample evidence that the delinquency of early borderland street gangs contained both benign mischief and serious delinquency, including extreme violence. But for most gang scholars, these are not their only or even primary defining characteristics. The reasons they exist and their social aspects are the main points of intrigue.

4. See appendix A for a complete listing of 1930s and 1940s era El Paso gangs.

5. Figure 1.9 in this chapter contains a 1960s-era map of gang turf in Chihuahuita and Segundo Barrio.

6. When El Paso County authorities implemented a gang injunction against the

Barrio Azteca in 2003, for example, it was issued solely in the Segundo Barrio (O'Deane 2011). The details are in chapter 5.

7. In 1936, District Attorney Roy Jackson estimated there were only about 100 gang-involved youth in south El Paso (i.e., the Mexican area), far less than Dickerson's account in 1925. In 1950, Walt Finley reported there were four major gangs in south El Paso. By 1953, 11 gangs were reported (Wegemer 1953), and by 1957, there were reportedly 52 gangs (*El Paso Herald Post* 1958a). Based on these divergent accounts, either there are frequent, radical shifts in the number of youth participating in gangs, or there are significantly differing assessments of the size of this population. Generally, due to inconsistent definitions, viewpoints, purposes, and methods used, estimates of gangs, gang members, and gang-related incidents in a large population center are notoriously unreliable. That remains so in the modern context as well (Jacobs 2009).

8. Either it never existed, or by 1938, Fourteenth Street was obsolete. While the Rio Linda neighborhood once had Eleventh, Twelfth, and Thirteenth Streets, it is in a different portion of south El Paso than the area described in the newspaper (see fig. 1.9). Parts of Rio Linda and the area referenced in the 1920 newspaper article were renegotiated to Mexican territory during the Chamizal dispute, lasting several decades and resolved in 1963. Thirteenth Street would have been the southernmost point closest to Juárez in 1920, but in a 1938 map, it is shown to be on the Juárez side, with Eleventh Street as the southernmost El Paso point (http://www.mapsofthepast.com/el-paso-texas-tx-city-western -map-co-1938.html). Such findings speak to the sister city narrative that has long been used to characterize El Paso and Juárez. Indeed, the border was once a mere formality and for most forms of social and cultural exchange, virtually nonexistent.

9. This group was likely the predecessor to x-14, a.k.a. Los del Catorce, as it was located in their 1950s turf (see fig. 1.7).

10. See Vigil 1988 for notes on the age-graded structure of barrio gangs.

11. Notes in Rahm (1958) state this gang didn't last very long, but he likely had them confused with another group or was given bad information. The OK 9s were one of El Paso's original barrio gangs, lasted well into the 1950s, and were considered one of El Paso's most feared groups (Birge 1962).

12. "OK" stood for the various neighborhood sectors between the parallel Oregon and Kansas Streets in Segundo Barrio (Morales 2017).

13. In 1925, a 23-year-old south El Paso man police and the newspapers referred to as "El Paso's super criminal" (*El Paso Herald Post*, 1925a) was jailed in LA after four different failed attempts to apprehend him in El Paso. The subject, Gabriel Ramirez, who was sought on murder charges, entered into a series of shootouts and up-close physical struggles with police before fleeing to LA and eventually being caught there.

14. See chapter 3 for details of a rather intense modern-day set of Tortilla Flats in Farmington, New Mexico.

15. Public commentators of the era expressed disdain for the pachuco youth subculture in El Paso, inventing their own definitions of the word to include "bum, shiftless, lazy, thug, thief . . . and hoodlum" (Conner 1943).

16. Now-obsolete maneuvers, such as grand jury probes, were political tools used by the district attorneys in large Texas cities to garner support for prosecuting youth gangs. See, for example, similar processes occurring around this time in San Antonio (*San Antonio Express News* 1951).

17. A gang by the same name emerged in Sunland Park, New Mexico, in the 1980s. It grew and migrated to Anthony in the 1990s; see chapter 3 for details.

18. For example, in 1958, a series of rumbles between young Ft. Bliss soldiers and El Paso "gang members" erupted at the Oasis Drive-In. The "gang" identified in this story were the Stompers, which is the region's youth slang term for *cowboy* or *[ran]chero* youth belonging to the Future Farmers Association in El Paso high schools.

19. Austin, Bowie, and El Paso High School principals banned the wearing of such jackets at their schools, naming some of the jacket-wearing groups including the Saints, the Knights, Roadrunners, and Aces.

20. This neighborhood is still considered a potent area for Chicano gang activity, with EPPD's Gang Unit currently listing Varrio Hacienda Heights as having 55 active members, a large, multigenerational gang by any standard.

21. Smooth cement walls 15 to 20 feet high in public parks resembling outdoor racquetball courts.

22. When demolition and remodeling of the Paisano Projects began in the early 2000s, members of the gang moved to the Missouri Avenue area between Copia and Piedras Avenues (Carrillo 2018).

23. Los Comancheros was erroneously listed in Campbell (2009, 86) as a nearby gang, presumably tied to a street name in that barrio. However, my research places them a few miles away at Lakeside in the lower valley (per interviewees, Tommy, Raul, and Hector).

24. One of Campbell's (2009, 86) interviewees claimed Clardy eventually merged with Valverde Frogs.

25. A 1970 newspaper article perhaps erroneously named a gang called La Muerta [*sic*] as belonging to Andress High School in the northeast part of the city (*El Paso Herald Post* 1970, February 26).

26. Fonce, Tammy, and Curtis Solis. 1993. "Supporters Approve of Enforcing U.S. Border." *The Prospector*, October 5, p. 6.

27. These apartments were also sarcastically known as "the Presidios" or more appropriately as "Los Cinco Infiernos" (Torres 2010). These are notoriously overcrowded, dilapidated tenements still in use today.

28. A third crossing with an aggressive resident gang was in Sunland Park–Anapra, about six miles to the west along the border. This group was from Colonia Buena Vista (a.k.a. El Rojo) located at El Puente Rojo (the Red Bridge).

29. Whereas *Tecato* is a generic Chicano slang term used to refer to intravenous drug users, this particular group of former inmates' clashes with the T-Birds served to unify and solidify them as a gang by that name.

30. Given the T-Birds' turf included several blocks of Ochoa Street, several offshoot pee-wee gangs were formed under them. One was the Ochoa Kreeps, identified in Campbell (2009) and in a blog about known El Paso gangs. Another was the South Side Ochoa gang, documented in Ahlgren (1981).

31. Del Sherman Territory is currently listed with 24 members in the EPPD gang database and the Sherman Park Locos with only three members.

32. In later years, sets appeared down in the lower valley just outside of the city limit (Carrillo 2018).

33. Morales (2017) notes a group from Chihuahuita who hung around La Tienda de Bucha at 911 South Chihuahua. In the 1930s the gang was called Los Pinochos. He also notes Los Tirilones, a 1930s group from the same area.

34. In 1994, a 16-year-old member of White Fence was shot in the head by the father of a rival gang while the former and a 13-year-old member attempted a drive-by shooting on their rival's home. After repeated drive-bys at the home, the family was armed and ready, killing the youth in a defensive posture (McDonnell 1994a).

CHAPTER TWO

1. This is the official version of the LCPD (Berg 2005); however, a newspaper article about a gang sweep in 1991 suggested that police efforts to combat them were consistent with the national trend. This taskforce was comprised of city, county, and federal officers. It began to hold community meetings due to community concerns about gang activity in October of that year (Dickson 1991). In the only published field research on youth gangs in Las Cruces, Mays, Winfree, and Jackson (1993) state there was a gang unit formed in the late 1980s but do not provide much detail.

2. One of several notable exceptions was that of Manuel Astorga, a local youth who was convicted of robbing J. A. Sweet's store just south of Las Cruces in 1940 when he was 16 years of age (*Las Cruces Sun News* 1943).

3. Mays et al.'s (1993) interviews of gang youth in Las Cruces note several second- and third-generation Chicano gang members but do not specify if their elder family members were also from Las Cruces. One of these youths specified his father was from Albuquerque.

4. According to a founding member of Natural High, they were fundamentally different from the founders of ESL in that the former "didn't party," hence they

chose the name "Natural High." One of the first splinter groups that formed within the ESL due to differences with leadership style was the East Side Dog Pound.

5. Las Cruces now hosts an annual festival in Kline Park (a.k.a. 45ers Park) that celebrates zoot suit and lowrider culture (Ruelas 2017).

6. One interviewee (Jane) stated the use of the color green by ESL was due to Las Cruces Public Schools banning the use of traditional gang colors (red and blue). However, another interviewee (Angel) stated that Natural High, which branched off from ESL in the late 1970s, also adopted green as its color, suggesting its origins predate such measures used in schools in the 1990s.

7. Los Pelones is also the name of a gang in Anthony, New Mexico, whose rivals were Varrio Berino Heights-13. According to the El Paso Intelligence Center (2011)—a multiagency nerve center for federal drug gang intelligence—*pelones* also refers to young hit men hired by the cartel or subcontracted by Barrio Azteca in the El Paso–Juárez area.

8. The Alcoholics Krew (AK), for example, who were located in the far West Side, used the color red. The AKs were an offshoot of the Varrio King Cobra, the most dominant red-affiliated group in Las Cruces since the 1980s.

9. A well-known ex-convict and member of Las Cruces's underworld going back to the 1960s was Manuel "Blackie" Madrid, of Doña Ana. As each of these families named had a large set of brothers, he was one of several but is the most well-known among them.

10. For this reason, no map of gang turf was ever produced for Las Cruces in the course of this study. No subject was ever willing or able to draft up a comprehensive map of gang turf, likely due to the fact that it was not well defined.

11. Chapter 3 focuses on the gangs of Anthony, New Mexico, and surrounding areas, more fully profiling the Mesquiteros (a.k.a. Varrio Mesquite Locos-13), Varrio Berino Heights (VBH-13), and others.

12. Unaffiliated with the various King Cobra gangs in Chicago and New Zealand.

13. The A-Ks from 50 miles away in El Paso, Texas, are the Alvarez Kings, which are not connected to the Las Cruces group.

14. One of the group's leaders, Adrian Vigil, stated that his conversion to Christianity as a young man led him to abandon his fascination with Satanism and gang life.

15. Several core members were arrested and deported to Mexico, for example.

16. At least one other borderland street gang, from Anthony, New Mexico, the West Side Dukes, is known to have ties to a Mexican drug cartel. Perhaps, by extension, older members of the ESL also have such ties, although this is not as well documented.

17. One version of SSRN's genesis is that a gang leader of the VKC and a reputable

West Sider formed the gang to grow in numbers to rival the ESL. While the West Siders and the VKC remained intact, the SSRN continued on independently of them. Nonetheless, El Paso's Lakeside area had a late 1970s gang either called the Royal Knights (*El Paso Times* 1972; *El Paso Herald Post* 1981) or the Royal Dukes (Tommy, Ben), or both. As there are several other reputable Las Cruces gangs with noted origins in El Paso, it is difficult to consider these name similarities pure coincidence, given its proximity. There was also a central Las Cruces gang called the Royal Chicanos in the 1970s–1980s.

18. Las Cruces was one of 11 original sites where the Gang Resistance, Education, and Training (GREAT) program was evaluated. This yielded survey data on a cohort of 8th graders from Las Cruces that researchers from NMSU analyzed and used to publish quantitative findings, but not much qualitative fieldwork was generated from the project.

19. United States v. Almaraz 2005.

20. In the borderland region, however, with its proximity to and strong ties to California in the Latino population, the purity of the transplantation process is often considerable. See in chapter 3, for example, the case of Varrio Berino Heights-13, who were said to be reprimanded by some larger Sureño authority for "not having permission" to start up a 13 set, unlike their enemies, the Varrio Anthony Locos (VALS-13), who were a sanctioned set.

21. The implication of 13 is a supposed connection to the California Mexican Mafia (EME) prison gang.

22. See United States v. Archuleta 2013.

23. In the southwestern Chicano gang subculture, *true-blue* is the adjective used to refer to "real" Sureños from proven SUR-13 sets in southern California. See Morales (2008) for an extensive description of each of these sets.

24. In late 2004, Police Lt. Todd Gregory stated the LCPD was putting together a gang database (Hopkins 2004).

25. *South Side* is a generic label often used by Sureños. Also, Las Cruces-based inmates will often tattoo the words *South Side* or *Down South* to identify with the southern part of the state. This may be a point of confusion with jail classification officers from whom the LCPD gets much of its information.

26. Federal statute (28 CFR, part 23) and Texas Code of Criminal Procedure Chapter 61 require removal of a person from the active gang database if he or she does not re-offend within a two-year timeframe for juveniles and five years for adults.

CHAPTER THREE

1. For example, a rash of gang-related shootings and other violence broke out in Anthony, New Mexico, from about 2005 to 2007. In the press, the Texas

side of the city was depicted as not having as bad of a gang or crime problem (*Albuquerque Journal* 2007; Meeks 2008). This continued to be echoed by persons interviewed in the current study. With one exception (theft), recent crime stats still reflect a slightly higher rate of major crimes on the New Mexico side (City Data 2017a, b).

2. Juárez gangs have a different numerical naming convention than US gangs. One of Juárez's most reputable gangs, for example, were/are Los Harpis-15.

   As in nearby Las Cruces, the Norte affiliation of the Teners has an ambiguous meaning. First, it is a reference to northern Mexico (i.e., *la Frontera*), a strong indicator of the Juárez influence on this Anthony-based gang. Perhaps as important is that *Norte* refers to an affiliation to the Norteño gang nation on the US side, who exclusively wear the color red. This is an example of the convoluted nature of youth gang subcultures as they search for identity when they are first forming. The reason for adopting this affiliation (aside from convenience) is that the Norteños are natural rivals of the Sureños, who favor the color blue and with whom the Teners' enemies, the VAL-13s, are allied.

3. Recall from chapter 2, this also occurred with a longstanding group from north of Las Cruces, Los Doñaneros. However, the split and resulting affiliations occurred in reverse order from those in Anthony in south Doña Ana County. The Doñaneros originally did not claim colors or a national affiliation. After a rift created two distinct groups within the gang, the original group adopted a blue rag and SUR-13 affiliation. The break-off group, the Doña Ana Boys, adopted a northern orientation and affiliation to the red rag 14s, eventually claiming North Side Doña Ana (NSDA). Their leadership, the Saenz family, is thought to have had preexisting ties to northern California, however. It thus appears to have been a natural progression to a Norte affiliation for them.

4. Chapter 1 notes that one of the biggest reputable gangs in nearby El Paso in the late 1940s and early 1950s was the Dukes, who had a female counterpart called the Duchesses (*El Paso Herald Post* 1950; Finley 1950). While this may be pure coincidence, it seems unlikely.

5. Many Teners also live in Berino, namely in the small neighborhood of Las Palmeras.

6. Numerous oral histories held in Special Collections at UT-El Paso Library also detail the close connections between El Paso and Los Angeles Chicano residents and families.

7. Based on the errors seen in local police agency gang rosters, this name ambiguity has even tripped up gang officers.

8. EPPD reported dramatic increases in gang-related crimes between 2016 and 2017. While some of the increase could be real, it is well known that arrest data is as much a product of changes in policing strategies as it is in the number of criminal incidents. In February 2017, the EPPD increased the size of the gang

unit by 10 officers and one sergeant. This was a full three months before the initial press releases on gang stats appeared. So the increase in arrests and investigations could simply be linked to the increase in officers focused on gangs. Moreover, the designation of a case as "gang related" is a judgement call by the police. The EPPD keeps a database of gang members, and if someone in that database gets arrested for any crime, the incident will likely be counted as "gang related," even if it was a case of domestic violence or theft from a store, for example. In short, changes in levels of gang crime can be a politicized issue to justify the allocation of greater resources to the police department.

9. Initially, the feds' Operation Stonegarden was particularly targeted at Barrio Azteca, the region's most powerful street-prison-cartel hybrid (Borunda 2014 b). However, as the feds' operation slowly moved toward an immigration control function, it became controversial, with public outcry. County officials continued to receive the funds despite the public criticism (Cook 2018).

10. Campbell (2009, 192) notes that law enforcement in the region often refrain from publicizing their busts in the media to maintain a strategic advantage against smugglers.

CHAPTER FOUR

1. See one anecdote in chapter 1 about an early member of El Paso's El Diablo gang who survived a shooting by the border patrol on a smuggling attempt in 1932, documented in Rojas (2007).

2. See a more recent organized version of this hustle with El Puente Negro gang in chapter 1.

3. See figure 0.1 in the introduction.

4. One major exception was the Porvenir massacre of 1918 near Juárez–El Paso (Mekelberg 2018).

5. Many published estimates for 2010 actually place the number of homicides at well over 3,000 (e.g., Molloy & Bowden 2012; Padilla 2013; Puig 2013; Quiñonez 2016; US Dept. of Justice 2011).

6. Barrio Chico Trece (BCT) was present in Juárez's Colonia Anahuac since the 1970s. It is interesting that El Paso's faction is in the Memorial Park area in the Five Points District, which is somewhat distant from Juárez (5–10 miles away), relative to other communities with Juárez gang influences.

7. By several accounts, 10 members of Los Rebeldes were scapegoated and falsely convicted for the brutal ritualistic murders of a dozen young females in the infamous Juárez femicides of the 1990s (e.g., Washington-Valdez 2006).

8. This is the rough estimate for both black and Latino males ages 15–29 in El Paso in 2011 using census data and police data. At this time, El Paso Police reported about 5,000 young gang members in their database out of 85,421 young males in the population (excluding whites). More details on these estimates appear in the section below.

9. A 2009 survey of youth in Juárez found that children as young as 9 years old aspired to become part of a drug gang (Luhnow 2010).

10. Triplett (1997) surveyed gang officers from Texas's 38 largest police departments. As the fifth largest metro area in the state, El Paso reported the second largest number of gangs at 491.

11. Compare 13 murders in 2009 in El Paso versus 2,400 in Juárez in 2009.

12. In late 2018, this author met with grant writers from governmental agencies in Las Cruces and El Paso to draft a funding proposal to the US Department of Justice to conduct gang intervention. The effort was a nonstarter because neither of these communities had high enough gang violence rates to qualify for grant funds per the grant solicitation's criteria.

CHAPTER FIVE

1. In fact, of 38 total murders in El Paso in 1983, only 2 were confirmed as gang related (Olvera 1984b).

2. See note 5 below and chapter 6 for more on Chuco Tango.

3. Street taxes from drug sales are also collected in the barrios of San Antonio by the Texas Mexican Mafia a.k.a. Mexikanemi or La Eme, but there is competition from the Texas Syndicate and other prison gangs, and resistance by their junior affiliates. This is unlike El Paso, where the Barrio Azteca is the only street tax enforcer.

4. This issue is taken up again later in the chapter where the strong presence of the Bloods, Crips, and Gangster Disciples in El Paso's northeastern section beginning in the early 2000s is discussed.

5. An interesting case study regarding ethnic identity and modern Chicano gangs is with a group called Chuco Tango, El Paso's seventh largest gang. The self-proclaimed raison d'être of the various Tango factions in Texas is in rebellion against overbearing prison gangs by employing a power in numbers strategy against their oppressors. One manner of doing so has been to shirk norms that respect the hierarchy and tradition of Chicano prison gangs. Tangos are also somewhat "post-racial" in that they accept white and black members to keep their number of members high. As a younger generation, the typical Tango orientation in places like Houston, Dallas, and San Antonio is decidedly more gangsta and less barrio. See chapter 6 for more on the uniqueness of Chuco Tango compared to those in the rest of the state.

6. See the Logan Heights gang's murder of a member of a central-northeast area gang called Straight Motherfuckin' Thugs (SMT) documented in Merritz (2009).

7. Historically, the "black" area of El Paso is in the central part of the city, situated around the Douglass School for blacks on Eucalyptus Street. Most of the black families from this area were indeed initially tied to Ft. Bliss. Interviewees Tony and Neto noted that in the 1960s the black youth of the Lincoln barrio hung

around the Mine and Mill dancehall (a.k.a. the Bel-Mar) and the Lincoln Theater at 3123 Alameda Avenue.

8. The Bishops, a predominantly black gang in northeast El Paso in the 1980s, was the predecessor to its more contemporary Blood-affiliated gangs.

9. These schools had gangs in them as early as the 1960s (*El Paso Herald Post* 1970).

10. It is also possible that some underwent name changes to modernize or to attempt to throw off law enforcement, but who still occupy the same turf and involve the same family networks of their predecessors.

11. Barrio Logan of San Diego, California—no relation to that of El Paso—once had a profile similar to that of the Barrio Azteca, as it was said to have become involved with the Tijuana Cartel for some time in the 1990s (Corcoran 2013; Sullivan 1999; United Gangs 2017).

12. Some detached but astute observers have referred to the BA as one of the world's most dangerous gangs (e.g., Casey 2010a). While this title is often given to MS-13 by the press, by comparison to the BA, it has proven to be a glib misnomer. Ward (2013) illustrates that the roots and evolution of MS-13 are not much different than those of most US Latino street gangs, for example. Under the Trump presidency, former Attorney General Jeff Sessions exploited the false sense of danger posed by MS-13 to the general public to further politicize the issue of Latinos and crime.

13. One version appearing in the *New York Times* was that Leslie Enriquez (Redelfs' wife) had taken bribes to regularly issue travel visas to members of a rival gang of the BA (Malkin 2010).

14. While this arrangement stood for well over a decade, the Juárez police has commented on the recent friction between the BA and La Linea, perhaps causing them to split up. On December 29, 2017, an executed corpse was hung from a bridge at the border between Santa Teresa and Anapra, with a *narcomanta* (message) scrawled on it. This prompted the comments from Juárez authorities to the press (*Tiempo* 2017). Also see Borunda (2019) and Esquivel (2018) for a detailed breakdown of the warring factions, some of whom were once allies depicted in figure 5.4.

15. There are active and former members of well-known California Sureño sets such as Colonia Watts, Gary Lomas, and Varrio Nuevo Estrada scattered across El Paso, but as individual groups, their presence is not as prominent as the others mentioned in this section.

16. A notable incident occurred in 2011 at Shooter's Billiards in the Devil's Triangle when a high-ranking Sureño/Eme transplant from California was assaulted, stabbed, shot, and left for dead by three members of the BA (Ortiz 2011). The intended message was essentially "this [El Paso–Juárez] is our turf."

1. For example, while visiting the city in 1977, the Director of the Texas Council of Crime and Delinquency, John Albach, referred to south El Paso's gangs as "unemployment gangs," reminiscent of those that roamed the streets during the Great Depression (Marston 1977).

2. Santana and Morales (2014) are gang investigators who have described the links between these groups and northern Mexican cartels as temporary and unreliable, prone to change with frequent shifts in alliances and other drug gang politics.

3. See the work of Guadalupe Correa-Cabrera (2013) and Rajeev Gundur (2019) for great exceptions.

4. There appears to be no decipherable pattern, for example, for the existence of "stash houses" that hold drugs or money throughout El Paso, where they seem to appear in various neighborhoods at random (Gundur 2017).

5. On January 24, 2019, this office held a press conference to highlight results from the first operation involving each of the nine law enforcement agencies housed in the center. It was a six-month investigation that resulted in the arrest of nine Sureño gang members, caught with a total of 47.1 grams of heroin, 2.7 grams of methamphetamine, and 4.3 grams of marijuana. The street value of this amount of drugs pales in comparison to the value of the resources, manpower, and other expenditures it took to make the bust.

6. As modern urban gang members place a high value on gangsta rap music (Kubrin 2005), the prominence of Houston's Chicano gang scene was propelled by the career of Carlos Coy, a.k.a. the Southpark Mexican, whose music captivated Texas's street youth since the mid-1990s. His was a unique style of "chopped & screwed" rap, produced under the label Dopehouse Records. His references to "Screwston," "H-Town" and "Hustletown," helped to establish Houston's gangsta rap scene among a widespread audience, giving rise to a larger "3rd Coast" rap style movement. Prior to adopting the name Tango Blast, the loose federation of nonprison gang inmates representing Houston (i.e., its original Tango) was known as Houstone. Similarly, Dallas and Ft. Worth Tangos went by D-town and Foritos, and Austin as La Capirucha (i.e., Capital of Texas). Today, they essentially are all affiliated with Tango Blast. Only San Antonio stands alone in this arrangement, as expounded in Tapia (2017).

7. In EPPD's current list of active gangs, Tango Blast is one of the largest, with 44 reported members. While some of these members may be from various cities east of El Paso, most Tango Blasters are from Houston.

8. El Syndicato de Nuevo Mexico (SNM), Los Carnales, and Los Padillas.

9. Most law enforcement and corrections professionals in the area place the formation of the Cruces Boys between 2008 and 2012. Uncertainty of their date

of origin is tied to the process of their formation as a gradual one. It comes by virtue of street gangs' general frustration with overbearing prison gangs inside incarceration facilities. The result is the formation of a street-to-prison hybrid that is organized around geography or, more specifically, the inmates' hometown.

10. Many major cities in the United States have a local gang that employs some version of this phrase in their gang name. The historical gang inventory in appendix A has at least three modern variations of this gang name with Carnales over Bitches (COB) and Money over Bitches (MOB) in El Paso and Men of Business (MOB) in Las Cruces.

APPENDIX A

1. As some of the information published in Ahlgren's (1981) four-part series on gangs appears to be incorrect, it is not certain this was accurate. This also applies to the following gangs he noted: Mesa Vista, Limas y Octubre, 13th and 14th Street gangs, the Heads, Barrio Gang, Huercos del diablo, and the Virgins. Either some of these never existed or they were not well-known gangs.

REFERENCES

Agren, David. 2017. "Mexico Maelstrom: How the Drug Violence Got so Bad." *The Guardian*, December 26.

Aguilar, Julian. 2013. "Participants Say Mérida Initiative Making a Big Difference in Juárez." *Texas Tribune*, December 4.

Ahlgren, Frank Jr. 1981. "Gang Life Has Lost its Glamour." *El Paso Herald Post*, December 16, A-1.

Ainsle, Ricardo. 2013. *The Fight to Save Juarez*. Austin: University of Texas Press.

Albuquerque Journal. 2008. "Gang Violence Has Anthony, N.M. on Edge." July 3. https://www.abqjournal.com/18625/835am-gang-violence-has-anthony-n-m-on-edge.html.

Albuquerque Journal. 2008. "Anthony Man Gets 18 Years in Vehicular Homicide." January 15. https://www.abqjournal.com/19870/640am-anthony-man-gets-18-years-in-vehicular-homicide.html.

Amarillo Globe News. 2001. "Search Continuing for Jail Escapee." March 25.

Anderson, Lindsey. 2014. "Autopsy Released in Fatal New Year's Day Fight at Joe Torrez Home." *Las Cruces Sun News*, June 26, 1.

Arellano, Raymundo P. 2017. "Encuentran 26 Osamentas en el Desierto del Valle de Juárez." Televisa News. http://noticieros.televisa.com/ultimas-noticias/estados/2017–04-08/encuentran-26-osamentas-desierto-valle-juarez-chihuahua/.

Associated Press. 1954. "L.A. Officer Sees No Nationwide Pachuco Tieup." *El Paso Herald Post*, September 2, 4.

———. 1998. "Authorities Hit Alleged Drug-Trafficking Street Gang." October 1.

Associated Press News. 2000. "Man Given Life for Student Killing." April 28. https://www.apnews.com/90a5e5f7f84601fab4c7ecd3ebccafb1.

Ball, Richard A., and G. David Curry. 1995. "Purposes and Methods for Defining 'Gangs.'" *Criminology* 33 (2): 225–45.

Barajas, Luis. 2002. "Drive By Shooting Response Team." El Paso Police Department. 1–14.

Barker, Tom (ed.). 2012. *North American Criminal Gangs*. Durham, NC: Carolina Academy Press.

Bender, Steven W. 2012. *Run for the Border: Vice and Virtue in U.S.-Mexico Crossings.* New York: New York University Press.

Berg, Jeff. 2005. "Ganging Up." *Desert Exposure*, November. http://www.desert exposure.com/200511/200511_gangs.html.

Birge, Bill. 1962. "Charms Fought Their Way Up." *El Paso Times*, December 3.

Bogardus, E. 1943. "Gangs of Mexican American Boys." *Sociology & Social Science Research* 28: 55–66.

Borunda, Daniel. 2006. "El Paso Gang Troubles Rise." *El Paso Times*, January 22.

———. 2008a. "223 Arrested in Crackdown." *Las Cruces Sun News*, June 30.

———. 2008b. "Ex-Azteca's Testimony Reveals His Ties to F B I." *El Paso Times*, November 4.

———. 2009. "Bloods Gang Dates Back to '80s in El Paso." *El Paso Times*, April 1.

———. 2009. "El Paso man Arrested by Mexican Army, Suspected of Being Hit Man for Juárez Drug Cartel." *Las Cruces Sun News*, September 11, B-1.

———. 2010. "Neighbors Fearful as Gang Feud Takes Root." *El Paso Times*, March 24.

———. 2011. "El Paso Police Report Big Drop in Gang Membership." *El Paso Times*, October 21.

———. 2014a. "Texas D P S Report: Sureño Street Gang Has Grown in El Paso." *El Paso Times*. April 22. Reprinted July 13, 2016. http://www.elpasotimes.com /story/archives/2016/07/13/texas-dps-report-sureo-street-gang-has-grown-el -paso/87033028/.

———. 2014b. "Operations Ome Ce, Stonegarden: Racketeering Investigation 'Disrupts' Barrio Azteca Gang." *El Paso Times*, October 12. A-1.

———. 2015. "Central El Paso, Freeway Shootings Linked to 'Gang Feud.'" *El Paso Times*, August 13.

———. 2017a. "U.S. Attorney General Calls Border 'Ground Zero.'" *El Paso Times*, April 20. A-1.

———. 2017b. "El Paso Woman Accused of Leading Drug Cell." *El Paso Times*, December 21.

———. 2018a. "Chuco Tango Gang Member Pleads Guilty in Drive-By Shooting Murder of Barrio Azteca Rival." *El Paso Times*, April 24.

———. 2018b. "Ysleta High School Student Killed in Juarez Shooting." *El Paso Times*, January 16.

———. 2019. "Mexico drug cartel violence flares as Mexicles, Gente Nueva war rattles Valley of Juárez." *El Paso Times*, June 19.

Bowden, Charles. 2002. *Down by the River: Drugs, Money, Murder, and Family.* New York: Simon & Schuster.

———. 2010. *Murder City: Cd. Juárez and the Global Economy's New Killing Fields.* New York: Nation Books.

Bracamontes, Raymond. 2009. "Injunction Clamps Down on Gang." *El Paso Times*, March 21, 1-B.

Braddy, Helen. 1960. "The *Pachucos* and Their Argot." *Southern Folklore Quarterly* 24: 225–71.

Bradshaw, B., D. Johnson, D. Cheatwood, and S. Blanchard. 1998. "A Historical Geographic Study of Lethal Violence in San Antonio." *Social Science Quarterly* 79 (4): 863–78.

Brotherton, David, and Luis Barrios. 2004. *The Almighty Latin King and Queen Nation*. New York: Columbia University Press.

Burciaga, Jose Antonio. 1992. *Drink Cultura: Chicanismo*. Santa Barbara, CA: Capra.

Burrus, Louie. 2017. Personal communication with author, May 25.

Buch, Jason. 2013. "Zetas and Prison Gang Members Enter Pleas in San Antonio." *San Antonio Express News*, January 11.

Bursik, Robert J. Jr., and Harold G. Grasmick. 1993. *Neighborhoods and Crime: The Dimensions of Effective Community Control*. New York: Lexington Books.

Campbell, H. 2009. *Drug War Zone: Frontline Dispatches from the Streets of El Paso and Juarez*. Austin: University of Texas Press.

Campoy, Ana, and Leslie Eaton. 2011. "City Hall Plotters Accused in Gun Smuggling Scheme." *Wall Street Journal*, March 14.

Carrigan, William D., and Clive Webb. 2003. "The Lynching of Persons of Mexican Origin or Descent in the U.S. 1848–1928." *Journal of Social History* 37 (2): 411–38.

Carrillo, Mary Lou (Det.). 2018. El Paso Intelligence Center (EPIC)/DEA. Personal communication with author, January 23.

Cartwright, Gary. 1998. *Dirty Dealing: Drug Smuggling on the Mexican Border*. El Paso: Cinco Puntos.

Casey, Nicholas. 2010a. "Gang Questioned in Mexico Killings." *Wall Street Journal*, March 19.

———. 2010b. "Mexican City's Deaths Rise Amid Border War." *Wall Street Journal*, May 25.

———. 2010c. "Cartel Wars Gut Juarez, A Onetime Boomtown." *Wall Street Journal*, March 20.

Castro, S., and M. Vargas. 2018. "Agosto el mas violento del año." *El Diario*, September 1.

Chavez, Adriana. 2009. "14 Alleged Aztecas Are Arrested in Drug Case." *El Paso Times*, May 16.

———. 2010. "Detective Says Murder Suspect on Crips List." *Las Cruces Sun News*, February 9.

———. 2019. "A Case Study of the El Paso/Juarez Prison Gang, Barrio Azteca." Master's thesis, New Mexico State University.

Chavez, Julio Cesar. 2017. "Juarez Back on List of Most Violent Cities." KVIA News, April 9. http://www.kvia.com/news/border/juarez-back-on-list-of-most-violent -cities/444930297.

Chessey, Bob. (2016). "Death on the Calle Del Diablo." *Password* 60 (2) (Summer): 53–64.

Chiechi, Dino. 1984. "Terrorized Neighborhoods: Families Fear Violence from Rival Gangs in Housing Complex." *El Paso Herald Post*, September 25, A-1.

City Data. 2019a. Anthony, New Mexico. http://www.city-data.com/city/Anthony -New-Mexico.html.

———. 2019b. Anthony, Texas. http://www.city-data.com/city/Anthony-Texas.html.

City of El Paso. 2017. "El Paso Texas Anti-Gang Center is in Full Operation." News Release, September 28.

Coltharp, Lurline. 1965. *The Tongue of the Tirilones: A Linguistic Study of a Criminal Argot*. Tuscaloosa: University of Alabama Press.

———. 1975. "Pachuco, Tirilon, and Chicano." *American Speech* 50 (1–2): 25–29.

Conner, B. U. L. 1935. Opinion-Editorial. *El Paso Herald Post*, September 27, 4.

———. 1943. "The Fence." Opinion-Editorial. *El Paso Herald Post*, January 23, 4.

Cook, Mike. 2018. "City Accepts Troublesome Federal Grant." *Las Cruces Bulletin*, March 30.

Copeland, Peter. 1983. "New Program is Transforming Juarez Gangs." *El Paso Times*, December 5, B-1.

Corcoran, Patrick. 2012. "Mexico Has 80 Drug Cartels: Attorney General." *Insight Crime*, December 20. https://www.insightcrime.org/news/analysis/mexico-has -80-drug-cartels-attorney-general/

Corchado, Alfredo. 2016. "Why El Paso Prospers as Juarez Struggles." *Dallas Morning News*, September 23.

Correa-Cabrera, Guadalupe. 2013. "Security, Migration and the Economy in the Texas-Tamaulipas Border Region." *Politics & Policy* 41 (1): 65–82.

Cummings, Laura. 2003. "Pachuco Culture in the Greater Southwest." *Journal of the Southwest* 45 (3): 329–48.

Curry, David G., and Scott Decker. 1997. "What's in a Name? A Gang by any Other Name Isn't Quite the Same." *Valparaiso University Law Review* 31: 501–14.

Davidson, Theodore. 1974. *Chicano Prisoners: The Key to San Quentin*. New York: Holt, Rinehart & Wilson.

Day, Jon. 2017. Captain, Dona Ana County Sheriff's Office. Personal communication with author, February 15.

Decker, Scott, and Barrick Van Winkle. 1996. *Life in the Gang*. Cambridge, UK: Cambridge University Press.

Delgado, Celeste. 1997. "Teens Rebel Against Authority." *Borderlands*, 15. El Paso Community College Library Research Guides.

Desmond, Scott, and Charis Kubrin. 2009. "The Power of Place: Immigrant Communities and Adolescent Violence." *Sociological Quarterly* 50 (4): 581–607.

Dibble, Sandra. 2018. "Control for Street Drug Trade Pushes Tijuana to Grisly New Record." *San Diego Union Tribune*, January 14. http://www.sandiegounion

tribune.com/news/border-baja-california/sd-me-homicides-tijuana -20180102-story.html.

Dickson, Gordon. 1991. "Las Cruces Gang Patrol Arrests 15." *Las Cruces Sun News*, October 2, B-1.

Dominguez, Elhiu. 2009. "Northeast Residents Protected By a New Gang Injunction Against Members of the Bloods." County of El Paso Press Release. October 20.

Durán, Robert. 2013. *Gang Life in Two Cities: An Insider's Journey*. New York: Columbia University Press.

———. 2018. *Gang Paradox: Inequality and Miracles on the U.S.–Mexico Border*. New York: Columbia University Press.

Duran, Robert, and Carlos Posadas. 2016. "The Policing of Youth on the U.S.–Mexico Border: A Law Enforcement Perception of Leniency. *Race and Justice* 6 (1), 57–83.

Eastaugh, Sophie. 2017. "The Future of the US–Mexican Border: Inside the "Split City" of El Paso–Juarez." *Guardian*, January 25. https://www.theguardian.com /cities/2017/jan/25/el-paso-juarez-us-mexican-border-life-binational-city.

Einhorn, Catrin. 2011. "And Then There Were Eight (on the FBI's List of Most Wanted Fugitives)." *New York Times*, June 24, 8.

El Diario. 2017a. "Fin de semana 'largo' deja 9 asesinatos." February 7.

El Diario. 2017b. "Septiembre, el mes mas violento en cuatro años." September 22.

El Diario de Juárez. 2018. "Tiene agosto inicio mas violento que meses previos." August 12. https: //diario.mx/Local/2018–08–11_dc4800dd/tiene-agosto -inicio-mas-violento-que-meses-previos-/.

El Diario de Juárez. 2019. "Ejecutan a 11 el fin de semana". March 19. https://diario .mx/juarez/ejecutan-a-11-el-fin-de-semana-20190318-1491487/

El Paso County Government. 2016. "Memorandum of Understanding (MOU)." County #16–0338, 1–17.

El Paso Herald Post. 1920. "Activities of El Paso Detectives Show Large Increases in Thefts Here." March 11, 4.

El Paso Herald Post. 1925a. "Career of Crime Believed Ended As El Paso Thug Apprehended in Los Angeles; Shot Finley as Effort Made to Capture Him." April 21, 4.

El Paso Herald Post. 1925b. "'Horse Face' Is Released in Juarez." August 25, 1.

El Paso Herald Post. 1928. "Juarez Man Is 'Taken for a Ride'; Body Is Found." October 2, 1.

El Paso Herald Post. 1931a. "Police Hunt Driver Endangering Lives: Charge Youth Frightening Children While Crossing the Street." April 22, 5.

El Paso Herald Post. 1931b. "Bandits Kill Farmer: Slayers Members of an American Gang." November 27, 1.

El Paso Herald Post. 1932a. "El Paso's 'Capone' Wants to Aid Police in Breaking up South Side Gang Beatings." October 15, 2.

El Paso Herald Post. 1932b. "Holdups and Robberies Under Investigation in Border Town." August 29, 1.

El Paso Herald Post. 1932c. "Seek Robber Gang." August 8, 7.

El Paso Herald Post. 1932d. "One Man Dies, Two Wounded in Gang War." March 19, 1.

El Paso Herald Post. 1932e. "Border Bandit Shot to Death." March 19, 10.

El Paso Herald Post. 1932f. "Night Life Women Moving." April 2, 3.

El Paso Herald Post. 1932g. "Rum Runners in Gang War: Mystery Fight Between Rival Gangs." October 22, 1.

El Paso Herald Post. 1933a. "May Hold Drive to Continue Good Will Club." May 19, 2.

El Paso Herald Post. 1933b. "Gang Rivalry Aids in Youth's Arrest." June 8, 1.

El Paso Herald Post. 1933c. "Eight Boys Arrested for Stealing Fruit." July 31, 1.

El Paso Herald Cargo. 1933d. "Hijackers Seize Ammunition Cargo." December 21, 1.

El Paso Herald Post. 1933e. "Bogus Money Gang Hunted in Juarez." January 6, 3.

El Paso Herald Post. 1933f. "Man Slain on 'Ride' Identified by Police." December 21.

El Paso Herald Post. 1933g. "Shot to Death by Gangsters." January 11, 1.

El Paso Herald Post. 1934a. "Gang Roundup Begun Following Stabbing." February 26, 3.

El Paso Herald Post. 1934b. "5 Boys Jailed for Burglaries: Two Found Hiding Under Bed in Home on Montana St." August 25, 2.

El Paso Herald Post. 1934c. "Identify Men Slain on River." October 31, 1.

El Paso Herald Post. 1935a. "Opium Seizure Bares Traffic." September 30, 1.

El Paso Herald Post. 1935b. "Gets 10 Years in Kidnapping." November 8, 1.

El Paso Herald Post. 1936a. "Gang Threats Curb Justice in E. P. Cases: Witnesses Afraid to Testify When South El Paso Youth Are Tried." February 3, 12.

El Paso Herald Post. 1936b. "South El Paso Gang Scored." May 27, 5.

El Paso Herald Post. 1936c. "Order Pool Hall Quiz; 30 Arrested in Raids." February 17, 1.

El Paso Herald Post. 1936d. "Two Are Jailed in Gang Slaying Threat Inquiry: Charge Youth Tried to Intimidate Trial Witnesses." February 19, 1.

El Paso Herald Post. 1936e. "Gang Attacks Man." April 8, 1.

El Paso Herald Post. 1937. "Elaborate Trap Laid to Crush Alcohol Ring." December 9, 8.

El Paso Herald Post. 1938a. "Judge Moves to Break Up Street Gangs." June 14, 5.

El Paso Herald Post. 1938b. "Assault Gang Here Smashed: Charge Young Girls Taken to Sand Hills by Boys and Attacked." July 6, 3.

El Paso Herald Post. 1939. "Pastor Asks Help Against Dope Gang." September 2, 4.

El Paso Herald Post. 1943a. "Police Investigate Young Hoodlum 'Pachuco' Gang: Organization of Thugs Spreads to West Coast Cities." January 21, 1.

El Paso Herald Post. 1943b. "City Detectives Unable to Link El Paso Gangs with 'Pachucos.'" January 29, 2.

El Paso Herald Post. 1944. "Juarez Zoot Suiters Riot." August 22, 1.

El Paso Herald Post. 1948. "Logan Heights Charges Neglect Since Annexation." November 30, 1

El Paso Herald Post. 1950. "Grand Jury Probes 'Rat Packs.'" June 22, 1.

El Paso Herald Post. 1951a. "2-x Gang Suspected of Stealing Grenades." August 27, 4.

El Paso Herald Post. 1951b. "EP Police Trail Suspect in Gang Shooting of Youth." August 24, 1.

El Paso Herald Post. 1956. "Gangs Are an Issue for Community Says School Chief." January 31, 1.

El Paso Herald Post. 1957a. "Girl Is Slashed at Dance in Home." August 12, 15.

El Paso Herald Post. 1957b. "Rival Girl Gangs Called 'Little Darlings' & 'Baby Dolls.'" August 22, 4.

El Paso Herald Post. 1957c. "Police Catch 2 Stealing Hubcaps." August 31, 20.

El Paso Herald Post. 1958a. "Youth Gang Wars Take 2nd Life in 16 Days." September 17, 1.

El Paso Herald Post. 1958b. "Drive Inn Parking Clash Leads to Gang Flare-Up." February 25, 1.

El Paso Herald Post. 1958c. "Two Stabbed, One Fatally in Juarez." February 17, 28.

El Paso Herald Post. 1959a. "Gang Clashes over Girl; Murder Charges Filed." June 3, 1.

El Paso Herald Post. 1959b. "Youth Chases His Enemy, Knifes Him." June 3, 1.

El Paso Herald Post. 1960. "Youth Shot During Fight." May 7.

El Paso Herald Post. 1961. "Gangs Fight At Drive-Ins." June 8.

El Paso Herald Post. 1965a. "Valley Thugs Keep Police on the Run." May 29.

El Paso Herald Post. 1965b. "Youth Stabbed in Gang Brawl." September 18.

El Paso Herald Post. 1965c. "Police Probe Shooting, Fight Link." April 5.

El Paso Herald Post. 1967. "Teenage Gangs Assault Four." May 7.

El Paso Herald Post. 1970. "Gang Fight Sends Youth to Hospital." February 26.

El Paso Herald Post. 2017. "Website Names El Paso 'Second Safest City in America.'" August 23. https://elpasoheraldpost.com/el-paso-named-second-safest-city -america/.

El Paso Intelligence Center (EPIC). 2011. "Language of the Cartels: Narco Terminology, Identifiers, and Clothing Style." Report of the Gang Intelligence Unit, 1–14.

El Paso Times. 1982. "Gang Members Booked in Assault." January 21, 8B.

El Paso Times. 2016. "Three Anthony, N.M. Men Arrested by Gang Unit." December 6. http://www.elpasotimes.com/story/news/crime/2016/12/06/three -anthony-nm-men-arrested-gang-unit/95040038/.

Epstein, David. 2015. "Devils, Deals, and the DEA." *Propublica*, December 17.

Esquivel, J. Jesus. 2018. "Cuidad Juárez, como es sus peores épocas." *Proceso*, September 15.

Farmer, Liz. 2016. "Man Jailed in El Paso Is Linked to Cartel Kidnapping, Murder of Drug Dealer Found with Hands Chopped Off." *Dallas Morning News*, May 4. https://www.dallasnews.com/news/crime/2016/05/04/man-jailed-in-el-paso -connected-to-cartel-kidnapping-murder-of-drug-dealer-found-with-hands- chopped-off.

Feldmeyer, Ben. 2009. "Immigration and Violence: The Offsetting Effects on Latino Violence." *Social Science Research* 38 (3): 717–31.

Ferrante, Lou. 2015. "Inside the Gangster's Code: S01E03 The Burqueños." http:// www.dailymotion.com/video/x2i66ns.

Fertig, Jillian. 2017. "Some El Paso Neighborhoods fed up with Gang Activity, Crime." KFOX14 News, June 6. http://kfoxtv.com/news/local/some-el-paso -neighborhoods-fed-up-with-gang-activity-crime.

Finley, Walt. 1950. "Girls in Rat Packs Carry Weapons." *El Paso Herald Post*, June 20, 1.

Fleisher, Mark. 1997. *Dead End Kids: Girls, Gangs, & the Boys They Know*. Madison: University of Wisconsin.

Flores, Aileen. 2017. "No 'Sense of Division' Before Fence." *Las Cruces Sun News*, July 17, 2-A.

Flores, Eric. 2017. Sgt., Dona Ana County Sheriff's Office. Personal communication with author, April.

Fonce, Tammy. 1994. "Police Want Ortiz Handed Over: Gang Brother Charged." *El Paso Herald Post*. August 16, A-1.

Fong, Robert. 1990. "The Organizational Structure of Prison Gangs: A Texas Case Study." *Federal Probation* 54 (1): 36–44.

Forsythe, Kimberly. 1998. "The Angel's Triangle." El Paso Police Department. June 28, 1–14.

Garcia, Mario T. 1995. *Memories of Chicano History: The Life & Narrative of Bert Corona*. Berkeley: University of California Press.

Garcia v. El Paso Limited Partnership. 2006. No. 08-05-00152-CV. http://caselaw .findlaw.com/tx-court-of-appeals/1251057.html.

Gerstein, Josh. 2006. "Army Transfers Could Trigger a Gang War." *New York Sun*, March 16. http://www.nysun.com/national/army-transfers-could-trigger-a -gang-war/29230/.

Gibson, Jeff. 2017. El Paso County Sheriff, Gang Task Force Officer. Personal communication with the author. February 24.

Gieryn, Thomas F. 2000. "A Space for Place in Sociology." *Annual Review of Sociology* 26: 463–96.

Gonzales, Jessica. 2017. "Gang-Related Crime Continues to Plague El Paso, EPPD Says." KFOX News, August 23. http://kfoxtv.com/news/local/gang-related-crime -continues-to-plague-el-paso-eppd-says.

Greene, J., & Pranis, K. 2007. Gang Wars: The Failure of Enforcement Tactics and the Need for Effective Public Safety Strategies. Justice Policy Institute. Washington, DC.

Guadian, Stephanie. 2017. "El Paso and Juarez Rekindling Official Sister City Status." KVIA News, October 30. http://www.kvia.com/news/el-paso/el-paso -and-juarez-rekindling-official-sister-citystatus/649086961.

Gundur, Rajeev. 2017. "Organizing Crime in the Margins: The Enterprises and People of the American Drug Trade." PhD diss., Cardiff University, Wales.

———. 2018. "The Changing Social Organization of Prison Protection Markets: When Prisoners Choose to Organize Horizontally Rather than Vertically." *Trends in Organized Crime.* February, 1–20. DOI: 10.1007/s12117-018-9332-0.

———. 2019. "Negotiating Violence and Protection in Prison and on the Outside: The organizational evolution of the transnational prison gang Barrio Azteca." *International Criminal Justice Review.* (Online first) doi:10.1177/1057567719836466.

Guzman, Romeo. 2017. "Mexico's Most Celebrated Pachuco: Tin Tan." KCET.org, February 23. https://www.kcet.org/shows/artbound/mexicos-most-celebrated -pachuco-tin-tan.

Hagedorn, John. 1988. *People and Folks: Gangs, Crime, and the Underclass in a Rustbelt City.* Chicago: Lakeview Press.

Herrera, Patricia. 2017. "A dos días de terminar diciembre van 79 ejecutados en Ciudad Juárez." *Tiempo,* December 29. http://tiempo.com.mx/noticia/111535-eje cutados_en_ciudad_juarez_ciudad_juarez_homicidios_fiscalia_zona_norte/1.

Hopkins, T. S. 2004. "Gov. Proposes Anti-Gang Plan." *Las Cruces Sun News.* December 7, 1-A.

Howell, James. 1999. "Youth Gang Homicide." *Crime and Delinquency* 45 (2): 208–41.

Howie, Patrick. 2017. Lt. Doña Ana County Detention Center. Personal communication with the author, May 15.

Instituto Nacional de Estadística y Geografía (INEGI). 2006. Anuario estadístico. Chihuahua, table 1.Victoria de Durango, Durango.

Jacobs, James B. 1974. Street Gangs Behind Bars. *Social Problems* 21: 395–409.

———. 2009. "Gang Databases: Context and Questions." *Criminology and Public Policy* 8 (4): 705–9.

Jasso, Juan Jose v. The State of Texas. 2001. No. 08-01-00231-CR. https://law.justia .com/cases/texas/eighth-court-of-appeals/2003/62444.html.

Kelling, George, and James Q. Wilson. 1982. "Broken Windows: The Police and Neighborhood Safety." *Atlantic* (March): 29–38.

Kennedy, David. 2009. "Constructing and Deconstructing Gang Databases." *Criminology and Public Policy* 8 (4): 710–16.

KFOX News. 2011. "Gang Activity up in Las Cruces." March 31. https://www .nationalgangcenter.gov/Gang-Related-News?st=NM&p=4.

Kirk, Harry. 1993. *An Historical Review of Gangs and Gang Violence in El Paso, Texas.* Sam Houston State University, Law Enforcement Management Institute report. 1–58.

Knox, George, James Houston, Ed Tromanhauser, Tom McCurrie, and John

Laskey. 1996. "Addressing and Testing the Migration Issue: A Summary of Recent Findings." In *Gangs: A Criminal Justice Approach*, edited by Mitch Miller and Jeff Rush (76–85). Cincinnati: ACJS/Anderson Monograph Series.

Kolb, Joe. 2013. "Troubled U.S. Marshall's '09 Execution Remains a Mystery." *Fox News*, December 16. http://www.foxnews.com/world/2013/12/16/troubled-us-marshal-0-execution-in-mexico-remains-mystery.html.

Kornhauser, Ruth. 1978. *Social Sources of Delinquency: Underlying Assumptions of Basic Models of Delinquency Theories.* Chicago: University of Chicago Press.

Kubrin, Charis. 2005. "Gangstas, Thugs, and Hustlas: Identity and the Code of the Street in Rap Music." *Social Problems* 52 (3): 360–78.

KVIA. 2017. "Chihuahua State Police Officer Arrested in Vado Allegedly in Possession of Marijuana." http://www.kvia.com/crime/chihuahua-state-police-officer-arrested-in-las-cruces-allegedly-in-possession-of-marijuana/553433344.

La Frontera Fluida. 2017. "Mexican Revolution." http://www.lafronterafluida.com/mexican-revolution/.

Las Cruces Sun News. 1943. "Youth Held After Theft from a Car." March 22, 1.

Las Cruces Sun News. 1959. "District Judge Lowers the Boom on Juveniles Here." September 15, 1.

Las Cruces Sun News. 1968. "Clothing Needed for Hernandez Benefit Drive." October 10, 2.

Las Cruces Sun News. 1969a. "Desert Rascals Open New Home." January 19, 2.

Las Cruces Sun News. 1969b. "Sheriff Seeks Hall Closing as Trouble Spot." August 4, 1.

Las Cruces Sun News. 1969c. "Gang Fight in Anthony Still Mystery." September 8, 2.

Las Cruces Sun News. 1971. "Autopsy Reveals Cause of Death of Young Man." August 18.

Las Cruces Sun News. 1972. "EP Police Probe Weekend Gang Fight." April 3, 1.

Las Cruces Sun News. 1977. "Officers Investigate Anthony Rape Report." April 18, 2-A.

Las Cruces Sun News. 2012. "Graffiti a Never-Ending Problem for Las Cruces Codes Officers." March 22. https://www.nationalgangcenter.gov/Gang-Related-News?st=NM&p=3.

Linthicum, Kate. 2017. "More and More People Are Being Murdered in Mexico—and Once More Drug Cartels are to Blame." *Los Angeles Times*, March 3. http://www.latimes.com/world/mexico-americas/la-fg-mexico-murders-20170301-story.html.

Lira Arredondo Sanchez, J., Z. Orozco, O. Ferreira Rodriguez, and D. Shirk. 2018. *The Resurgence of Violent Crime in Tijuana.* Justice in Mexico. Policy Brief, February, University of San Diego.

Llorente, Elizabeth. 2011. "Texas Attorney General Says Mexico Drug Violence Spilling Over." Fox News, November 2. http://www.foxnews.com/politics/2011/11/02/texas-attorney-general-says-mexico-cartel-violence-is-spilling-into-lone-star.html.

Lopez, Carlos Andres. 2017. "Authorities Charge 28 Cartel Affiliated Suspects." *Las Cruces Sun News*, April 28. http://www.lcsun-news.com/story/news/crime/2017/04/28/authorities-charge-28-cartel-affiliated-suspects/101051842/.

Lopez, Iris. 2016. "Police: Hikers Robbed, Assaulted on Mt. Cristo Rey." October 23. http://www.kvia.com/news/top-stories/reports-of-possible-robbery-assault-at-mount-cristo-rey/130352586.

Lopez-Stafford, Gloria. 1996. *A Place in El Paso*. Albuquerque: University of New Mexico Press.

Luhnow, David. 2010. "Youth Suspected as Cartel Hitman." *Wall Street Journal*, December 4.

MacArthur, Betsy. 1996. "3 Die in Gang Shootout, 2 Arrested." *El Paso Times*, February 26. 1-A.

Males, Mike. 2017. "California Continue Steep Decline in Arrests." Center for Juvenile and Criminal Justice (CJCJ) Brief. December. 1–3.

Malkin, Elizabeth. 2010. "Drug Gang Leader is Arrested." *New York Times*, November 29, 5.

Marston, Janis. 1977. "Southside EP Gangs Likened to Depression-Era Youth." *El Paso Times*, April 2.

Martinez, Aaron. 2016. "Men Allegedly Sold Drugs to FBI Informant." September 28. http://www.elpasotimes.com/story/news/2016/09/28/men-allegedly-sold-drugs-fbi-informant/91229040/.

Martinez, Jesse. 2014. "Man Arrested, Suspect Sought in Deadly Drive-by Shooting." KFOX News, December 3. http://kfoxtv.com/news/local/man-arrested-suspect-sought-in-deadly-drive-by-shooting.

Martinez, Jose M., and Abel Montilla. 2018. "Gangs on the U.S. Border." Presentation, Texas Gang Investigator's Association, San Antonio, June 25.

Martinez, Ramiro. 2002. *Latino Homicide*. New York: Routledge.

——. 2014. *Latino Homicide*, 2nd ed. New York: Routledge.

Maxson, Cheryl L. 1993. "Investigating Gang Migration: Contextual Issues for Intervention." *Gang Journal* 1: 1–8.

Maxson, Cheryl L., Kristi J. Woods, and Malcolm W. Klein. 1996. "Street Gang Migration: How Big a Threat?" *National Institute of Justice Journal* 230: 26–31.

Mays, Larry, Thomas Winfree, and Stacy Jackson. 1993. "Youth Gangs in Southern New Mexico: A Qualitative Analysis." *Journal of Contemporary Criminal Justice* 9 (2): 134–45.

McArthur, Betsy. 1996. "3 Die in Gang Shootout, 2 Arrested." *El Paso Times*, February 26, sec. A.

McCaffrey, Barry, and Robert Scales. 2011. *Texas Border Security: A Strategic Military Assessment*. A Colgen Report. September 20, 1–182.

McDonnell, Patrick. 1994a. "Man Fires Back at Youths." *El Paso Herald Post*, June 4, A-1.

——. 1994b. "8 More Arrested in Attack." *El Paso Herald Post*, May 13, A-1.

McKinley, James. 2010a. "Fleeing Extreme Gun Violence, Mexican Families Pour into U.S." *New York Times*, April 18.

———. 2010b. "Suspect Says Juárez Killers Pursued Jail Guard." *New York Times*, March 31. http://www.nytimes.com/2010/04/01/world/americas/01mexico.html ?mcubz=1.

McVicar, Jim. 1960. "EP Juvenile Gang Wars Exist, But Underground." *El Paso Herald Post*, February 16, 3.

Medina, Jose. 2007. "Police Counter Anthony Gangs." *Las Cruces Sun News*, July 2, 1.

Meeks, Ashley. 2008. "Gangs in Dona Ana County: What Can We Do?" *Las Cruces Sun News*, December 30.

———. 2011. "Jury Hears Opening Arguments for Murder Case." *Las Cruces Sun News*, August 8.

Merritz, Darren. 2009. "Lawyer Paints Self-Defense Scenario in Murder Trial." *Las Cruces Sun News*, August 12.

Miller, Jody. 2001. *One of the Guys: Girls, Gangs, and Gender*. New York: Oxford University Press.

Millman, Joel 2007. "Politics and Economics: A Shift is afoot at the Mexican Border." *Wall Street Journal*, October 25.

Mirandé, Afredo. 1987. *Gringo Justice*. South Bend, IN: University of Notre Dame Press.

Molloy, Molly. 2017. Personal communication with the author, October 17.

Molloy, Molly, and Charles Bowden. 2012. *El Sicario*. New York: Nation Books.

Montejano, David. 2010. *Quixote's Soldiers: A Local History of the Chicano Movement, 1966–1981*. Austin: University of Texas Press.

Montgomery, Bill. 1956. "Juvenile Authorities Say 50 Teen-Age Gangs Active." *El Paso Times*, October 20.

Moore, Bill. 1976. "20 Years ago the Southside was a Battleground." *El Paso Times*, September 20.

Moore, Joan, Diego Vigil, and Robert Garcia. 1983. "Residence and Territoriality in Chicano Gangs." *Social Problems* 31 (2): 182–94.

Morales, Fred 2007. *La Chihuahuita*. El Paso, TX: El Paso/Juarez Historical Museum. OCLC 174149696.

———. 2017. Personal communication with the author, May 20–December 30.

Morales, Gabriel. 2008. "The Sureño Influence on Southern California Gangs." In *Sureños 2008*. Rocky Mountain Info Network. 17–33.

Moreno, Mark E. 2006. "Mexican American Street Gangs, Migration, and Violence in the Yakima Valley." *Pacific Northwest Quarterly* 97 (3): 131–38.

Moreno, Ruben. 1999. "El Pecas: Una Semblanca Biografica." *Semanario El Meridiano* 107 (Ed. Sur): 10–17.

Morenoff, Jeffrey D. 2005. "Racial and Ethnic Disparities in Crime and Delinquency in the U.S." In *Ethnicity and Causal Mechanisms*, edited by M. Tienda and M. Rutter (139–73). New York: Cambridge University Press.

Nassif, Alberto A. 2012. "Violencia y destrucción en una periferia urbana: El caso de Ciudad Juárez, México." *Gestion y Politica Publica* 21: 227–68.

National Gang Center. 2013. "Gang Related Offenses." https://www.national gangcenter.gov/Survey-Analysis/Gang-Related-Offenses.

National Gang Intelligence Center. 2016. *National Gang Report 2015*. Washington, DC, 1–64.

Nielsen, Amie L., Matthew T. Lee, and Ramiro Martinez Jr. 2005. "Integrating Race, Place and Motive in Social Disorganization Theory: Lessons from a Comparison of Black and Latino Homicide Types in Two Immigrant Destination Cities." *Criminology* 43 (August 18): 837–72.

Obregon-Pagan, Eduardo. 2003. *Murder at the Sleepy Lagoon: Zoot Suits, Race, and Riots in Wartime L.A.* Chapel Hill: University of North Carolina Press.

O'Deane, Matthew. 2011. *Gang Injunctions and Abatement: Using Civil Remedies to Curb Gang Related Crimes*. New York: CRC Press.

Olson, E., D. Shirk, and A. Selee, eds. 2010. *Shared Responsibility: U.S.–Mexico Policy Options for Confronting Organized Crime*. Woodrow Wilson International Center for Scholars.

Olvera, Joe. 1983. "Parents Worried about Gang Violence Against Children." *El Paso Herald Post*, December 5, B-2.

———. 1984a. "Professor: Cholos are Misunderstood." *El Paso Herald Post*, August 17, B-2.

———. 1984b. "We Could Conquer El Paso: With 1,000 Members, Gangs Continue to Roam City Neighborhoods." *El Paso Herald Post*, February 22, 1-A.

Ornstein, J. 1983. Linguistic and Social Aspects of Pachuco Caló: A Bilingual Variety of the U.S.–Mexico Border. In *Proceedings of the Thirteenth International Congress of Linguistics*, edited by S. Hattori et al., 832–36. Tokyo: Gakushuin University.

Ortiz, Fernie. 2011. "Police Arrest 3 Men in Shooting at Shooters Billiards." KVIA News, November 2. http://www.kvia.com/news/police-arrest-3-men-in-shooting -at-shooters-billiards/53341254.

Ortiz Uribe, Monica. 2014. "Vicious Gang, Barrio Azteca, Gets its Start in El Paso." NPR, March 25. http://www.npr.org/2014/03/25/294133885/vicious-gang-barrio -azteca-gets-its-start-in-el-paso.

Padilla, Hector. 2013. "Cd. Juarez: Militarizacion, discursos, y paisajes." In *Vida, muerte, y resistencia en Ciudad Juarez*, coordinated by Salvador Cruz-Sierra, 105–42. Tijuana: El Colegio de la Frontera-Norte.

Parker, Asmann. 2018. "Barrio Azteca Leader's Arrest Casts Doubt on Trump's Border Rhetoric." *InSight Crime*, July 3. https://www.insightcrime.org/news/brief /barrio-azteca-leader-arrest-casts-doubt-trump-border-rhetoric/.

Peach, James, and James Williams. 1994. "Demographic Changes in the El Paso– Juarez–Las Cruces Region." *Estudios Fronterizos* 34, 117–37.

Peerman, Lucas. 1999. "Welcome Inn Allegedly the Scene of Numerous Illegal Acts." *Las Cruces Sun News*, October 21, A-5.

Perez, Elida. 2017. "Duranguito Buildings Spared from Immediate Demolition after Flurry of Court Actions." *El Paso Times*, September 11. http://www.elpasotimes .com/story/news/local/2017/09/11/fencing-going-up-duranguito-demolition -may-begin-Tuesday/654616001/.

Persio, Sofia L. 2017. "Crime in Mexico: Murder Rate Reaches Record High and Nobody is Talking About It." *Newsweek*, June 22. http://www.newsweek.com /crime-mexico-murder-rate-reaches-record-high-and-nobody-talking- about-it-628193.

Proceso. 2006. "Pandillas al servicio del Narco." February 5. http://www.proceso .com.mx/97085/pandillas-al-servicio-del-narco.

Puig, Carlos. 2013. "Crime and No Punishment." *New York Times*, November 20.

Quiñones, Sam. 2014. "The End of Gangs." *Pacific Standard*, December 29. http:// www.psmag.com/politics-and-law/the-end-of-gangs-los-angeles-southern -california-epidemic-crime-95498.

———. 2016. "Once the World's Most Dangerous City, Juárez Returns to Life." *National Geographic*, June. http://www.nationalgeographic.com/magazine /2016/06/juarez-mexico-border-city-drug-cartels-murder-revival/.

Rahm, Harold J., and J. Robert Weber. 1958. *Office in the Alley: Report on a Project with Gang Youngsters*. Austin: University of Texas Austin Hogg Foundation.

Renteria, Ramon. 1979. "Sunland Park Residents Protest Area Gang Violence." *El Paso Times*. July 21.

Richardson, Chad. 2012. *The Informal and Underground Economy of the South Texas Border*. Austin: UT Press.

Rivera, Jose. n.d. *American Wetback*. Unpublished Manuscript.

Rivera, Kristopher. 2016. "6 arrested in Chuco Tango case." *El Paso Times*, August 20, 1-A.

Roberts, Matthew. 2008. "Gang Warfare." *American Conservative*, May 5. http:// www.theamericanconservative.com/articles/gang-warfare/.

Rodriguez, Nestor. 1993. "Economic Restructuring and Latino Growth in Houston." In *In the Barrios: Latinos and the Underclass Debate*, edited by Joan Moore and Raquel Pinderhughes, 101–27. New York: Russell Sage Foundation.

Rojas, Raymundo E. 2007. "Where Devils Fear to Tread: The Good, the Bad, and the Ugly of El Paso Historic Diablo Territory." *Pluma Fronteriza blog* (Spring), Part 1.

Rooker, Bob. 1957. "Kenneth Barhill Says Juvenile Delinquency in Las Cruces Area Is by no Means 'Out Of Hand.'" *Las Cruces Sun News*, October 20.

Ruelas, Renee. 2017. "Zoot Suit Pachanga Celebrates Culture, History." *Las Cruces Sun Times*, June 6. http://www.lcsun-news.com/story/news/local/2017/06/04 /zoot-suit-pachanga-celebrates-culture-history/368565001/.

Salazar, Bert. 1972. "Area Respects Unwritten Law." *El Paso Times*, April 24.

Sampson, R., J. Morenoff, and E. Raudenbush. 2005. "Social Anatomy of Racial and Ethnic Disparities in Violence." *American Journal of Public Health* 95 (2): 225–32.

San Antonio Express-News. 1951. "Judge Gives DA Credit for Youth 'Gang' Inquiry." August 5, 1.

San Antonio Light. 1955. "Cop Spikes Rugcutters." January 13, 23.

Sanchez, Carlos. 2016. "El Pachuco Nunca Pasa de Moda." *El Diario de Juárez*, September 19.

Sanchez, Stephanie. 2009. "FBI Links Fugitive to Hundreds of Cartel Hits." *El Paso Times*, October 22 1-A.

Santana, Juan, and Gabriel Morales. 2014. *Don't Mess with Texas: Gangs in the Lonestar State*. Columbia, SC: Create Space.

Santiago Baca, Jimmy. 1986. *Martín & Meditations on the South Valley*. New York: New Directions.

Schoville, Chuck. 2008. "Sureños 2008." Rocky Mountain Information Network. Phoenix, AZ.

Sellers, Joe Bob. 2017. Las Cruces PD (ret.). Personal communication with author, May 7.

Serrano, Xavier. 2017. DEA Special Agent in Charge, El Paso Intelligence Center (EPIC). Personal communication with author, October 27.

Sierra, Salvador C. 2014. "Violencia y jóvenes: pandilla e identidad compton en Ciudad Juárez." *Revista Mexicana de Sociologia* 76 (4): 613–37.

Sikes, Gini. 1997. *8-Ball Chicks*. New York: Doubleday.

Skarbeck, David. 2012. "Prison Gangs, Norms, and Organizations." *Journal of Economic Behavior and Organization* 82 (1): 702–16.

Smith, Laun. 1969. "Desert Rascals Really Wanted?" *Las Cruces Sun News*, December 17, 1.

Sotomayor, Ernie. 1976. "'Police not the answer', residents say." *El Paso Herald Post*. August 26.

Soular, Diana A. 2017. "Doña Ana County to Accept Federal Border-Security Funds Through Operation Stonegarden." *Las Cruces Sun News*, September 26.

Southern New Mexico-Texas Gang Update. 2008. https://www.yumpu.com/en /document/view/15571538/southern-new-mexico-texas-gang-update-nmsu-web -hosting-/7

Statistical Atlas. 2017. "Race and Ethnicity in El Paso, Texas." https://statisticalatlas .com/place/Texas/El-Paso/Race-and-Ethnicity.

Sullivan, John. 1999. "Gangs, Hooligans, and Anarchists." In *Networks and Netwars: The Future of Terror, Crime, and Militancy*, edited by John Arquilla and David Ronfeldt, 99–128. Santa Monica, CA: Rand.

Tapia, Mike. 2013. "Texas Latino Gangs and Large Urban Jails: Intergenerational Conflict and Issues in Management." *Journal of Crime and Justice* 37 (2): 256–74.

———. 2014. "Latino Street Gang Emergence in the Midwest: Strategic Franchising or Natural Migration?" *Crime and Delinquency* 60 (4): 592–618.

———. 2015. "San Antonio's Barrio Gangs: Size, Scope, and Other Characteristics." *Deviant Behavior* 36 (9): 691–701.

———. 2017. *The Barrio Gangs of San Antonio, Texas, 1915–2015*. Fort Worth: Texas Christian University Press.

Tapia, Mike, Corey Sparks, and J. Mitchell Miller. 2014. "Texas Latino Prison Gangs: An Exploration of Generational Shift and Rebellion." *Prison Journal* 94 (2): 159–79.

Tessneer, Marvin. 1973. "Down by the Levee: A Season of Headaches." *Las Cruces Sun News*, May 13, 6.

Texas Comptroller. 2017. "Port of Entry: El Paso, Economic Impact 2015." https://comptroller.texas.gov/economy/economic-data/ports/el-paso.php.

Texas Department of Public Safety. 2015. *Texas Gang Threat Assessment*. Texas Fusion Center, Intelligence and Counter Terrorism Division.

Texas Department of Public Safety. 2018. *Texas Gang Threat Assessment*. Texas Joint Crime Information Center, Intelligence and Counter Terrorism Division.

Thrasher, Frederic. 1927. *The Gang*. Chicago: University of Chicago Press.

Thompson, Bill. 1984. "Shooting Leaves Man Hospitalized." *El Paso Herald Post*, October 17.

Timmons, W. H. 1990. *El Paso: A Borderlands History*. El Paso: Texas Western Press/University of Texas at El Paso.

Tinsley, Jesse. 1982. "One Dead, Four Wounded in Southside Dispute." *El Paso Herald Post*, September 11.

Thorsby, Devon. 2016. "10 Places with the Highest Rates of Auto Theft in the U.S." *U.S. News*, December 29. https://realestate.usnews.com/real-estate/articles /10-places-with-the-highest-rates-of-car-theft-in-the-us.

Torres, Jaime. 2010. *Pachuco: Out of El Segundo Barrio*. Bloomington, IN: Xlibris.

Triplett, Ruth, 1997. "Youth Gangs in Texas, Part II." *Texas Law Enforcement Management and Administrative Statistics Program* 4 (4): 1–11.

Uhl, David, and Moses Meglorino. 1993. "Chihuahuita in the 1930s: Tough Times in the Barrio." *Borderlands* 12. El Paso Community College, Library Guides. http://epcc.libguides.com/content.php?pid=309255&sid=2621839.

United Gangs. 2010. "Compton Varrio Tortilla Flats." https://unitedgangs.com/2010 /05/06/compton-varrio-tortilla-flats/.

———. 2017. "Logan Heights Gang." https://unitedgangs.com/barrio-logan-heights -gang/.

United States v. Ruben Almaraz. 2005. No. 04–2227. December 20.

United States v. Nathan Archuleta. 2013. No. 12–2026. December 17.

University of Texas at El Paso (UTEP). 1974. Institute of Oral History Interview with Guillermo Balderas by Oscar Martinez. Interview 148, April 18.

———. 1978. Institute of Oral History Interview with Anonymous by Wendy Thomson. Interview 724, April 8.

———. 1979. Institute of Oral History Interview with Francisco Martinez Parga by Virgilio H. Sanchez Saucedo. Interview 384, February 2.

US Census Bureau. 1982. "General Population Characteristics, New Mexico." Report PC80-1-B33. May.

———. 2019a. "Quick Facts, Las Cruces city, New Mexico." https://www.census.gov/quickfacts/fact/table/lascrucescitynewmexico/PST045217.

———. 2019b. "Quick Facts, El Paso County, Texas." https://www.census.gov/quickfacts/fact/table/elpasocountytexas/PST045216.

US Customs and Border Patrol. 2017. "Acting CBP Deputy Commissioner Visits Texas/Mexico Border to Promote Cross-Border Relations with Mexico." October 19. https://www.cbp.gov/newsroom/local-media-release/acting-cbp-deputy-commissioner-visits-texasmexico-border-promote-cross.

US Department of Justice. 2011. "West Texas High Intensity Drug Trafficking Area (HIDTA) Drug Market Analysis." National Drug Intelligence Center, Washington, DC.

———. 2015. "Folk Nation/Gangster Disciples Gang Member Receives Life Sentences for Federal Sex Trafficking Violations." Press release, June 25.

———. 2017a. Federal Bureau of Investigation Uniform Crime Report. El Paso, Texas Police Department, Number of Violent Crimes, 1990; 2006. https://www.ucrdatatool.gov/Search/Crime/Local/RunCrimeOneYearofData.cfm.

———. 2017b. Drug Enforcement Agency. "National Drug Threat Assessment." October. https://www.dea.gov/sites/default/files/2018-07/DIR-040-17_2017-NDTA.pdf

———. 2017c. "Federal and State Authorities in Las Cruces Arrest Members and Associates of the 'Cruces Boys' on Drug Trafficking Charges." Press release, June 8.

Valdemar, Richard. 2008. "Chuckie, Midget, and the Compton Tortilla Flats Gang." Police, January 25. http://www.policemag.com/blog/gangs/story/2008/01/chuckie-midget-and-the-compton-tortilla-flats-gang.aspx.

Valdez, Al, and Rene Enriquez. 2011. Urban Street Terrorism: The Mexican Mafia and the Sureño Trece. Santa Ana, CA: Police & Fire Publishing.

Valdez, Avelardo. 1993. "Persistent Poverty, Crime, and Drugs: U.S. Mexican Border Region." In In the Barrios: Latinos and the Underclass Debate, edited by Joan Moore and Raquel Pinderhughes, 173–94. New York: Russell Sage Foundation.

———. 2005. "Toward a Typology of Contemporary Mexican American Youth Gangs." In Gangs and Society: Alternative Perspectives, edited by Louis Kontos, David Brotherton, and Luis Barrios, 12–40. New York: Columbia University Press.

———. 2007. Mexican-American Girls & Gang Violence: Beyond Risk. New York: Palgrave MacMillan.

Valdez, Avelardo, Alice Cepeda, and Charles Kaplan. 2009. "Homicidal Events Among Mexican American Street Gangs: A Situational Analysis." Homicide Studies 13: 288–306.

Valenzuela, Jose Manuel. 2013. "Juaritos: Prohibicionismo, violencia, y frontera." In *Vida, muerte, y resistencia en Ciudad Juárez*, coordinated by Salvador Cruz-Sierra, 91–104. Tijuana: El Colegio de la Frontera-Norte.

Valenzuela, Tony. 2017. Personal communication with the author. January 1–August 31.

Vargas, Robert. 2014. "Criminal Group Embeddedness and the Adverse Effects of Arresting a Gang's Leader: A Comparative Case Study." *Criminology* 52 (2): 143–68.

Vigil, James Diego. 1988. *Barrio Gangs: Street Life and Identity in Southern California*. Austin: Texas University Press.

Vila, Pablo. 2000. *Crossing Borders, Reinforcing Borders: Social Categories, Metaphors, and Narrative Identities on the U.S.–Mexico Frontier*. Austin: University of Texas Press.

Villalobos, Ramon. 1972. "Baby-Faced 'El Raton' Terrorizing Elderly in South El Paso." *El Paso Times*. August 19.

Villalpando, Ruben. 2004. "Bandas juarenses, responsables de 70% de delitos en el municipio." *La Jornada*, December 9. http://www.jornada.unam.mx/2004/12/09/034n1est.php.

———. 2011. "Al menos de 950 Pandillas Operan en Ciudad Juárez advierte edil." *La Jornada*, July 13. http://www.jornada.unam.mx/2011/07/13/estados/035n1est.

Waldorf, Dan. 1993. "When the Crips Invaded San Francisco: Gang Migration." *Gang Journal* 1: 11–16.

Ward, T. W. 2013. *Gangsters Without Borders: Ethnography of a Salvadoran Street Gang*. New York: Oxford University Press.

Washington-Valdez, Diana. 2006. *The Killing Fields: The Truth About Mexico's Bloody Border Legacy*. Burbank, CA: Peace at the Border.

Wegemer, Al. 1953. "Police Fear Flare-Ups of Juvenile Delinquency." *El Paso Herald Post*, November 16, 1.

Xie, Min, and Eric Baumer. 2018. "Reassessing the Breadth of the Protective Benefit of Immigrant Neighborhoods." *Criminology* 56 (2): 302–32.

Yablonsky, Lewis. 1959. "The Delinquent Gang as a Near-Group." *Social Problems* 7: 108–17.

Yearwood, Douglass, and Alison Rhyne. 2007. "Hispanic/Latino Gangs: A Comparative Analysis of Nationally Affiliated and Local Gangs. *Journal of Gang Research* 14: 1–18.

Zea, Maria del Sol Morales. 2012. "Migracion en Cd. Juárez (1950–2000)." *Anatemas y Apologias*, February 13. https://anatemasyapologias.wordpress.com/2012/02/13/migracion-en-ciudad-juarez-1950-2000-pasos-hacia-la-complejizacion-de-una-sociedad-fronteriza/

INDEX

Page numbers in italic text indicate illustrations.